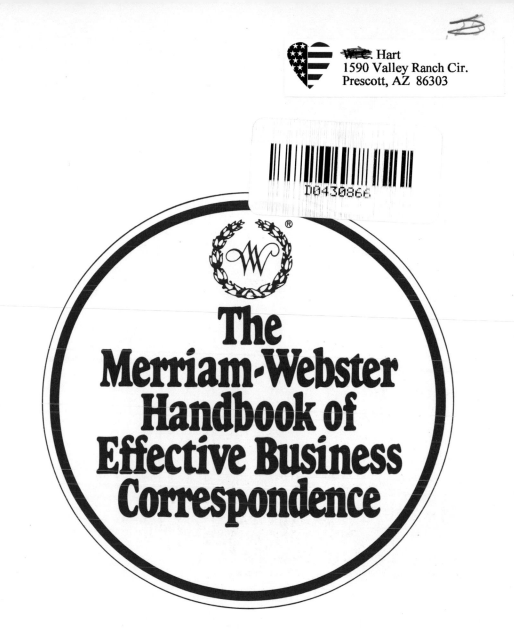

The Merriam-Webster Handbook of Effective Business Correspondence

A WALLABY BOOK
PUBLISHED BY POCKET BOOKS NEW YORK

POCKET BOOKS, a Simon & Schuster division of
GULF & WESTERN CORPORATION
1230 Avenue of the Americas, New York, N.Y. 10020

ISBN: 0-671-79081-1

10 9 8 7 6 5 4 3

TABLE OF CONTENTS

1
STYLE IN BUSINESS CORRESPONDENCE • 1

2
A GUIDE TO EFFECTIVE BUSINESS ENGLISH • 92

PREFACE

The book that you are reading is a compact guide to more effective business-letter writing. It is intended not only for secretaries and executives but also for students enrolled in Business Education curricula and general users. *The Merriam-Webster Handbook of Effective Business Correspondence* comprises two major parts: the first part deals exclusively with the mechanical styling of business letters, while the second part treats the grammatical and stylistic conventions of Business English.

Among the book's most useful characteristics are its illustrative features. For example, the text is illustrated with over 30 facsimiles showing the correct format for the Block Letter, the AMS Simplified Letter, the Modified Block Letter, the Modified Semi-block Letter, the Official Letter, the Hanging-indented Letter, and the Half-sheet Letter. In addition, the book contains charts providing over 250 rules for the proper use of abbreviations, capitalization, italics, numerals, punctuation, and spacing in typewritten letters and other business documents. Each rule is exemplified by at least one verbal illustration from the Merriam-Webster file of over 12 million printed examples of English usage. Another feature is the 30-page chart giving the appropriate forms of address for over 150 individuals whose offices, ranks, or professions warrant special courtesy titles, salutations, and complimentary closes. These persons include members of the bar and the judiciary, the government, the consular and diplomatic corps, the armed forces, the academic and medical communities, and the clergy. A fourth feature is the detailed, illustrated discussion of the components of discourse — the eight parts of speech, the phrase, the clause, the sentence, and the paragraph — found in the second part of the book.

The Merriam-Webster Handbook of Effective Business Correspondence offers comprehensive guidance for achieving the concise, accurate, and effective written communication required by men and women in the business sector today.

The Editor

1

STYLE IN BUSINESS CORRESPONDENCE

CONTENTS

1.1

THE BUSINESS LETTER AS AN IMAGE-MAKER

The word *style* as applied to business-letter writing encompasses format, grammar, stylistics, and word usage. All of these elements conjoin in a letter to produce a tangible reflection on paper not only of the writer's ability and knowledge and the typist's competence, but also of an organization's total image. For example, a corporation may spend considerable sums on advertising to promote its products and services and to advance a positive image; yet, this image may be seriously eroded or negated altogether by massive output of carelessly prepared letters especially when produced over a long time span. On a smaller scale, a few letters of that kind may create such negative impressions on their recipients that they will have second thoughts about pursuing business relationships with the writer or his organization —a situation that has special impact on small businesses. The letter, then, is actually an exponent of overall organizational style, regardless of the size of the firm. And if there appears to be no pride in or concern for the quality of something as basic as one's business correspondence, how then can there be concern for or pride in the quality of one's products and services? Thus, the initial impression created by an attractively and accurately typed, logically oriented, and clearly written letter can be a crucial factor in its ultimate effectiveness.

Letters—whether mass-produced by word processors or typed individually—are still the most personal method of written business communication. An executive may devote as much as 50 percent or more of the workday to correspondence, be it planning and thinking out the direction, tone, and content of his or her own letters or reading and acting on incoming letters. Secretaries spend even more of their time on correspondence. And time costs money.

Therefore, if both writer and typist keep in mind the following simple aids to good letter production, the time and money involved will have been well spent:

1. Stationery should be of high-quality paper having excellent correcting or erasing properties.
2. Typing should be neat and accurate with any corrections or erasures rendered invisible.
3. The essential elements of a letter (such as the date line, inside address, message, and signature block) and any other included parts should conform in page placement and format with one of the generally acceptable, up-to-date business-letter stylings (as the Simplified Letter, the Block Letter, the Modified Block Letter, the Modified Semi-block Letter, or the Hanging-indented Letter).
4. The language of the letter should be clear, concise, grammatically correct, and devoid of padding and clichés.
5. The ideas in the message should be logically oriented, with the writer always keeping in mind the reader's reaction.
6. All statistical data should be accurate and complete.

Style in business correspondence, like language itself, is not a static entity: it has changed over the years to meet the varying needs of its users, and it is continuing to change today. For example, the open punctuation pattern and the Simplified Letter have gained wide currency. On the other hand, the closed punctuation pattern and the Indented Letter, once considered standard formats, are now little used in the United States. General diversification and the multinational character of modern business have rendered fast, clear, lean communication in all media essential. The following two chapters have been prepared with all of these factors in mind.

1.2

TOTAL-LETTER CONSIDERATIONS

It has often been said that an attractive letter should look like a symmetrically framed picture with even margins working as a frame for the typed lines that are balanced under the letterhead. But how many letters really do look like framed pictures? Planning ahead before starting to type is the real key to letter symmetry:

1. Estimate the approximate number of words in the letter or the general length of the message by looking over the writer's rough draft or one's shorthand notes, or by checking the length of a dictated source.

2. Make mental notes of any long quotations, tabular data, long lists or footnotes, or of the occurrence of scientific names and formulas that may require margin adjustments, a different typeface, or even handwork within the message.
3. Set the left and right margin stops according to the estimated letter length: about one inch for very long letters, about one and one-half inches for medium-length ones, and about two inches for very short ones.
4. Use a guide sheet as a bottom margin warning.
5. Continuation-sheet margins should match those of the first sheet, and at least three lines of the message should be carried over to the continuation sheet.

The following illustrations show how letters of varying sizes may be balanced on a page.

A Quick Guide to Attractive Letter Placement on the Page

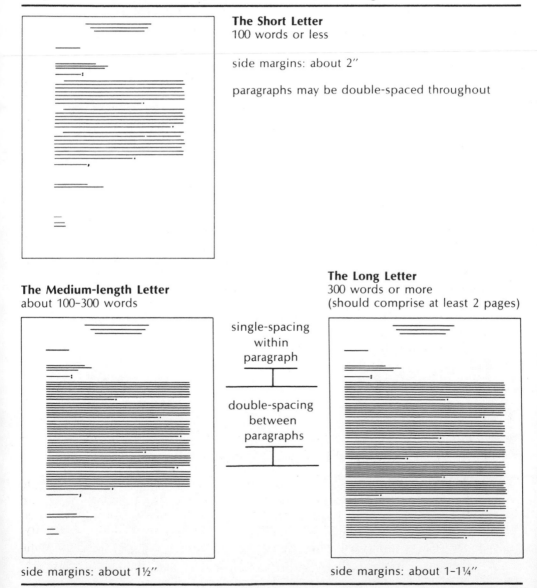

The Short Letter
100 words or less

side margins: about 2"

paragraphs may be double-spaced throughout

The Medium-length Letter
about 100–300 words

The Long Letter
300 words or more
(should comprise at least 2 pages)

single-spacing
within
paragraph

double-spacing
between
paragraphs

side margins: about 1½"

side margins: about 1–1¼"

1.3

LETTERHEAD DESIGN AND LETTER BALANCE

Letterhead designs vary with one's organization. Some letterheads are positioned dead-center at the top of the page, others are laid out across the top of the page from the left to the right margin, and still others are more heavily balanced right or left of center. Sometimes a company's name and logo appear at the top of the page, while its address and other data are printed at the bottom.

Regardless of layout and design, a typical business letterhead contains all or some of the following elements, with the asterisked items being essential:

logo
*full legal name of the firm, company, corporation, institution, or group
*full street address
 suite, room, or building number, if needed—post office box number, if applicable
*city, state, and ZIP Code
 Area Code and telephone number(s)
 other data (as telex or cable references)

The names of particular departments, plants, groups, or divisions may be printed on the letterhead of extremely large or diversified companies or institutions. Other organizations such as large law firms may have the full names of their partners and staff attorneys all listed on the letterhead. Elaborate letterhead layouts require especially careful letter planning to avoid an unbalanced look.

Personalized or executive letterhead for high corporate officers is widely used: the standard company letterhead design is supplemented with the name of the office (as "Office of the President") or with the full name and business title of the officer (as "John M. Jones, Jr., President") printed or engraved in small letters one or two lines beneath the letterhead at or near the left margin. The officer's business title may appear on the same line as his or her name if space permits and if both name and title are short, or it may be blocked directly below the name. Executive stationery is often not printed but instead engraved on a better grade of paper than that of the standard, printed company stationery. Executive stationery is also smaller than the standard, as shown in the table on page 5.

1.4

ALL ABOUT PAPER

Paper and envelope size, quality, and basis weight vary according to application. The table on page 5 lists various paper and envelope sizes along with their uses.

Good-quality paper is an essential element in the production of attractive, effective letters. When one assesses paper quality, one should ask these questions:

1. Will the paper withstand corrections and erasures without pitting, buckling, or tearing?
2. Will the paper accept even and clear typed characters?
3. Will the paper permit smooth written signatures?
4. Will the paper perform well with carbons and in copying machines?
5. Will the paper withstand storage and repeated handling and will its color wear well over long time periods?

Stationery and Envelope Sizes and Applications

Stationery	Stationery Size	Application	Envelope	Envelope Size
Standard	8½″ × 11″ also 8″ × 10½″	general business correspondence	*commercial* No. 6¾ No. 9 No. 10	3⅝″ × 6½″ 3⅞″ × 8⅞″ 4⅛″ × 9½″
			window No. 6¾ No. 9 No. 10	3⅝″ × 6½″ 3⅞″ × 8⅞″ 4⅛″ × 9½″
			airmail No. 6¾ No. 10	3⅝″ × 6½″ 4⅛″ × 9½″
Executive *or* Monarch	7¼″ × 10½″ *or* 7½″ × 10″	high-level corporate officers' correspondence; usually personalized	*regular* Executive *or* Monarch	3⅞″ × 7½″
			window Monarch	3⅞″ × 7½″
Half-sheet *or* Baronial	5½″ × 8½″	extremely brief notes	*regular* Baronial	3⅝″ × 6½″

An important characteristic of paper is its fiber direction or grain. When selecting paper, one should ensure that the grain will be parallel to the direction of the type-written lines, thus providing a smooth surface for clear and even characters, an easy erasing or correcting surface, and a smooth fit of paper against the typewriter platen. Every sheet of paper has what is called a felt side: this is the top side of the paper from which a watermark may be read, and it is from this side of the sheet that the letterhead should be printed or engraved. The table below illustrates various paper weights according to their specific uses.

Weights of Paper for Specific Business Correspondence Applications

Application: letter papers and envelopes	Basis Weight: letter papers and envelopes
Standard (*i.e., corporate correspondence*)	24 *or* 20
Executive	24 *or* 20
Airmail (*especially for overseas correspondence*)	13
Branch-office *or* salesmen's stationery	20 *or* 16
Form letters	20 *or* 24
Continuation sheets	match basis weight of first sheet
Half-sheets	24 *or* 20

Continuation sheets, although blank, must match the letterhead sheet in color, basis weight, texture, size, and quality. Envelopes should match both the first and continuation sheets. Therefore, these materials should be ordered along with the letterhead to ensure a good match.

1.5

GENERAL PUNCTUATION PATTERNS IN BUSINESS CORRESPONDENCE

As with letterhead designs, the choice of general punctuation patterns in business correspondence is usually determined by the organization. However, it is important that specific punctuation patterns be selected for designated letter stylings, and that these patterns be adhered to for the sake of consistency and fast output. The two most common patterns are *open punctuation* and *mixed punctuation.* Their increased popularity in recent years is yet another reflection of the marked trend toward streamlining correspondence, for these patterns have all but totally replaced the older and more complex *closed punctuation* requiring a terminal mark at the end of each element of a business letter—a pattern that was used most often with the now outmoded Indented Letter styling.

OPEN PUNCTUATION PATTERN

1. The end of the date line is unpunctuated, although the comma between day and year is retained.
2. The ends of the lines of the inside address are unpunctuated, unless an abbreviation such as *Inc.* terminates a line, in which case the period after the abbreviation is retained.
3. The salutation if used is unpunctuated.
4. The complimentary close if used is unpunctuated.
5. The ends of the signature block lines are unpunctuated.
6. This pattern is always used with the Simplified Letter (see pages 32–33) and is often used with the Block Letter (see pages 34–35).

Open Punctuation Pattern

The Simplified Letter   **The Block Letter**

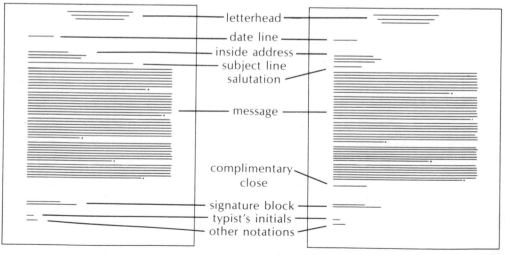

letterhead
date line
inside address
subject line
salutation
message
complimentary close
signature block
typist's initials
other notations

MIXED PUNCTUATION PATTERN

1. The end of the date line is unpunctuated, although the comma between the day and year is retained.
2. The ends of the lines of the inside address are unpunctuated unless an abbreviation such as *Inc.* terminates a line, in which case the period after the abbreviation is retained.
3. The salutation is punctuated with a colon.
4. The complimentary close is punctuated with a comma.
5. The end(s) of the signature block line(s) are unpunctuated.
6. This pattern is used with either the Block, the Modified Block, Modified Semi-block, or the Hanging-indented Letters.

Mixed Punctuation Pattern Illustrated in Four Letter Stylings

The Block Letter · **The Modified Block Letter**

The Modified Semi-block Letter **The Hanging-indented Letter**

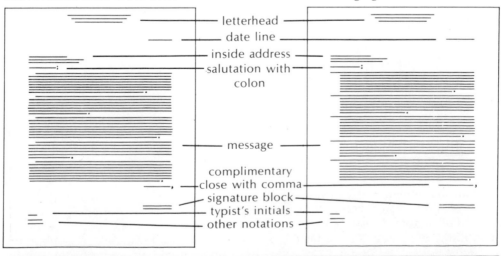

CLOSED PUNCTUATION PATTERN

Although the closed punctuation pattern is not used in the United States today, it is, nevertheless, employed in some European business correspondence. This pattern exhibits these characteristics:

1. A period terminates the date line.
2. A comma terminates each line of the inside address except the last which is ended by a period.
3. A colon punctuates the salutation.
4. A comma punctuates the complimentary close.
5. A comma terminates each line of the signature block except the last which is terminated by a period.
6. This pattern is used chiefly with the Indented Letter.

Closed Punctuation Pattern

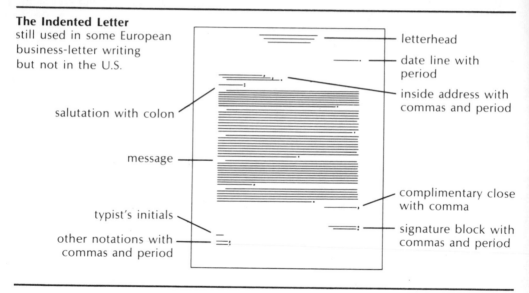

The Indented Letter
still used in some European business-letter writing but not in the U.S.

letterhead

date line with period

inside address with commas and period

salutation with colon

message

complimentary close with comma

typist's initials

signature block with commas and period

other notations with commas and period

It should be added that the above illustration is the only description given in this book of the Indented Letter. It is shown here only as a point of reference for secretaries who may encounter it, especially in foreign correspondence.

1.6

THE INDIVIDUAL PARTS OF A BUSINESS LETTER: A Discussion of Each

The various elements of a business letter are listed below in the order of their occurrence. While asterisked items are essential elements of any letter regardless of its general styling, those items that are unmarked may or may not be included, depending on general styling (as the Simplified Letter or the Block Letter) and on the nature of the letter itself (as general or confidential correspondence):

*date line
  reference line
  special mailing notations
  on-arrival notations
*inside address
  attention line
  salutation
  subject line

*message
  complimentary close
*signature block
  identification initials
  enclosure notation
  carbon copy notation
  postscript

DATE LINE

The date line may be typed two to six lines below the last line of the printed letter-head; however, three-line spacing is recommended as a standard for most letters. Spacing may be expanded or contracted, depending on letter length, space available, letterhead design, and organization policy. In the Simplified Letter, the date is typed six lines below the letterhead at the left margin. The date line consists of the month, the day, and the year: January 1, 19--

The use of an abbreviation or an Arabic numeral for the month is not permitted in date lines, although the day and the month may be reversed and the comma dropped in United States Government correspondence or in British correspondence, where this styling is common: 1 January 19--

The following page placements of date lines are all acceptable, and the choice depends on the general letter styling or the letterhead layout; however, the date line should never overrun either right or left margins.

date line blocked flush with the left margin used with the Block Letter (see letter facsimile, pages 34–35 for full-page views).

date line blocked flush with the right margin so that the last digit of the date is aligned exactly with the margin: may be used with the Modified Block, the Modified Semi-block, and the Hanging-indented Letters.

In order to align a date at the right margin, the typist moves the typewriter carriage to the right margin stop and then backspaces once for each keystroke and space that will be required in the typed date. The secretary can then set the tab stops when typing the first of several letters that will bear the same date.

date line centered directly under the letterhead may be used with the Modified Block or the Modified Semi-block Letters.

date line positioned about five spaces to the right of dead center may be used with the Modified Block or the Modified Semi-block Letters (see page 36).

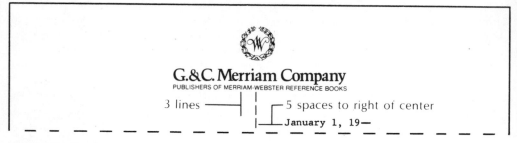

REFERENCE LINE

A reference line with file, correspondence, control, order, invoice, or policy numbers is included in a letter when the addressee has specifically requested that correspondence on a subject contain a reference, or when it is needed for filing. It may be centered and typed one to four lines below the date, although some offices require that it be typed and single-spaced directly above or below the date. With the Block Letter, the reference line should be aligned flush left, regardless of its position either above or below the date. With the Modified Block and the Modified Semi-block Letters, the reference line may be centered on the page or blocked under or above the date line wherever it has been typed.

reference line blocked left	**reference line blocked right**
January 1, 19--	January 1, 19--
X-123-4	X-123-4
or	or
X-123-4	X-123-4
January 1, 19--	January 1, 19--

Reference Line Blocked with Date Line to Right of Dead Center

Reference Number Centered on Page Four Lines Beneath Date Line

Reference lines on the first sheet must be carried over to the heading of a continuation sheet or sheets. The styling of the date line and the reference line on a continuation sheet should match the one on the first page as closely as possible; for example, if the reference line appears on a line below the date on the first sheet, it should be so typed on the continuation sheet. The first setup below illustrates a continuation-sheet reference line as used with the Simplified or Block Letters:

Mr. John B. Jones
January 1, 19--
X-123-4
Page 2

The second example illustrates the positioning of a reference line on the continuation sheet of a Modified Block, a Modified Semi-block, or a Hanging-indented Letter:

Mr. John B. Jones   -2-   January 1, 19--
                                                                             X-123-4

See page 19 for continuation-sheet facsimiles.

SPECIAL MAILING NOTATIONS

If a letter is to be sent by any method other than by regular mail, that fact is indicated on the letter itself and on the envelope (see pages 41–48 for details on envelope styling). The all-capitalized special mailing notation (as CERTIFIED MAIL or SPECIAL DELIVERY) is aligned flush left about four lines below the line on

Special Mailing Notation vis-à-vis Inside Address and Date Line

G.&C. Merriam Company
PUBLISHERS OF MERRIAM-WEBSTER REFERENCE BOOKS

January 1, 19—
                    ———— 4 lines

SPECIAL DELIVERY
                    ———— 2 lines
Mr. John B. Jones
XYZ Corporation
1234 Smith Boulevard
Smithville, ST 56789

which the date appears, and about two lines above the first line of the inside address. While some organizations prefer that this notation appear on the original and on all copies, others prefer that the notation be typed only on the original.

Vertical spacing (as between the date line and the special mailing notation) may vary with letter length, i.e., more space may be left for short or medium letter lengths.

ON-ARRIVAL NOTATIONS

The on-arrival notations that may be included in the letter itself are PERSONAL and CONFIDENTIAL. The first indicates that the letter may be opened and read only by its addressee; the second, that the letter may be opened and read by its addressee and/or any other person or persons authorized to view such material. These all-capitalized notations are usually positioned four lines below the date line and usually two but not more than four lines above the first line of the inside address. They are blocked flush left in all letter stylings. If a special mailing notation has been used, the on-arrival notation is blocked one line beneath it. Spacing between the date line and the on-arrival notation may be increased to as much as six lines if the letter is extremely brief.

If either PERSONAL or CONFIDENTIAL appears in the letter, it must also appear on the envelope (see pages 41–44 for envelope styling).

On-arrival Notation vis-à-vis Date Line, Special Mailing Notation, and Inside Address

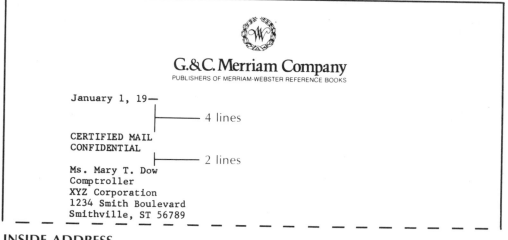

INSIDE ADDRESS

An inside address typically includes:

1. *if letter is directed to a particular individual*
   addressee's courtesy title + full name
   addressee's business title if required
   full name of addressee's business affiiliation
   full geographical address   .
2. *if letter is addressed to an organization in general*
   full name of the firm, company, corporation, or institution
   individual department name if required
   full geographical address

It is placed about three to eight, but not more than 12 lines below the date. The inside address in the Simplified Letter is typed three lines below the date. Inside-address page placement relative to the date may be expanded or contracted according to letter length or organization policy. The inside address is always single-spaced internally. In all of the letters discussed in this book, the inside address is blocked flush with the left margin.

Inside Address Styling Used with the Block Letter

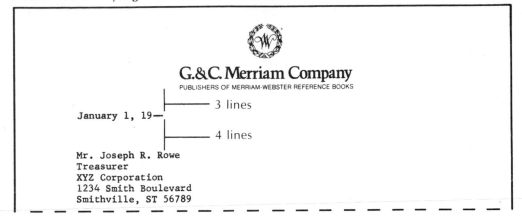

A courtesy title (as *Mr., Ms., Mrs., Miss,* or *Dr.*) should always be typed before the addressee's full name, even if a business title (as *Treasurer*) is also included after the surname (see the Forms of Address chart on pages 45–75 of this chapter for a full list and discussion of special titles).

Before typing the addressee's full name, the secretary should, if possible, refer to the signature block of previous correspondence from that individual to ascertain the exact spelling and styling of the name. This information may also be obtained from printed executive letterhead. A business title, if included, should also match the styling in previous correspondence or in official literature (such as an annual report). Business titles should not be abbreviated. If an individual holds several offices (as *Vice-president and General Manager*) within an organization, the title shown in the signature block of previous correspondence should be copied, or the title of the individual's highest office (in this case, *Vice-president*) may be selected. If a business title is so long that it might overrun the center of the page, it may be typed on two lines with the second line indented two spaces, as

Mr. John P. Hemphill, Jr.
Vice-president and Director
  of Research and Development

The following are acceptable inside-address stylings for business titles; however, care should be taken to choose the one that will enhance and not detract from the total balance of the letter on the page:

Mr. Arthur O. Brown
News Director
Radio Station WXYZ
1234 Peters Street
Jonesville, ZZ 56789

In the above example, the business title forms line 2 of the inside address. This format is acceptable with all letter styles.

Ms. Ann B. Lowe, Director
Apex Community Theater
67 Smith Street
North Bend, XX 12345

Here, the business title ends line 1 and is separated from the addressee's surname by a comma—a format recommended for short names and titles that may be used with all letter styles: the Simplified, the Block, the Modified Block, the Modified Semi-block, and the Hanging-indented Letters.

Mrs. Joyce A. Cavitt
President, C & A Realty
Johnson Beach, ZZ 56789

The business title heads line 2 and is separated from the addressee's business affiliation by a comma. This format is recommended for short titles and short business-affiliation names, and may be used with all letter styles: the Simplified, the Block, the Modified Block, the Modified Semi-block, and the Hanging-indented Letters.

If an individual addressee's name is unknown or irrelevant and the writer wishes to direct a letter to an organization in general or to a unit within that organization, the organization name is typed on line 1 of the inside address, followed on line 2 by the name of a specific department if required. The full address of the organization is then typed on subsequent lines, as

XYZ Corporation
Consumer Products Division
1234 Smith Boulevard
Smithville, ST 56789

The organization name should be styled exactly as it appears on the letterhead of previous correspondence, or as it appears in printed sources (as annual reports or business directories).

Street addresses should be typed in full and not abbreviated unless window envelopes are being used (as in mass automated office mailings). Arabic numerals should be used for all building and house numbers except *one*, which should be typed out in letters, as

One Bayside Drive
but
6 Link Road
1436 Freemont Avenue

and Arabic numerals should be used for all numbered street names above *twelve*, as

145 East 14th Street

but numbered street names from *one* through *twelve* should be spelled out:

167 West Second Avenue   One East Ninth Street

If a numbered street name over *twelve* follows a house number with no intervening word or words (as a compass direction), a spaced hyphen is inserted between the house number and the street-name number, as

2018 – 14th Street

An apartment, building, or suite number if required should follow the street address on the same line with two spaces or a comma separating the two:

62 Park Towers Suite 9   62 Park Towers, Suite 9

Names of cities (except those following the pattern of *St. Louis* or *St. Paul*) should be typed out in full. The name of the city is followed by a comma and then by the name of the state and the ZIP Code. Names of states (except for the District of Columbia which is always styled *DC* or *D.C.*) may or may not be abbreviated: if a window envelope is being used, the all-capitalized, unpunctuated two-letter Postal Service abbreviation followed by <u>one space</u> and the ZIP Code must be used; on the other hand, if a regular envelope is being used, the name of the state may be typed out in full followed by one space and the ZIP Code, or the two-letter Postal Service abbreviation may be used. For the sake of fewer keystrokes and consistency, it is recommended that the Postal Service abbreviations be used throughout the material.

An inside address should comprise no more than five typed lines. No line should overrun the center of the page. Lengthy organizational names, however, like lengthy business titles, may be carried over to a second line and indented two spaces from the left margin.

ATTENTION LINE

If the writer wishes to address a letter to an organization in general but also to bring it to the attention of a particular individual at the same time, an attention line may be typed two lines below the last line of the inside address and two lines above the salutation if there is one. The attention line is usually blocked flush with the left margin; it must be so blocked in the Simplified and Block Letters. On the other hand, some organizations prefer that the attention line be centered on the page: this placement is acceptable with all letters except the Simplified and the Block. However, for the sake of fast output, it is generally recommended that the attention line be aligned with the left margin. This line should be neither underlined nor entirely capitalized; only its main elements are capitalized. Placement of a colon after the word *Attention* is optional unless the open punctuation pattern is being followed throughout the letter, in which case the colon should be omitted:

Attention Mr. John P. Doe   *or*   Attention: Mr. John P. Doe

The salutation appearing beneath the attention line should be "Gentlemen" even though the attention line routes the letter to a particular person. Such a letter is actually written to the organization; hence, the collective-noun salutation.

Page Placement of an Attention Line in a Block Letter with Open Punctuation

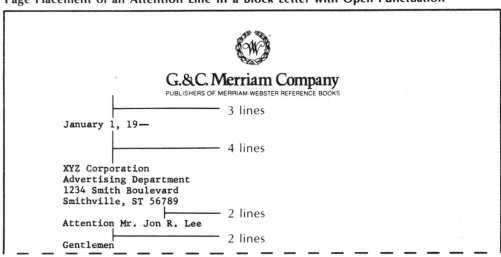

SALUTATION

The salutation—used with all letter stylings except the Simplified—is typed flush with the left margin, usually two to four lines beneath the last line of the inside address or two lines below the attention line if there is one. Additional vertical lines of space may be added after the inside address of a short letter which is to be enclosed in a window envelope. The first letter of the first word of the salutation is capitalized, as are the first letters of the addressee's courtesy title and surname.

If the mixed punctuation pattern is being followed in the letter, the salutation is followed by a colon; if open punctuation is being observed, the salutation is unpunctuated. The following are typical examples of various salutations, the last four of which are used in letters to high-level personages (as in the government, the diplomatic corps, or the clergy):

most commonly used
Gentlemen
Dear Mr. (*or* Ms., Mrs., Miss, Dr., Professor) Smith
Dear Bob
reserved for high-level personages
My dear Justice Roberts
Your Excellency
Excellency
Right Reverend and dear Father

The salutation "Dear Sir" is rarely used today except in form letters and in letters to high-level personages (as the President-elect of the U.S.). Although the salutation "Dear Sirs" is now considered archaic in American business writing, it is still used in Great Britain.

With the advent of the Women's Rights Movement and the ensuing national interest in equal rights and equal opportunity, some writers—both male and female—have discarded the conventional salutation "Gentlemen" and have coined what they feel are more neutral, non-sexist replacements for letters addressed to organizations whose officers may be both male and female. Although a number of writers have used the following salutations, widespread general usage over a long time span has not yet been achieved and these expressions are therefore still not considered conventional:

Gentlepeople   Gentlepersons   Dear People   Dear Sir, Madam, or Ms.

The most conventional way of addressing a male-female group is to write

Ladies and Gentlemen   *or*   Dear Sir or Madam

although the latter expression has become less popular in recent years since the use of *Madam* in a letter to an unmarried woman may offend her. The most convenient way to avoid the problem of sexual semantics altogether is to use the salutationless Simplified Letter styling.

When a letter is addressed to an all-female organization, the following salutations may be used:

Ladies   *or*   Mesdames

The salutation for a married couple is styled as

Dear Mr. and Mrs. Hathaway
Dear Dr. and Mrs. Simpson

Salutations for letters addressed to two or more persons having the same or different surnames may be found in the Forms of Address section, page 75. Salutations in letters addressed to persons with specialized titles may also be found in the Forms of Address section, pages 45–74.

SUBJECT LINE
A subject line gives the gist of the letter. Its phrasing is necessarily succinct and to the point: it should not be so long as to require more than one line. The subject line serves as an immediate point of reference for the reader as well as a convenient filing tool for the secretaries at both ends of the correspondence.

In the salutationless Simplified Letter, the subject line (an essential element) is positioned flush left, three lines below the last line of the inside address. The subject line may be entirely capitalized and not underlined. As an alternative, the main words in the subject line may be capitalized and every word underlined.

   If a subject line is included in a letter featuring a salutation, it is positioned flush left, two lines beneath the salutation, and may be entirely capitalized. Also, the word *subject* may be used to introduce the line as follows:

SUBJECT: CHANGE IN TRAFFIC ROUTE

Page Placement of the Subject Line in the Simplified Letter

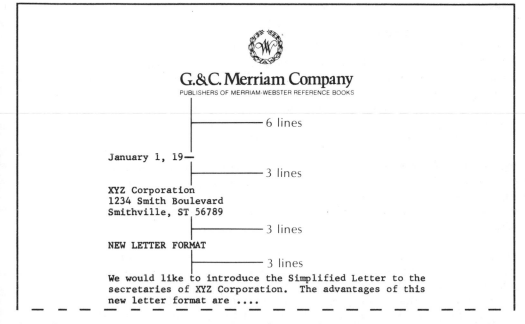

Page Placement of the Subject Line with a Short Block Letter, Open Punctuation

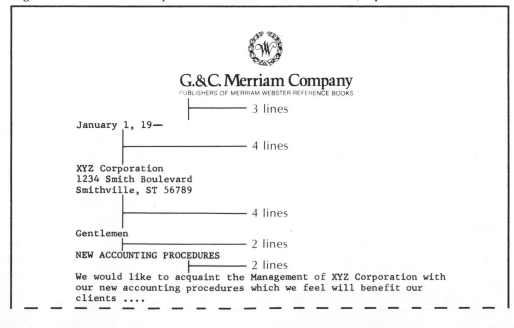

While the subject-line headings *In re* and *Re* are now seldom recommended for general business letters, they are nevertheless often used in legal correspondence. Some offices still prefer use of the headings

SUBJECT: *or*   Subject: *or*   Reference:

followed by the rest of the subject line, but the unheaded line is the most common except in government and military correspondence (see pages 84 and 87). Headings should not be used if one is following the Simplified Letter styling.

MESSAGE

The body of the letter—the message—should begin about two lines below the salutation or two lines below the subject line if there is one in all letter stylings except the Simplified Letter, where the message is typed three lines below the subject line.

Paragraphs are single-spaced internally and double-spaced between each other. If a letter is extremely brief, its paragraphs may be double-spaced throughout the letter. Indentations then identify paragraphs.

Equal margins measuring one inch for long letters, about one and one-half inches for medium-length letters, and at least two inches for short letters should be kept (see Section 1.2 for a discussion of attractive letter page placement).

The first lines of indented paragraphs (as in the Modified Semi-block Letter) should begin five to ten spaces from the left margin; however, the five-space pattern is the most common. With the Hanging-indented Letter, the first lines of the paragraphs are blocked flush left, while subsequent lines are indented and blocked five spaces from the left margin. All other letter stylings require flush-left paragraph alignment.

Long quotations should be indented and blocked five to ten spaces from the left and right margins with internal single-spacing and top-and-bottom double-spacing so that the material will be set off from the rest of the message. Long enumerations should also be indented: enumerations with items requiring more than one line apiece may require single-spacing within each item, followed by double-spacing between items. Tabular data should be centered on the page.

Page Placement of a Long Quotation   **Page Placement of an Enumeration**

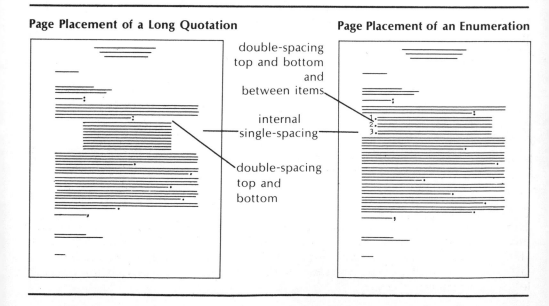

If a letter is long enough to require a continuation sheet or sheets, at least three message lines must be carried over to the next page. The complimentary close and/or typed signature block should never stand alone on a continuation sheet. The last word on a page should not be divided. Continuation-sheet margins should match those of the first sheet. At least six blank lines equaling one inch should be maintained at the top of the continuation sheet. The two most common continuation-sheet headings are described below.

Continuation-sheet Heading: Simplified and Block Letters

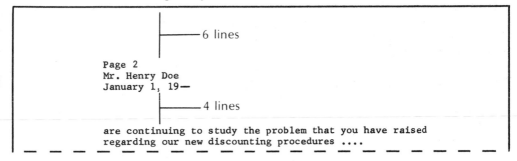

The format shown above is used with the Simplified and Block Letters. It features a flush-left heading beginning with the page number, followed on the next line by the addressee's courtesy title and full name, and ending with the date on the third line. Some companies prefer that the page number appear as the last line of the continuation-sheet heading, especially if a reference number is included.

Another way to type the heading of a continuation sheet is to lay the material out across the page, six lines down from the top edge of the sheet. The addressee's name is typed flush with the left margin, the page number in Arabic numerals is centered on the same line and enclosed with spaced hyphens, and the date is aligned flush with the right margin—all on the same line. This format is often used with the Modified Block, the Modified Semi-block, and the Hanging-indented Letters.

Continuation-sheet Heading: Used with Modified Block, Modified Semi-block, and Hanging-indented Letters

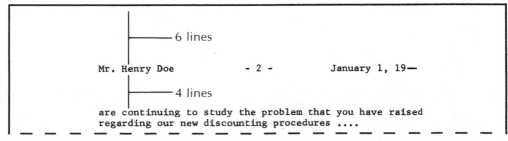

COMPLIMENTARY CLOSE

There is no complimentary close in the Simplified Letter. However, a complimentary close is used with the Block, Modified Block, Modified Semi-block, and Hanging-indented Letters. The complimentary close is typed two lines below the last line of the message in all letters. Its page placement depends on the general letter styling being used:

complimentary close with the Block Letter the complimentary close is blocked flush with the left margin.

Open Punctuation Pattern Shown in Block Letter Format for Complimentary Close

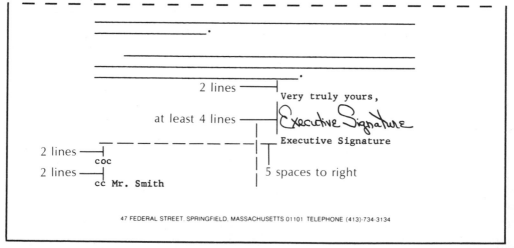

complimentary close with the Modified Block, the Modified Semi-block, and the Hanging-indented Letters the complimentary close may be aligned directly under the date line (e.g., about five spaces to the right of dead center, or flush with the right margin) or under some particular part of the printed letterhead. It should never overrun the right margin.

Complimentary Close Five Spaces to Right of Center as in a Modified Block Letter with Mixed Punctuation

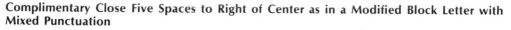

Only the first word of the complimentary close is capitalized. If the open punctuation pattern is being followed, the complimentary close is unpunctuated. If the mixed punctuation pattern is being followed, a comma terminates the complimentary close. The following chart lists the most often used complimentary closes, and also groups them according to general tone and degree of formality. For a complete list of complimentary closes for letters addressed to high-level officials and to persons with specialized titles, see Forms of Address.

General Tone & Degree of Formality	Complimentary Close
highly formal—usually used in diplomatic, governmental, or ecclesiastical correspondence to show respect and deference to a high-ranking addressee	Respectfully yours Respectfully Very respectfully
politely neutral—usually used in general correspondence	Very truly yours Yours very truly Yours truly
friendly and less formal—usually used in general correspondence	Most sincerely Very sincerely Very sincerely yours Sincerely yours Yours sincerely Sincerely
more friendly and informal—often used when writer and reader are on a first-name basis but also often used in general business correspondence	Most cordially Yours cordially Cordially yours Cordially
most friendly and informal—usually used when writer and reader are on a first-name basis	As ever Best wishes Best regards Kindest regards Kindest personal regards Regards
British	Yours faithfully Yours sincerely

The typist should always use the complimentary close that is dictated because the writer may have a special reason for the choice of phrasing. If the dictator does not specify a particular closing, the typist may wish to select the one that best reflects the general tone of the letter and the state of the writer-reader relationship.

SIGNATURE BLOCK
With the Simplified Letter, the name of the writer is typed entirely in capitals flush left at least five lines below the last line of the message. If the writer's business title is not included in the printed letterhead, it may be typed on the same line as the name entirely in capitals and separated from the last element of the name by a spaced hyphen, as

JOHN P. HEWETT - DIRECTOR

although some organizations prefer to use a comma in place of the hyphen, as

JOHN P. HEWETT, DIRECTOR

or a combination of the two punctuation marks may be used if the title is complex, as

JOHN P. HEWETT - DIRECTOR, TECHNICAL INFORMATION
or
JOHN P. HEWETT · DIRECTOR
TECHNICAL INFORMATION CENTER

Page Placement of Signature Block, Simplified Letter

With the Block Letter, the signature block is aligned flush left at least four lines below the complimentary close. Only the first letter of each element of the writer's name is capitalized, and only the first letter of each major element of the writer's business title and/or department name are capitalized if they are included. The business title and the department name may be omitted if they appear in the printed letterhead:

John D. Russell, Director	*if title and department name*
Consumer Products Division	*are needed for identification*
or	
John D. Russell	*if department name is already*
Director	*printed on the letterhead*
or	
John D. Russell	*if both title and department*
	name appear in printed letterhead

Signature Block in the Block Letter

With the Modified Block, the Modified Semi-block, and the Hanging-indented Letters, the signature block begins with the name of the writer typed at least four lines below the complimentary close. The first letter of the first element of each line in the signature block is aligned directly below the first letter of the first element of the complimentary close, unless this alignment will result in an overrunning of the right margin, in which case the signature block may be centered under the complimentary close. Only the first letter of each of the major elements of the writer's name, title (if used), and department name (if used) are capitalized:

(Ms.) Sarah L. Talbott, Director   *or*   (Ms.) Sarah L. Talbott   *or*   (Ms.) Sarah L. Talbott
Marketing Division   Director

Signature Block Five Spaces to Right of Center as in a Modified Block Letter with Mixed Punctuation

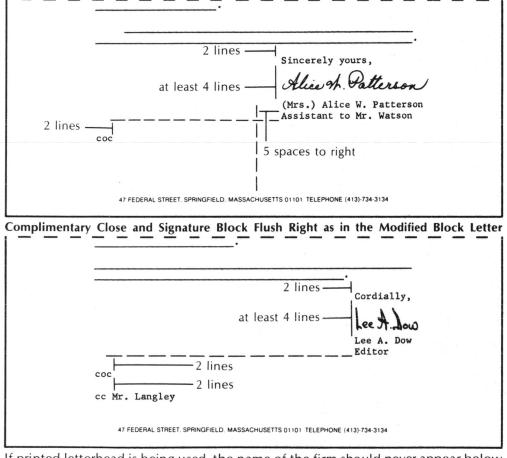

If printed letterhead is being used, the name of the firm should <u>never</u> appear below the complimentary close. If printed letterhead is <u>not</u> being used, the name of the firm may be typed all in capitals two lines beneath the complimentary close with the first letter of the firm's name aligned directly underneath, as

Very truly yours,

AJAX VAN LINES, INC.

Samuel O. Lescott
Dispatcher

with the writer's name typed in capitals and lowercase at least four lines below the firm's name. The writer's title if needed is typed in capitals and lowercase on a line directly underneath the signature line.

If the company name is long enough to overrun the right margin, it may be centered beneath the complimentary close in the Modified Block and the Modified Semi-block Letters, as

---

Very truly yours,

JOHNSON AEROSPACE ENGINEERING ASSOCIATES

Sidney C. Johnson

Sidney C. Johnson, Ph.D.
President

Regardless of page placement and letter styling, the name of the writer should be typed exactly as he signs his name. If applicable, any academic degrees (as *Ph.D.*) or professional ratings (as *P.E.*) that the writer holds should be included after his surname so that the recipient of the letter will know the proper form of address to use in his or her reply. For example:

Typed Signature	**Salutation in Reply**
Francis E. Atlee, M.D.	Dear Dr. Atlee:
Ellen Y. Langford, Ph.D. Dean of Women	Dear Dr. Langford *or* Dear Dean Langford
Carol I. Etheridge, C.P.A. *or* (Mrs.) Carol I. Etheridge, C.P.A.	Dear Ms. Etheridge Dear Mrs. Etheridge

These academic and professional degrees and ratings need not be repeated in the signature line if they are already included in the printed letterhead, and they are never included in the written signature.

The only titles that may precede a typed signature are *Ms., Mrs.,* and *Miss,* even though they are not included in the writer's written signature. These titles are enclosed in parentheses and are blocked flush left in the Simplified and the Block Letters, and they are aligned with or centered under the complimentary close in the Modified Block, the Modified Semi-block, and the Hanging-indented Letters.

**Signature Stylings
for Unmarried Women**   or   or

Sincerely yours	Sincerely yours	Sincerely yours
Joan Dunn	*Joan Dunn*	*Joan Dunn*
Joan Dunn Vice-president	(Ms.) Joan Dunn Vice-president	(Miss) Joan Dunn Vice-president

---

Signature Stylings for Women who Consider their Marital Status Irrelevant

Sincerely yours   or   Sincerely yours

[signature: Joan Dunn]

(Ms.) Joan Dunn
Vice-president

[signature: Joan Dunn]

Joan Dunn
Vice-president

Signature Stylings for Married Women Using Given Name + Maiden Name Initial + Husband's Surname

Sincerely yours   or   Sincerely yours

[signature: Joan M. Dunn]

(Mrs.) Joan M. Dunn
Vice-president

[signature: Joan M. Dunn]

(Ms.) Joan M. Dunn
Vice-president

Signature Stylings for Married Woman Using her Husband's Full Name

Sincerely yours

[signature: Joan Dunn]

Mrs. Robert A. Dunn
Vice-president

A widow may use either her first name and her maiden name initial and her late husband's surname with the courtesy title *Mrs.* or *Ms.* enclosed in parentheses, or she may use her husband's full name with *Mrs.*, as

Sincerely yours   Sincerely yours

[signature: Joan M. Dunn]   *[signature: Joan Dunn]*

(Mrs.) Joan M. Dunn   Mrs. Robert A. Dunn
or (Ms.)

A divorcee may use her maiden name if it has been legally regained, along with the courtesy title *Ms.* or *Miss* enclosed by parentheses or she may omit the title:

Sincerely yours   Sincerely yours

[signature: Joan M. Dunn]   *[signature: Joan M. Dunn]*

(Ms.) Joan M. Dunn   Joan M. Dunn
or (Miss)

or she may use her maiden name and her former husband's surname with *Mrs.*:

Sincerely yours

Joan Dunn

Mrs. Matthews Dunn

If the secretary signs a letter for the dictator or writer, his name is followed by the typist's initials immediately below and to the right of the surname, or centered under the full name, as

David R. Robins lc   *David R. Robins* lc

If the secretary signs a letter in her own name for someone else, that individual's courtesy title and surname <u>only</u> are typed directly below, as

Sincerely yours   Sincerely yours

Janet A. Smith   *Seymour T. Barnes*

(Miss) Janet A. Smith   Seymour T. Barnes
Assistant to Mr. Wood   Assistant to Senator Ross

Sincerely yours

Lee L. Linden

Lee L. Linden
Secretary to Ms. Key

IDENTIFICATION INITIALS

The initials of the typist and sometimes those of the writer are placed two lines below the last line of the signature block, and are aligned flush left in all letter stylings. There is a marked trend towards complete omission of the writer's initials if the name is already typed in the signature block or if it appears in the printed letterhead. In the Simplified Letter, the writer and/or dictator's initials are usually omitted, and the typist's initials if included on the original are typed in lowercase. Many organizations indicate the typist's initials only on carbons for record-keeping purposes, and they do not show the dictator's initials unless another individual signs the letter. These are common stylings:

FCM/HL	FCM:HL	Franklin C. Mason:HL
FM/hl	FCM:HOL	
		Franklin C. Mason
hol	FCM:hl	HL
hl	FCM:hol	
	fcm:hol	

A letter dictated by one person (as an administrative secretary), typed by another (as a corresponding secretary), and signed by yet another person (as the writer) may show (1) the writer/signer's initials entirely in capitals followed by a colon and (2) the dictator's initials entirely in capitals followed by a colon and (3) the transcriber/typist's initials in lowercase, as AWM:COC:ls

ENCLOSURE NOTATION

If a letter is to be accompanied by an enclosure or enclosures, one of the following expressions should be aligned flush left and typed one to two lines beneath the identification initials, if there are any, or one to two lines beneath the last line of the signature block, if there is no identification line:

Enclosure   *or if more than one*   Enclosures (3)
or
enc. *or* encl.   *or if more than one*   3 encs.

If the enclosures are of special importance, each of them should be numerically listed and briefly described with single-spacing between each item:

Enclosures: 1. Annual Report (19--), 2 copies
2. List of Major Accounts
3. Profit and Loss Statement (19--)

The following type of notation then may be typed in the top right corner of each page of each of the enclosures:

Enclosure (1) to <u>company name</u> letter No. 1-234-X,
dated January 1, <u>19--</u>, page 2 of 8
(if enclosure has more than one page)

If the enclosure is bound, a single notation attached to its cover sheet will suffice.

CARBON COPY NOTATION

A carbon copy notation showing the distribution of courtesy copies to other individuals should be aligned flush left and typed two lines below the signature block if there are no other notations or initials, or two lines below any other notations. If space is very tight, the carbon copy notation may be single-spaced below the above-mentioned items. The most common stylings are:

cc   cc: Copy to   Copies to

This notation may appear on the original and all copies or only on the copies.

Multiple recipients of copies should be listed alphabetically. Sometimes only their initials are shown, as

cc: WPB
TLC
CNR

or the individuals' names may be shown, especially if the writer feels that such information can be useful to the addressee:

cc: William L. Carton, Esq.   *or*   cc: Ms. Lee Jamieson
45 Park Towers, Suite 1   Copy to Mr. John K. Long
Smithville, ST 56789   Copies to Mr. Houghton
                                                     Mr. Ott
Dr. Daniel I. Maginnis   Mr. Smythe
1300 Dover Drive
Jonesville, ZZ 12345

If the recipient of the copy is to receive an enclosure or enclosures as well, that individual's full name and address as well as a description of each enclosure and the total number of enclosed items should be shown in the carbon copy notation:

cc: Ms. Barbra S. Lee (2 copies, Annual Report)
      123 Jones Street
      Smithville, ST 56789

      Ms. Sara T. Tufts
      Ms. Laura E. Yowell

If the writer wishes that copies of the letter be distributed without this list being shown on the original, the blind carbon copy notation   bcc   or   bcc: followed by an alphabetical list of the recipients' initials or names may be typed on the carbons in the same page position as a regular carbon copy notation. The *bcc* notation may also appear in the upper left-hand corner of the carbon copies.

Page Placement of Identification and Enclosure Notations

```
      Sincerely yours

      Executive Signature

      Executive Signature
      Business Title if Needed
      ├───────────────── 2 lines
coc
      ├───────────────── 2 lines
      Enclosures (7)




              47 FEDERAL STREET, SPRINGFIELD, MASSACHUSETTS 01101 TELEPHONE (413)-734-3134
```

POSTSCRIPT
A postscript is aligned flush left and is typed two to four lines (depending on space available) below the last notation. If the letter's paragraphs are strict-block, the postscript reflects this format. If the paragraphs within the letter are indented, the first line of the postscript is also indented. If the Hanging-indented Letter styling is used, the first line of the postscript is flush left and all subsequent lines are indented five spaces. All postscripts are single-spaced. Their margins conform with those maintained in the letters themselves. The writer should initial a postscript. While it is not incorrect to head a postscript with the initials *P.S.* (for an initial postscript) and *P.P.S.* (for subsequent ones), these headings are redundant and require extra keystrokes; therefore, it is recommended that they be omitted.

1.7

ESSENTIAL LETTER STYLES FOR TODAY'S BUSINESS CORRESPONDENCE

LETTER FACSIMILES
The following is a list of full-page letter facsimiles of the five most often used business-letter formats:

The Simplified Letter
The Block Letter
The Modified Block Letter
The Modified Semi-block Letter
The Hanging-indented Letter

In addition, the section contains facsimiles of the following letters:

The Official Letter Styling (Executive)
The Official Letter Styling (plain bond)
The Half-sheet

Each facsimile contains a detailed description of letter format and styling.

The Official Letter Styling with Printed Executive Letterhead

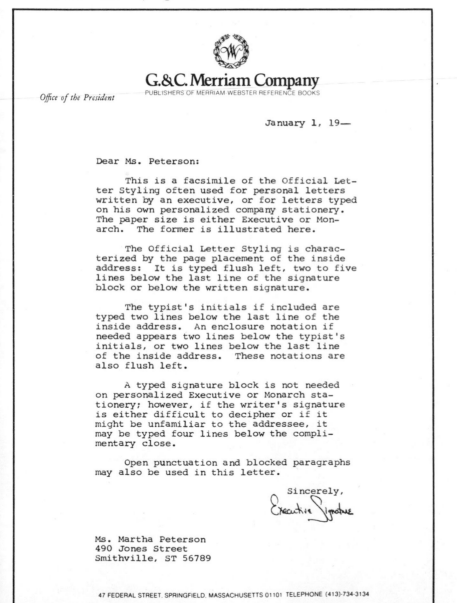

Letter facsimile text:

G.&C. Merriam Company

PUBLISHERS OF MERRIAM-WEBSTER REFERENCE BOOKS

Office of the President

January 1, 19—

Dear Ms. Peterson:

This is a facsimile of the Official Letter Styling often used for personal letters written by an executive, or for letters typed on his own personalized company stationery. The paper size is either Executive or Monarch. The former is illustrated here.

The Official Letter Styling is characterized by the page placement of the inside address: It is typed flush left, two to five lines below the last line of the signature block or below the written signature.

The typist's initials if included are typed two lines below the last line of the inside address. An enclosure notation if needed appears two lines below the typist's initials, or two lines below the last line of the inside address. These notations are also flush left.

A typed signature block is not needed on personalized Executive or Monarch stationery; however, if the writer's signature is either difficult to decipher or if it might be unfamiliar to the addressee, it may be typed four lines below the complimentary close.

Open punctuation and blocked paragraphs may also be used in this letter.

Sincerely,

Executive Signature

Ms. Martha Peterson
490 Jones Street
Smithville, ST 56789

47 FEDERAL STREET. SPRINGFIELD. MASSACHUSETTS 01101 TELEPHONE (413)-734-3134

The Official Letter Styling with Plain Executive Letterhead

                                        4400 Ambler Boulevard
                                        Smithville, ST 56789
                                        January 1, 19—

Dear Bob

This is a facsimile of a letter typed on plain
Executive or Monarch stationery. The basic
format is the same as that of the Official Letter Styling. The block paragraphs and the open
punctuation pattern are illustrated here.

The heading which includes the writer's full
address and the date may be positioned six lines
from the top edge of the page and flush with the
right margin as shown here. Approximately six
vertical lines may be placed after the date line
down to the salutation.

The complimentary close is typed two lines below the last line of the message. The inside
address is flush left, two to five lines below
the last line of the signature block or below
the written signature.

Typist's initials, if included, should be positioned two lines beneath the last line of the
inside address. An enclosure notation or any
other notation if required should be typed two
lines below the typist's initials or two lines
below the last line of the inside address if
there are no initials.

                                        Sincerely

                                        Executive Signature

Mr. Robert Y. Owens
123 East Second Avenue
Jonesville, ST 45678

The Hanging-indented Letter

G.&C. Merriam Company
PUBLISHERS OF MERRIAM-WEBSTER REFERENCE BOOKS

January 1, 19—

Mrs. Althea Nance
Assistant to the President
XYZ Corporation
1234 Smith Boulevard
Smithville, ST 56789

Dear Mrs. Nance:

This is a facsimile of the Hanging-indented Letter which is not ordinarily used
    in general business correspondence but rather in advertising letters as an
    attractive way of catching the reader's eye. Its main feature is the para-
    graph alignment: The first line of each paragraph is aligned flush left,
    but all subsequent lines are indented five spaces from the left margin.
    The paragraphs are single-spaced internally and double-spaced between each
    other. Either the open or the mixed punctuation pattern may be used in
    the Hanging-indented Letter: This facsimile illustrates the mixed pattern.

The date line, usually typed three lines below the last line of the letterhead,
    is aligned flush right. The inside address and salutation are blocked
    flush left. Spacing between these elements parallels the Modified Block
    and the Modified Semi-block Letters.

Continuation sheets must contain at least three message lines, and the last word
    on the first sheet must not be divided. Continuation-sheet headings may be
    blocked left as in the Block Letter or laid out across the top of the page
    as in the Modified Semi-block Letter. Six blank lines are left from the
    top edge of the page to the first line of the heading and four blank lines
    are left before typing the message. Margins and paragraph alignment par-
    allel those of the first sheet.

The complimentary close and the signature block are aligned under the date.
    Double-spacing is needed between the last message line and the complimen-
    tary close. At least four lines should be left for the written signature.

Identification initials, and enclosure and carbon copy notations are blocked
    flush left at least two lines below the last line of the signature block.
    Postscripts, if needed, are also hanging-indented.

Cordially,

Executive Signature

coc

47 FEDERAL STREET, SPRINGFIELD, MASSACHUSETTS 01101 TELEPHONE (413)-734-3134

The Simplified Letter

G.&C. Merriam Company
PUBLISHERS OF MERRIAM-WEBSTER REFERENCE BOOKS

January 1, 19—

Ms. Sarah H. Smith
Director of Marketing
XYZ Corporation
1234 Smith Boulevard
Smithville, ST 56789

SIMPLIFIED LETTER

Ms. Smith, this is the Simplified Letter recommended by the Administrative Management Society. Its main features—block format,
open punctuation, and fewer internal parts—reduce the number of
keystrokes and typewriter adjustments your secretary must make,
thus cutting costs, saving time, and increasing overall letter
output.

The date line is typed six lines below the last letterhead line.
The inside address, also flush left, appears three lines below the
date line. Since the placement of the inside address is designed
for window envelopes, it is suggested that the all-capitalized,
unpunctuated Postal Service State abbreviation be typed after the
city name, followed by one space and the ZIP Code.

The traditional salutation has been dropped and replaced by an unheaded, all-capitalized subject line typed flush left, three lines
beneath the last inside-address line. The subject line summarizes
the message.

The first message line begins three lines below the subject line.
The first sentence serves as a greeting to the reader. The addressee's name should appear in the first paragraph, preferably in
the first sentence as shown above. Inclusion of the name adds a
personal touch. All paragraphs are blocked flush left, single-
spaced internally, and double-spaced between each other. Tabular
data and numbered lists are also blocked flush left but are set
off from the rest of the message by double-spacing. Long quotations and unnumbered lists should be indented five to ten spaces
from the left and right margins and set off from the rest of the
message by top and bottom double-spacing.

47 FEDERAL STREET, SPRINGFIELD, MASSACHUSETTS 01101 TELEPHONE (413) 734-3134

Ms. Smith
Page 2
January 1, 19—

If a continuation sheet is required, at least three message lines
must be carried over. Continuation-sheet format and margins match
those of the first sheet. At least six blank lines are left from
the top edge of the page to the first line of the heading which is
blocked flush left, single-spaced internally, and typically composed of the addressee's courtesy title and name, the page number,
and the applicable date. The rest of the message begins four lines
beneath the last heading line.

There is no complimentary close in the Simplified Letter, although
closing sentences such as "You have my best wishes," and "My best
regards are yours" may end the message. The writer's name (and
business title if needed) is aligned flush left and typed all in
capitals at least five lines below the last message line. Although
the Administrative Management Society uses a spaced hyphen between
the writer's surname and his business title, some companies prefer
a comma. The writer's department name may be typed flush left all
in capitals, one line below the signature line.

The identification initials, flush left and two lines below the
last line of the signature block, comprise the typist's initials
only. An enclosure notation may be typed one line below the identification initials and aligned flush left. Carbon copy notations
may be typed one or two lines below the last notation, depending
on available space. If only the signature block and/or typist's
initials appear before it, the carbon copy notation is typed two
lines below.

EXECUTIVE SIGNATURE - BUSINESS TITLE

coc
Enclosures (12)

cc Dr. Alice L. Barnes

The Block Letter

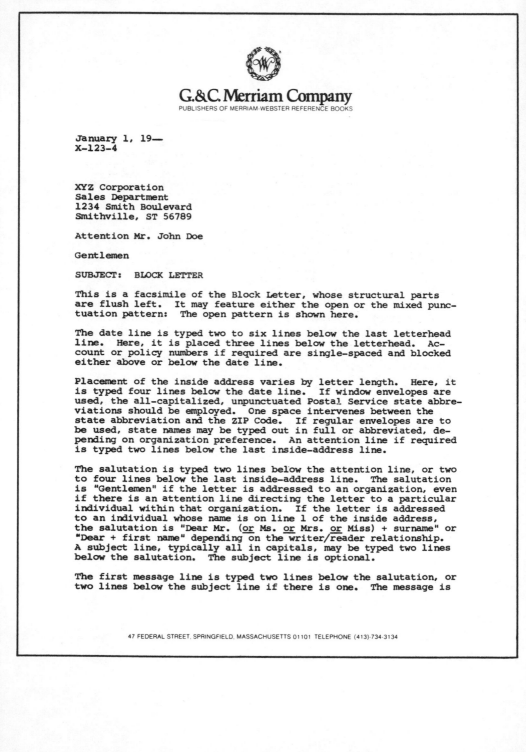

G.&C. Merriam Company

PUBLISHERS OF MERRIAM-WEBSTER REFERENCE BOOKS

January 1, 19—
X-123-4

XYZ Corporation
Sales Department
1234 Smith Boulevard
Smithville, ST 56789

Attention Mr. John Doe

Gentlemen

SUBJECT: BLOCK LETTER

This is a facsimile of the Block Letter, whose structural parts
are flush left. It may feature either the open or the mixed punctuation pattern: The open pattern is shown here.

The date line is typed two to six lines below the last letterhead
line. Here, it is placed three lines below the letterhead. Account or policy numbers if required are single-spaced and blocked
either above or below the date line.

Placement of the inside address varies by letter length. Here, it
is typed four lines below the date line. If window envelopes are
used, the all-capitalized, unpunctuated Postal Service state abbreviations should be employed. One space intervenes between the
state abbreviation and the ZIP Code. If regular envelopes are to
be used, state names may be typed out in full or abbreviated, depending on organization preference. An attention line if required
is typed two lines below the last inside-address line.

The salutation is typed two lines below the attention line, or two
to four lines below the last inside-address line. The salutation
is "Gentlemen" if the letter is addressed to an organization, even
if there is an attention line directing the letter to a particular
individual within that organization. If the letter is addressed
to an individual whose name is on line 1 of the inside address,
the salutation is "Dear Mr. (or Ms. or Mrs. or Miss) + surname" or
"Dear + first name" depending on the writer/reader relationship.
A subject line, typically all in capitals, may be typed two lines
below the salutation. The subject line is optional.

The first message line is typed two lines below the salutation, or
two lines below the subject line if there is one. The message is

47 FEDERAL STREET, SPRINGFIELD, MASSACHUSETTS 01101 TELEPHONE (413)-734-3134

XYZ Corporation
Sales Department
January 1, 19—
X-123-4
Page 2

single-spaced internally and double-spaced between paragraphs.
At least three message lines must be carried over to a continuation sheet: At no time should the complimentary close and the
signature block stand alone. The last word on a sheet should not
be divided. The continuation-sheet heading is typed six lines
from the top edge of the page. Account or policy numbers if used
on the first sheet must be included in the continuation-sheet
headings. The message begins four lines below the last line of
the heading.

The complimentary close is typed two lines below the last message
line, followed by at least four blank lines for the written signature, followed by the writer's name in capitals and lowercase.
The writer's business title and/or name of his department may be
included in the typed signature block, if they do not appear in
the printed letterhead.

Identification initials may comprise only the typist's initials if
the same person dictated and signed the letter. These initials
are typed two lines below the last signature-block line. The enclosure notation if used is typed one line below the identification line. The carbon copy notation if needed is placed one or
two lines below any other notations, depending on available space.

Sincerely yours

Executive Signature
Business Title

coc
Enclosures (2)

cc Mr. Howard T. Jansen

The Modified Block Letter

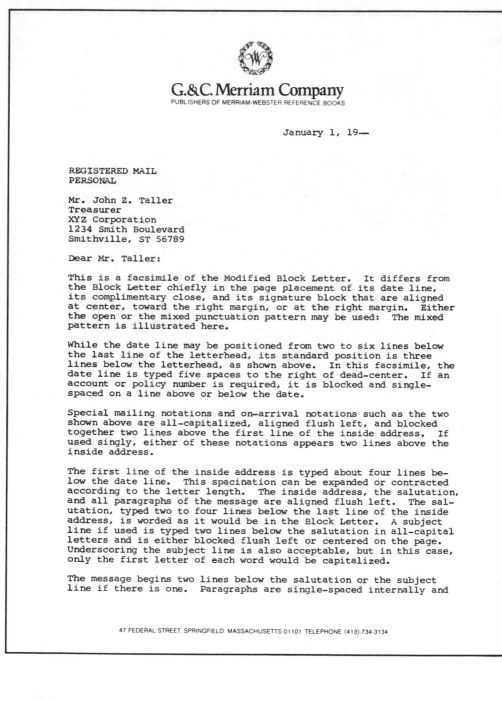

G.&C. Merriam Company
PUBLISHERS OF MERRIAM-WEBSTER REFERENCE BOOKS

January 1, 19—

REGISTERED MAIL
PERSONAL

Mr. John Z. Taller
Treasurer
XYZ Corporation
1234 Smith Boulevard
Smithville, ST 56789

Dear Mr. Taller:

This is a facsimile of the Modified Block Letter. It differs from
the Block Letter chiefly in the page placement of its date line,
its complimentary close, and its signature block that are aligned
at center, toward the right margin, or at the right margin. Either
the open or the mixed punctuation pattern may be used: The mixed
pattern is illustrated here.

While the date line may be positioned from two to six lines below
the last line of the letterhead, its standard position is three
lines below the letterhead, as shown above. In this facsimile, the
date line is typed five spaces to the right of dead-center. If an
account or policy number is required, it is blocked and single-
spaced on a line above or below the date.

Special mailing notations and on-arrival notations such as the two
shown above are all-capitalized, aligned flush left, and blocked
together two lines above the first line of the inside address. If
used singly, either of these notations appears two lines above the
inside address.

The first line of the inside address is typed about four lines below the date line. This spacination can be expanded or contracted
according to the letter length. The inside address, the salutation,
and all paragraphs of the message are aligned flush left. The salutation, typed two to four lines below the last line of the inside
address, is worded as it would be in the Block Letter. A subject
line if used is typed two lines below the salutation in all-capital
letters and is either blocked flush left or centered on the page.
Underscoring the subject line is also acceptable, but in this case,
only the first letter of each word would be capitalized.

The message begins two lines below the salutation or the subject
line if there is one. Paragraphs are single-spaced internally and

47 FEDERAL STREET, SPRINGFIELD, MASSACHUSETTS 01101 TELEPHONE (413)-734-3134

double-spaced between each other; however, in very short letters,
the paragraphs may be double-spaced internally and triple-spaced
between each other.

Continuation sheets should contain at least three message lines.
The last word on a sheet should not be divided. The continuation-
sheet heading may be blocked flush left as in the Block Letter or
it may be laid out across the top of the page as shown above. This
heading begins six lines from the top edge of the page, and the
message is continued four lines beneath it.

The complimentary close is typed two lines below the last line of
the message. While the complimentary close may be aligned under
some portion of the letterhead, directly under the date line, or
even flush with but not overrunning the right margin, it is often
typed five spaces to the right of dead-center as shown here.

The signature line is typed in capitals and lowercase at least four
lines below the complimentary close. The writer's business title
and department name may be included if they do not already appear
in the printed letterhead. All elements of the signature block
must be aligned with each other and with the complimentary close.

Identification initials need include only those of the typist, providing that the writer and the signer are the same person. These
initials appear two lines below the last line of the signature
block. An enclosure notation is typed one line below the identification line, and the carbon copy notation if required appears
one or two lines below any other notations, depending on space
available.

                                      Very truly yours,

                                      Executive Signature

                                      Executive Signature
                                      Business Title

coc
Enclosures (5)

cc Mr. Doe
   Mr. Franklin
   Mr. Mason
   Ms. Watson

The Modified Semi-block Letter

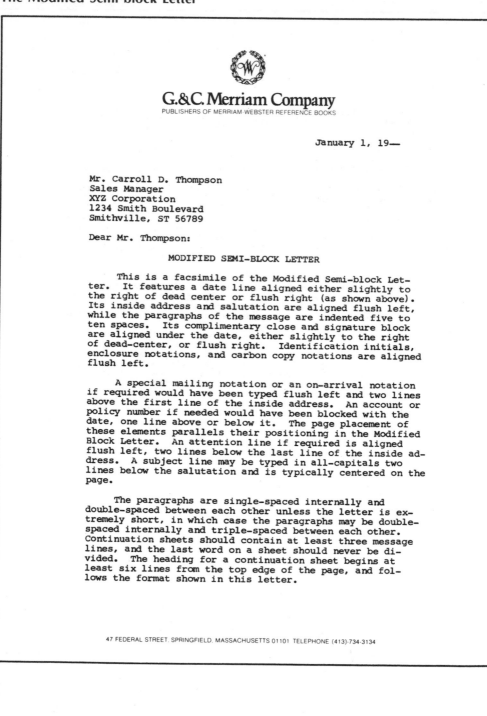

January 1, 19—

Mr. Carroll D. Thompson
Sales Manager
XYZ Corporation
1234 Smith Boulevard
Smithville, ST 56789

Dear Mr. Thompson:

MODIFIED SEMI-BLOCK LETTER

This is a facsimile of the Modified Semi-block Letter. It features a date line aligned either slightly to the right of dead center or flush right (as shown above). Its inside address and salutation are aligned flush left, while the paragraphs of the message are indented five to ten spaces. Its complimentary close and signature block are aligned under the date, either slightly to the right of dead-center, or flush right. Identification initials, enclosure notations, and carbon copy notations are aligned flush left.

A special mailing notation or an on-arrival notation if required would have been typed flush left and two lines above the first line of the inside address. An account or policy number if needed would have been blocked with the date, one line above or below it. The page placement of these elements parallels their positioning in the Modified Block Letter. An attention line if required is aligned flush left, two lines below the last line of the inside address. A subject line may be typed in all-capitals two lines below the salutation and is typically centered on the page.

The paragraphs are single-spaced internally and double-spaced between each other unless the letter is extremely short, in which case the paragraphs may be double-spaced internally and triple-spaced between each other. Continuation sheets should contain at least three message lines, and the last word on a sheet should never be divided. The heading for a continuation sheet begins at least six lines from the top edge of the page, and follows the format shown in this letter.

47 FEDERAL STREET, SPRINGFIELD, MASSACHUSETTS 01101 TELEPHONE (413)-734-3134

Mr. Thompson   - 2 -   January 1, 19—

    The complimentary close is typed at two lines below
the last line of the message. The signature line, four
lines below the complimentary close, is aligned with it
if possible, or centered under it if the name and title
will be long. In this case, it is better to align both
date and complimentary close about five spaces to the
right of dead-center to ensure enough room for the signature block which should never overrun the right margin.
The writer's name, business title and department name (if
not already printed on the stationery), are typed in capitals and lowercase.

    Although open punctuation may be followed, the mixed
punctuation pattern is quite common with the Modified
Semi-block Letter, and it is the latter that is shown
here.

                      Sincerely yours,

                    Executive Signature

                    Executive Signature
                    Business Title

coc

Enclosures: 2

cc: Dr. Bennett P. Oakley
     Addison Engineering Associates
     91011 Jones Street
     Smithville, ST 56789

    A postscript if needed is typically positioned two
to four lines below the last notation. In the Modified
Semi-block Letter, the postscript is indented five to ten
spaces to agree with message paragraphing. It is not
necessary to head the postscript with the abbreviation
P.S. The postscript should be initialed by the writer.

The Half-Sheet

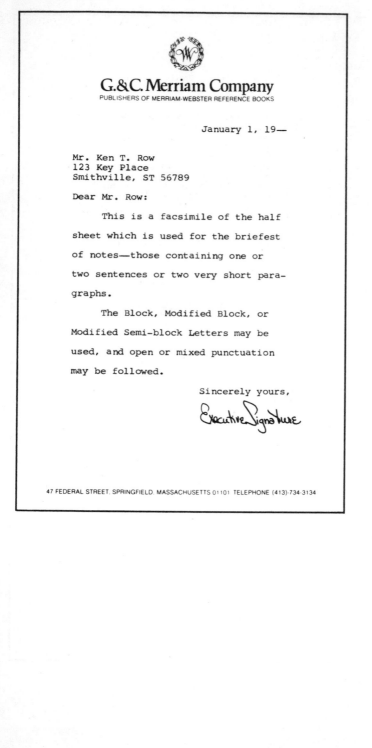

G.&C. Merriam Company
PUBLISHERS OF MERRIAM-WEBSTER REFERENCE BOOKS

January 1, 19—

Mr. Ken T. Row
123 Key Place
Smithville, ST 56789

Dear Mr. Row:

This is a facsimile of the half
sheet which is used for the briefest
of notes—those containing one or
two sentences or two very short paragraphs.

The Block, Modified Block, or
Modified Semi-block Letters may be
used, and open or mixed punctuation
may be followed.

Sincerely yours,

Executive Signature

47 FEDERAL STREET, SPRINGFIELD, MASSACHUSETTS 01101 TELEPHONE (413)-734-3134

ENVELOPES

The following information may appear on any envelope regardless of its size. Asterisked items are essential and those that are unmarked are optional, depending on the requirements of the particular letter:

*1. The addressee's full name and full geographical address typed approximately in the vertical and horizontal center

2. Special mailing notation or notations typed below the stamp

3. On-arrival notation or notations typed about nine lines below the top left

*4. Sender's full name and geographical address printed or typed in the upper left corner.

The typeface should be block style. The Postal Service does not recommend unusual or italic typefaces. The typewriter keys should be clean.

The address block on a regular envelope should encompass no more than 1½" × 3¾" of space. There should be ⅝" of space from the bottom line of the address block to the bottom edge of the envelope. The entire area from the right and left bottom margins of the address block to the right and left bottom edges of the envelope as well as the area under the center of the address block to the bottom center edge of the envelope should be free of print. With regular envelopes, most address blocks are begun about five spaces to the left of horizontal center to admit room for potentially long lines. The address block should be single-spaced. Block styling should be used throughout.

If a window envelope is being used, all address data must appear within the window space, and at least ¼" margins must be maintained between the address and the right, left, top, and bottom edges of the window space.

Address-block data on a regular envelope should match the spelling and styling of the inside address. Address-block elements are positioned as follows:

first line

If the addressee is an individual, that person's courtesy title + full name are typed on the first line.	*Examples:* Mr. Lee O. Idlewild, President *or* Mr. Lee O. Idlewild
If the addressee is an organization, its full name is typed on the first line.	President *or, addressed for automation* MR LEE O IDLEWILD
If an individual addressee's business title is included in the inside address, it may be typed either on the first line of the address block with a comma separating it from the addressee's name, or it may be typed alone on the next line, depending on length of title and name.	PRES *or* MR L O IDLEWILD PRES *and* XYZ Corporation Sales Department *or, addressed for automation*
If a particular department within an organization is specified, it is typed on a line under the name of the organization.	XYZ CORP SALES DEPT

next line

The full street address should be typed out (although it is acceptable to abbreviate such designations as *Street, Avenue, Boulevard,* etc.). In mass mailings that will be presorted for automated handling, it is correct to capitalize all elements of the address block and to use the unpunctuated abbreviations for streets and street-designations that are recommended by the U.S. Postal Service. Room, suite, apartment, and building numbers are typed immediately following the last element of the street address and are positioned on the same line with it.

last line

The last line of the address block contains the city, state, and the ZIP Code number. Only <u>one space</u> intervenes between the last letter of the state abbreviation and the first digit of the ZIP Code. The all-capitalized, unpunctuated, two-letter Postal Service state abbreviations are mandatory, as is the ZIP Code.

Examples:

Mr. John P. Smith
4523 Kendall Place, Apt. 8B
Smithville, ST 56789

or

Mr. John P. Smith
4523 Kendall Pl., Apt. 8B
Smithville, ST 56789
or, addressed for automation
MR J P SMITH
4523 KENDALL PL APT 8B
SMITHVILLE ST 56789
or
CAMERON CORP
ATTN MR J P SMITH
765 BAY ST ROOM 100
SMITHVILLE ST 56789

When typing a foreign address, the secretary should refer first to the return address on the envelope of previous correspondence to ascertain the correct ordering of the essential elements of the address block. Letterhead of previous correspondence may also be checked if an envelope is not available. If neither of these sources is available, the material should be typed as it appears in the inside address of the dictated letter. The following guidelines may be of assistance:

1. All foreign addresses should be typed in English or in English characters: if an address must be in foreign characters (as Russian), an English translation should be interlined in the address block.
2. Foreign courtesy titles <u>may</u> be substituted for the English; however, it is unnecessary.
3. The name of the country should be typed in all-capital letters. Canadian addresses always carry the name CANADA, even though the name of the province is also given.
4. When applicable, foreign postal district numbers should be included.

Some samples of foreign corporate abbreviations are shown in the following table.

Foreign Corporate Abbreviations: A Brief Sampling of Commonly Used Terms

Language	Type of Business	Abbreviation
Danish	Partnership	I/S
	Limited Partnership	K/S
	Limited-liability Company	A/S
	Private Limited-liability Company	Ap/S
Dutch	Private Company	B.V.
	Public Corporation	N.V.
French	Limited-liability Company	SARL
	Corporation	SA
German	Partnership	OHG
	Limited Partnership	KG
	Limited-liability Company	G.m.b.H.
	Corporation	AG
Italian	Corporation	S.p.A.
	Limited-liability Company	S.r.l.
Portuguese	Corporation	SARL
Spanish	Stock Company	SA
	Corporation	S/A
	Company	CIA
Swedish	Joint Stock Company	SA

On-arrival notations such as PERSONAL or CONFIDENTIAL must be typed entirely in capital letters, about nine lines below the left top edge of the envelope. Any other on-arrival instructions such as <u>Hold for Arrival</u> or <u>Please Forward</u> may be typed in capitals and lowercase, underlined, and positioned about nine lines from the left top edge of the envelope.

If an attention line is used in the letter itself, it too must appear on the envelope. Attention lines are typed in capitals and lowercase for regular mailings using commercial envelopes, and they are typed entirely in capitals for mass mailings that will be presorted for automatic handling. The attention line may be placed anywhere in the address block so long as it is directly above the next-to-last line, as

XYZ Corporation
Sales Department
Attention Mr. E. R. Bailey
1234 Smith Boulevard
Smithville, ST 56789

XYZ CORP
SALES DEPT
ATTN MR E R BAILEY
1234 SMITH BLVD
SMITHVILLE ST 56789

Facsimile of a Commercial Envelope Showing On-arrival and Special Mailing Notations

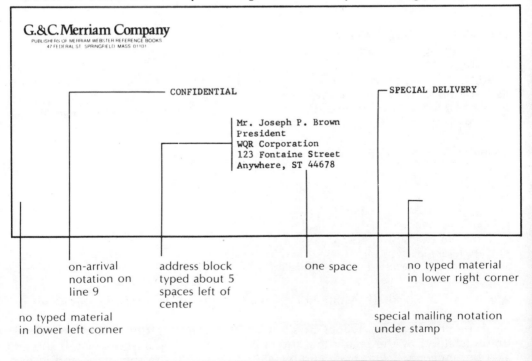

A special mailing notation (as CERTIFIED, REGISTERED MAIL, or SPECIAL DELIVERY) is typed entirely in capitals just below the stamp or about nine lines from the right top edge of the envelope. It should not overrun a ½" margin.

The printed return address (as of a company) may be supplemented by the name of the writer typed in at the top. The return address on a plain envelope should be styled as

Stephen P. Lemke
123 Ann Street
Jonesville, XX 12345

with at least two blank lines between the return address and the left and top edges of the envelope.

See page 5 for the chart showing stationery and envelope sizes and applications.

1.8

FORMS OF ADDRESS

It has already been emphasized that the initial impression created by a letter is vital to the letter's ultimate effectiveness. It follows that proper use of the conventional forms of address is essential, especially since these forms appear in conspicuous areas of the letter: on the envelope, in the inside address, and in the salutation.

FORMS OF ADDRESS CHART

The following pages contain a chart of alphabetically grouped and listed forms of address for individuals whose offices, ranks, or professions warrant special courtesy titles, salutations, and complimentary closes. The chart also indicates in its last column how these individuals should be addressed orally (as in an introduction or in a conversation) and how they should be referred to in a written text (such as in a letter, a report, or an article).

The main categories covered in the chart are listed below in the order of their appearance:

Clerical and Religious Orders
College and University Faculty and Officials
Consular Officers
Diplomats
Foreign Heads of State
Government Officials
Military Ranks
Miscellaneous Courtesy, Business, and Professional Titles
United Nations Officials

A special chart headed "Multiple Addressees" immediately follows the Forms of Address Chart.

When two or more stylings are shown in the Forms of Address Chart, it should be understood by the reader that the most formal styling appears first. It should also be understood that male and female addressees (as in the clergy and in the armed forces) are addressed alike unless stated otherwise. An acute space problem within this chart has precluded mention of both male and female addressees in every single instance. The fact that female addressees are not shown throughout the material in no way suggests that women may not hold these positions or ranks.

Addressee	Form of Address	Salutation	Complimentary Close	(1) Oral Reference (2) Written Reference
CLERICAL AND RELIGIOUS ORDERS				
abbot	The Right Reverend John R. Smith, O.S.B. Abbot of ----	Right Reverend and dear Father Dear Father Abbot Dear Father	Respectfully yours Sincerely yours	(1) Father Abbot (2) Father Smith
apostolic delegate	His Excellency, The Most Reverend John R. Smith Archbishop of ---- The Apostolic Delegate or The Apostolic Delegation	Your Excellency My dear Archbishop Gentlemen	Respectfully yours Respectfully Sincerely yours	(1) Your Excellency (2) the Apostolic Delegate (1 and 2) the Apostolic Delegation
archbishop	The Most Reverend Archbishop of ---- or The Most Reverend John R. Smith Archbishop of ----	Your Excellency Your Excellency Dear Archbishop Smith	Respectfully yours Respectfully yours Sincerely yours	(1) Your excellency (2) the Archbishop of ---- (1) Archbishop Smith (2) Archbishop Smith
archdeacon	The Venerable The Archdeacon of ---- or The Venerable John R. Smith	Venerable Sir Venerable Sir My dear Archdeacon	Respectfully yours Respectfully yours Sincerely yours	(1) Archdeacon Smith (2) the Archdeacon of ---- (1 and 2) Archdeacon (or if having doctorate Dr.) Smith
bishop, Catholic	The Most Reverend John R. Smith Bishop of ----	Your Excellency Dear Bishop Smith	Respectfully yours Sincerely yours	(1 and 2) Bishop Smith

Addressee	Form of Address	Salutation	Complimentary Close	(1) Oral Reference (2) Written Reference
bishop, Episcopal Presiding	The Most Reverend John R. Smith Presiding Bishop	Most Reverend Sir Dear Bishop Dear Bishop Smith	Respectfully yours Sincerely yours	(1 and 2) Bishop Smith
bishop, Episcopal	The Right Reverend The Bishop of ---- or The Right Reverend John R. Smith Bishop of ----	Right Reverend Sir Right Reverend Sir Dear Bishop Smith	Respectfully yours Respectfully yours Sincerely yours	(1) Bishop Smith (2) the Episcopal Bishop of ----
bishop, Methodist	The Reverend John R. Smith Methodist Bishop	Reverend Sir Dear Bishop Smith	Respectfully yours Sincerely yours	(1 and 2) Bishop Smith
brotherhood, member of	Brother John, S.J.	Dear Brother John	Respectfully yours Sincerely yours	(1) Brother John (2) Brother John, S.J.
brotherhood, superior of	Brother John, S.J., Superior	Dear Brother John	Respectfully yours Sincerely yours	(1) Brother John (2) Brother John, S.J., Superior of ----
canon	The Reverend John R. Smith Canon of ---- Cathedral	Dear Canon Smith	Respectfully yours Sincerely yours	(1 and 2) Canon Smith
cardinal	His Eminence John Cardinal Smith Archbishop of ---- or His Eminence Cardinal Smith Archbishop of ----	Your Eminence My dear Cardinal Smith Dear Cardinal Smith	Respectfully yours Sincerely yours	(1) Your Eminence or Cardinal Smith (2) His Eminence Cardinal Smith or Cardinal Smith

chaplain, college or university—see COLLEGE AND UNIVERSITY FACULTY AND OFFICIALS

Personage	Envelope and Letter Address	Salutation	Complimentary Close	Informal Address
clergyman, Protestant (excluding Episcopal)	The Reverend John R. Smith *or if having doctorate*	Dear Mr. Smith	Respectfully yours Sincerely yours	*(1)* Mr. Smith *(2)* The Reverend Mr. Smith *or* The Reverend John R. Smith *or* Mr. Smith
	The Reverend Dr. John R. Smith	Dear Dr. Smith	Respectfully yours Sincerely yours	*(1)* Dr. Smith *(2)* The Reverend Dr. Smith *or* Dr. Smith
dean (of a cathedral)	The Very Reverend John R. Smith ––– Cathedral *or* Dean John R. Smith ––– Cathedral	Very Reverend Sir Dear Dean Smith	Respectfully yours Sincerely yours	*(1 and 2)* Dean *(or if having doctorate Dr.)* Smith
		Very Reverend Sir Dear Dean Smith	Respectfully yours Sincerely yours	
moderator, Presbyterian	The Moderator of ––– *or* The Reverend John R. Smith *or if having doctorate* The Reverend Dr. John R. Smith	Reverend Sir My dear Sir Dear Mr. Moderator My dear Mr. Smith	Respectfully yours Sincerely yours Respectfully yours Sincerely yours	*(1 and 2)* the Moderator of ––– *(1 and 2)* Mr. Smith
		My dear Dr. Smith	Respectfully yours Sincerely yours	*(1 and 2)* Dr. Smith
monsignor **domestic prelate**	The Right Reverend Monsignor John R. Smith *or* The Rt. Rev. Msgr. John R. Smith	Right Reverend and dear Monsignor Smith	Respectfully yours	*(1 and 2)* Monsignor Smith
		Dear Monsignor Smith	Sincerely yours	
papal chamberlain	The Very Reverend Monsignor John R. Smith *or* The Very Rev. Msgr. John R. Smith	Very Reverend and dear Monsignor Smith	Respectfully yours	*(1 and 2)* Monsignor Smith
		Dear Monsignor Smith	Sincerely yours	

Addressee	Form of Address	Salutation	Complimentary Close	(1) Oral Reference (2) Written Reference
patriarch (of an Eastern Orthodox Church)	His Beatitude the Patriarch of ----	Most Reverend Lord	Respectfully yours	(1) Your Beatitude (2) John R. Smith, the Patriarch of ---- or The Patriarch
pope	His Holiness the Pope *or* His Holiness Pope ----	Your Holiness Most Holy Father	Respectfully yours	(1) Your Holiness (2) His Holiness the Pope or His Holiness, Pope ---- or The Pope
president, Mormon	The President Church of Jesus Christ of Latter-Day Saints	My dear President Dear President Smith	Respectfully yours Sincerely yours	(1 and 2) Mr. Smith
priest, Catholic	The Reverend John R. Smith *or if having doctorate* The Reverend Dr. John R. Smith	Dear Father Smith Dear Father Smith	Respectfully yours Sincerely yours Respectfully yours Sincerely yours	(1 and 2) Father Smith (1 and 2) Father Smith
priest, Episcopal	The Reverend John R. Smith *or if having doctorate* The Reverend Dr. John R. Smith	Dear Mr. Smith Dear Father Smith Dear Dr. Smith Dear Father Smith	Respectfully yours Sincerely yours Respectfully yours Sincerely yours	(1 and 2) Mr. (or Father) Smith (1 and 2) Dr. (or Father) Smith
priest/president—see COLLEGE AND UNIVERSITY FACULTY AND OFFICIALS (of a college or university)				
rabbi	Rabbi John R. Smith *or if having doctorate* Rabbi John R. Smith, D.D.	Dear Rabbi Smith Dear Dr. Smith	Respectfully yours Sincerely yours	(1 and 2) Rabbi Smith (1 and 2) Dr. (or Rabbi) Smith

COLLEGE AND UNIVERSITY FACULTY AND OFFICIALS

Personage	Envelope	Salutation	Complimentary close	Speaking
sisterhood, member of	Sister Mary Angelica, S.C.	Dear Sister / Dear Sister Mary Angelica	Respectfully yours / Sincerely yours	(1 and 2) Sister Mary Angelica
sisterhood, superior of	The Reverend Mother Superior, S.C.	Reverend Mother / Dear Reverend Mother	Respectfully yours / Sincerely yours	(1) Reverend Mother (2) The Reverend Mother Superior or The Reverend Mother
chancellor (of a university)	Dr. John } / Amelia } R. Smith, Chancellor	Sir Madam / Dear Dr. Smith	Very truly yours / Sincerely yours	(1) Dr. Smith (2) Dr. Smith or John / Amelia } R. Smith, Chancellor of ---- University
chaplain (of a college or university)	The Reverend John / Amelia } R. Smith, Chaplain	Dear Chaplain Smith / Dear Mr. / Miss / Mrs. } Smith / Dear Father Smith	Respectfully / Sincerely yours	(1 and 2) Chaplain Smith or Mr., Miss, Mrs. Smith or Father Smith
dean (of a college or university)	Dean John / Amelia } R. Smith or Dr. John / Amelia } R. Smith, Dean	Sir Madam / Dear Dr. Smith / Dear Dean Smith	Very truly yours / Sincerely yours	(1) Dean or Dr. Smith (2) Dean or Dr. Smith or Dr. Smith, Dean of ----
instructor	Mr., Dr. John R. Smith / Ms., Miss, Mrs., Dr. } Amelia R. Smith, Instructor	Dear Mr., Dr. Smith / Dear Ms., Miss, Mrs., Dr. Smith	Very truly yours / Sincerely yours	(1 and 2) Mr., Ms., Miss, Mrs., Dr. Smith

Addressee	Form of Address	Salutation	Complimentary Close	(1) Oral Reference / (2) Written Reference
president	Dr. John ⎱ R. Smith Amelia ⎰ President or President John ⎱ R. Smith Amelia ⎰ ----	Sir Madam Dear Dr. Smith Dear President Smith	Very truly yours Sincerely yours Very truly yours Sincerely yours	(1) Dr. Smith (2) Dr. Smith or Dr. Smith, the President of ----
president/priest	The Very Reverend John R. Smith, S.J. President	Sir Dear Father Smith	Respectfully yours Sincerely yours	(1) Father Smith (2) Father Smith, President of ----
professor, assistant or associate	Mr., Dr. John R. Smith Ms., Mrs., Miss, Dr. Amelia R. Smith Assistant/Associate Professor of ----	Dear Mr., Dr. Smith Dear Ms., Mrs., Miss, Dr. Smith or Dear Professor Smith	Very truly yours Sincerely yours	(1) Mr., Ms., Mrs., Miss, Dr. Smith (2) Professor Smith
professor, full	Professor John ⎱ R. Smith Amelia ⎰ or Dr. John ⎱ R. Smith Amelia ⎰ Professor of ----	Dear Professor Smith Dear Dr. Smith	Very truly yours Sincerely yours	(1 and 2) Professor or Dr. Smith
CONSULAR OFFICERS				
consulate, American	The American Consulate (foreign city, country) or if in Central or South America The Consulate of the United States of America (foreign city, country)	Gentlemen Gentlemen	Very truly yours Very truly yours	(1) ---- (2) the American Consulate in ---- (1) ---- (2) the United States Consulate in ----

	Address	Salutation	Complimentary Close	In Conversation or Reference
consuls, American (covers all consular grades such as Consul General, Consul, Vice-Consul and Consular Agent)	The American Consul (foreign city, country) or if in Central or South America	Sir	Respectfully yours Very truly yours	(1) ---- (2) the American Consul in ----
	The Consul of the United States of America (foreign city, country) or if individual name is known	Sir	Respectfully yours Very truly yours	(1) ---- (2) the United States Consul in ----
	John } R. Smith, Esq. Amelia } American Consul or if in Central or South America Consul of the United States of America	Sir Madam Dear Mr. Ms. Mrs. Miss } Smith	Respectfully yours Very truly yours	(1) Mr., Ms., Mrs., Miss Smith (2) the American or United States Consul in ----
NOTE: Since these officers are frequently transferred it is advisable to address letters to the office and not to the individual.				
consulate, foreign	The ---- Consulate or The Consulate of ---- (U.S. city, state, ZIP)	Gentlemen	Very truly yours	(1) ---- (2) the ---- Consulate or the Consulate of ----
consuls, foreign (covers all consular grades)	The ---- Consul or The Consul of ---- (U.S. city, state, ZIP) or if individual name is known	Sir	Respectfully yours Sincerely yours	(1) ---- (2) the ---- Consul in (city) or the Consul of ---- in (city)
	The Honorable John } R. Smith Amelia } ---- Consul or Consul of ---- (U.S. city, state, ZIP)	Sir Madame Dear Mr. Ms. Mrs. Miss } Smith	Respectfully yours Sincerely yours	(1) Mr., Ms., Mrs., Miss Smith or Mr., Ms., Mrs., Miss Smith, the ---- Consul (2) Mr., Ms., Mrs., Miss Smith, the ---- Consul in (city)
NOTE: Since these officers are frequently transferred it is advisable to address letters to the office and not to the individual.				

Addressee	Form of Address	Salutation	Complimentary Close	(1) Oral Reference (2) Written Reference
DIPLOMATS				
ambassador, American	The Honorable John } R. Smith Amelia } American Ambassador or if in Central or South America The Ambassador of the United States of America	Sir Madam Dear Mr. } Ambassador Madam }	Very truly yours Sincerely yours	(1) Mr., Madam Ambassador or Mr., Ms., Mrs., Miss Smith (2) the American Ambassador or the Ambassador of the United States or the United States Ambassador or Mr., Ms., Mrs., Miss Smith, the American Ambassador or the Ambassador
ambassador, foreign	His } Excellency Her } John } R. Smith Amelia } Ambassador of ――― or if from Great Britain His Excellency The Right Honorable John R. Smith British Ambassador	Excellency Dear Mr. } Ambassador Madame } Excellency Dear Mr. Ambassador	Respectfully yours Sincerely yours Respectfully yours Sincerely yours	(1) Mr., Madame Ambassador (2) the Ambassador of ――― or the Ambassador or Mr., Ms., Mrs., Miss Smith (1) Mr. Ambassador (2) the British Ambassador or The Honorable Mr. Smith, the British Ambassador
chargé d'affaires ad interim, American	John } R. Smith, Esq. Amelia } American Chargé d'Affaires ad Interim or if in Central or South America United States Chargé d'Affaires ad Interim	Sir Madam Dear Mr. } Ms. } Smith Mrs. } Miss }	Very truly yours Sincerely yours	(1) Mr., Ms., Mrs., Miss Smith (2) the American Chargé d'Affaires in ――― or the United States Chargé d'Affaires in ――― or Mr., Ms., Mrs., Miss Smith

chargé d'affaires ad interim, foreign	Mr. Ms. Mrs. Miss } John } R. Smith Amelia } Chargé d'Affaires ad Interim of ----	Sir Madame Dear Mr. Ms. Mrs. Miss } Smith	Respectfully yours Sincerely yours	(1) Mr., Ms., Mrs., Miss Smith (2) the ---- Chargé d'Affaires or Mr., Ms., Mrs., Miss Smith
chargé d'affaires (de missi) foreign	Mr. Ms. Mrs. Miss } John } R. Smith Amelia } Chargé d'Affaires of ----	Sir Madame Dear Mr. Ms. Mrs. Miss } Smith	Respectfully yours Sincerely yours	(1) Mr., Ms., Mrs., Miss Smith (2) the ---- Chargé d'Affaires or Mr., Ms., Mrs., Miss Smith
minister, American	The Honorable John } R. Smith Amelia } American Minister or if in Central or South America Minister of the United States of America	Sir Madam Dear Mr. Madam } Minister	Very truly yours Sincerely yours	(1) Mr., Madam Minister or Mr., Ms., Mrs., Miss Smith (2) the American (or the United States) Minister, Mr., Ms., Mrs., Miss Smith or the Minister or Mr., Ms., Mrs., Miss Smith
minister, foreign	The Honorable John } R. Smith Amelia } Minister of ----	Sir Madame Dear Mr. Madame } Minister	Respectfully yours Sincerely yours	(1) Mr., Madame Minister or Mr., Ms., Mrs., Miss Smith (2) the Minister of ---- or the Minister or Mr., Ms., Mrs., Miss Smith

Addressee	Form of Address	Salutation	Complimentary Close	(1) Oral Reference (2) Written Reference
FOREIGN HEADS OF STATE: A BRIEF SAMPLING				
premier	His } Excellency Her } John } R. Smith Amelia } Premier of ----	Excellency Dear Mr. } Premier Madame }	Respectfully yours Sincerely yours	(1) Your Excellency or Mr., Ms., Mrs., Miss Smith (2) the Premier of ---- or the Premier or Mr., Ms., Mrs., Miss Smith
president of a republic	His } Excellency Her } John } R. Smith Amelia } President of ----	Excellency Dear Mr. } President Madame }	Respectfully yours Sincerely yours	(1) Your Excellency (2) President Smith or Mr., Ms., Mrs., Miss Smith
prime minister	His } Excellency Her } John } R. Smith Amelia }	Excellency Dear Mr. } Prime Minister Madame }	Respectfully yours Sincerely yours	(1) Mr., Madame Prime Minister or Mr., Ms., Mrs., Miss Smith (2) the Prime Minister of ---- or the Prime Minister or Mr., Ms., Mrs., Miss Smith
GOVERNMENT OFFICIALS—FEDERAL				
attorney general	The Honorable John R. Smith The Attorney General	Sir Dear Mr. Attorney General	Very truly yours Sincerely yours	(1) Mr. Attorney General or Attorney General Smith or Mr. Smith (2) the Attorney General, Mr. Smith or the Attorney General or Mr. Smith

	Envelope and Letter Address	Salutation	Complimentary Close	In Speaking and Referring To
cabinet officer(s) addressed as "Secretary"	The Honorable The Secretary of ---- *or* The Honorable John ⎱ R. Smith Amelia ⎰ Secretary of ---- *or* The Secretary of ----	Sir Madam Sir Madam Dear Mr. ⎱ Madam ⎰ Secretary Sir Madam	Very truly yours Very truly yours Sincerely yours	(1) Mr., Madam Secretary or Secretary Smith or Mr., Ms., Mrs., Miss, Dr. Smith (2) the Secretary of ----, John ⎱ R. Smith or Amelia ⎰ the Secretary or Mr., Ms., Mrs., Miss, Dr. Smith
cabinet officer, former	The Honorable John ⎱ R. Smith Amelia	Dear Mr. ⎫ Ms. ⎬ Smith Mrs. ⎪ Miss ⎭	Very truly yours Sincerely yours	(1 and 2) Mr., Ms., Mrs., Miss Smith
chairman of a (sub) committee, U.S. Congress (stylings shown apply to House of Representatives & Senate)	The Honorable John ⎱ R. Smith Amelia ⎰ Chairman Committee on ---- United States Senate	Dear Mr. ⎱ Chairman Madam ⎰ Dear Senator Smith	Very truly yours Sincerely yours	(1) Mr., Madam Chairman or Senator Smith or Senator (2) *(title)* Smith, the Chairman of the ---- Committee on ---- or the Chairman or Senator Smith
chief justice—see SUPREME COURT, FEDERAL; STATE				
commissioner	*if appointed* The Honorable John ⎱ Amelia ⎰ R. Smith Commissioner *if career* Mr. ⎫ John Ms. ⎬ ⎱ R. Smith Mrs. ⎪ Amelia ⎰ Miss ⎭ Commissioner	Dear Mr. ⎱ Commissioner Madam ⎰ Dear Mr. ⎫ Ms. ⎬ Smith Mrs. ⎪ Miss ⎭ Dear Mr. ⎫ Ms. ⎬ Smith Mrs. ⎪ Miss ⎭	Very truly yours Sincerely yours Very truly yours Sincerely yours	(1) Mr., Ms., Mrs., Miss Smith (2) Mr., Ms., Mrs., Miss Smith, the ---- Commissioner or the Commissioner of ---- (1) Mr., Ms., Mrs., Miss Smith (2) Mr., Ms., Mrs., Miss Smith or the Commissioner of ----

Addressee	Form of Address	Salutation	Complimentary Close	(1) Oral Reference (2) Written Reference
congressman—see REPRESENTATIVE, U.S. CONGRESS				
director (as of an independent federal agency)	The Honorable John ⎱ R. Smith Amelia ⎰ Director ---- Agency	Dear Mr. ⎱ Ms. ⎰ Smith Mrs. Miss	Very truly yours Sincerely yours	(1) Mr., Ms., Mrs., Miss Smith (2) John ⎱ R. Smith Amelia ⎰ Director of ---- Agency or The Honorable Mr., Ms., Mrs., Miss Smith
district attorney	The Honorable John ⎱ R. Smith Amelia ⎰ District Attorney	Dear Mr. ⎱ Ms. ⎰ Smith Mrs. Miss	Very truly yours Sincerely yours	(1) Mr., Ms., Mrs., Miss Smith (2) District Attorney Smith or the District Attorney or Mr., Ms., Mrs., Miss Smith
federal judge	The Honorable John ⎱ R. Smith Amelia ⎰ Judge of the United States District Court for the ---- District of ----	Sir Madam My dear Judge Smith Dear Judge Smith	Very truly yours Very sincerely yours	(1) Judge Smith (2) the Judge or Judge Smith
justice—see SUPREME COURT, FEDERAL; STATE				
librarian of congress	The Honorable John R. Smith Librarian of Congress	Sir Dear Mr. Smith	Very truly yours Sincerely yours	(1) Mr. Smith (2) the Librarian of Congress or the Librarian or The Honorable Mr. Smith or Mr. Smith

	Address	Salutation	Complimentary close	Reference
postmaster general	The Honorable John R. Smith The Postmaster General	Sir Dear Mr. Postmaster General	Very truly yours Sincerely yours	(1) Mr. Postmaster General or Postmaster General Smith or Mr. Smith (2) the Postmaster General, Mr. Smith or the Postmaster General or Mr. Smith
president-elect of the United States	The Honorable John R. Smith President-elect of the United States (local address)	Dear Sir Dear Mr. Smith	Very truly yours Sincerely yours	(1) Mr. Smith (2) the President-elect or President-elect Smith or Mr. Smith
president of the United States	The President The White House or The Honorable John R. Smith President of the United States The White House	Mr. President My dear Mr. President Dear Mr. President Mr. President My dear Mr. President Dear Mr. President	Respectfully yours Very respectfully yours Respectfully yours Very respectfully yours	(1) Mr. President (2) The President or President Smith or The Chief Executive or Mr. Smith
president of the United States (former)	The Honorable John R. Smith (local address)	Sir Dear Mr. Smith	Respectfully yours Very truly yours Sincerely yours	(1) Mr. Smith (2) former President Smith or Mr. Smith
press secretary to the President of the United States	Mr. John R. Smith Press Secretary to the President The White House	Dear Mr. Smith	Very truly yours Sincerely yours	(1) Mr. Smith (2) the President's Press Secretary, John Smith or Presidential Press Secretary John Smith or White House Press Secretary John Smith or Mr. Smith

Addressee	Form of Address	Salutation	Complimentary Close	(1) Oral Reference / (2) Written Reference
representative, United States Congress	The Honorable John / Amelia } R. Smith United States House of Representatives	Dear Sir / Dear Madam — Dear Representative Smith — Dear Mr. / Ms. / Mrs. / Miss } Smith	Very truly yours — Sincerely yours	(1) Mr., Ms., Mrs., Miss Smith — (2) John / Amelia } R. Smith, U.S. Representative from ---- or Congressman, Congressperson, Congresswoman ---- Smith
representative, United States Congress (former)	The Honorable John / Amelia } R. Smith (local address)	Dear Mr. / Ms. / Mrs. / Miss } Smith	Very truly yours — Sincerely yours	(1 and 2) Mr., Ms., Mrs., Miss Smith
senator, United States Senate	The Honorable John / Amelia } R. Smith United States Senate	Sir Madam — Dear Senator Smith	Very truly yours — Sincerely yours	(1) Senator Smith or Senator — (2) Senator Smith or the Senator from ---- or the Senator
senator-elect	The Honorable John / Amelia } R. Smith Senator-elect (local address)	Dear Mr. / Ms. / Mrs. / Miss } Smith	Very truly yours — Sincerely yours	(1) Mr., Ms., Mrs., Miss Smith — (2) Senator-elect Smith or Mr., Ms., Mrs., Miss Smith
senator (former)	The Honorable John / Amelia } R. Smith (local address)	Dear Senator Smith	Very truly yours — Sincerely yours	(1) Senator Smith or Senator or Mr., Ms., Mrs., Miss Smith — (2) Senator Smith or former Senator Smith

	Envelope / Address	Salutation	Complimentary Close	Informal Introduction or Reference
speaker, United States House of Representatives	The Honorable The Speaker of the House of Representatives *or* The Honorable Speaker of the House of Representatives *or* The Honorable John R. Smith Speaker of the House of Representatives	Sir; Sir; Sir; Dear Mr. Speaker; Dear Mr. Smith	Very truly yours; Very truly yours; Very truly yours; Sincerely yours	(1) Mr. Speaker *or* Mr. Smith (2) the Speaker, Mr. Smith *or* Speaker of the House John R. Smith *or* John R. Smith, Speaker of the House or the Speaker *or* Mr. Smith
speaker, United States House of Representatives (former)	The Honorable John R. Smith (local address)	Sir; Dear Mr. Smith	Very truly yours; Sincerely yours	(1) Mr. Smith (2) Mr. Smith or John R. Smith, former Speaker of the House
supreme court, associate justice	Mr. Justice Smith The Supreme Court of the United States	Sir or Mr. Justice; My dear Mr. Justice; Dear Mr. Justice; Dear Mr. Justice Smith	Very truly yours; Sincerely yours	(1) Mr. Justice Smith or Justice Smith (2) Mr. Justice Smith or John R. Smith, an associate Supreme Court justice or John R. Smith, an associate justice of the Supreme Court
supreme court, chief justice	The Chief Justice of the United States The Supreme Court of the United States *or* The Chief Justice The Supreme Court	Sir; My dear Mr. Chief Justice; Dear Mr. Chief Justice; Sir; My dear Mr. Chief Justice; Dear Mr. Chief Justice	Respectfully; Very truly yours; Respectfully; Very truly yours	(1) Mr. Chief Justice (2) the Chief Justice or Chief Justice John R. Smith or John R. Smith, Chief Justice of the U.S. Supreme Court

Addressee	Form of Address	Salutation	Complimentary Close	(1) Oral Reference (2) Written Reference
supreme court, retired justice	The Honorable John R. Smith (local address)	Sir Dear Justice Smith	Very truly yours Sincerely yours	(1) Mr. Justice Smith or Justice Smith (2) Mr. Justice Smith or retired Supreme Court Justice John R. Smith
special assistant to the President of the United States	Mr. / Ms. / Mrs. / Miss } John / Amelia } R. Smith	Dear Mr. / Ms. / Mrs. / Miss } Smith	Very truly yours Sincerely yours	(1 and 2) Mr., Ms., Mrs., Miss Smith
territorial delegate	The Honorable John / Amelia } R. Smith Delegate of ---- House of Representatives	Dear Mr. / Ms. / Mrs. / Miss } Smith	Very truly yours Sincerely yours	(1) Mr., Ms., Mrs., Miss Smith (2) Mr., Ms., Mrs., Miss Smith, Territorial Delegate of ----
undersecretary of a department	The Honorable John / Amelia } R. Smith Undersecretary of ----	Dear Mr. / Ms. / Mrs. / Miss } Smith	Very truly yours Sincerely yours	(1) Mr., Ms., Mrs., Miss Smith (2) Mr., Ms., Mrs., Miss Smith or ---- Smith, Undersecretary of ---- or the Undersecretary of ----, ---- Smith
vice president of the United States	The Vice President of the United States United States Senate or The Honorable John R. Smith Vice President of the United States Washington, DC ZIP	Sir My dear Mr. Vice President Sir My dear Mr. Vice President Dear Mr. Vice President	Respectfully Very truly yours Respectfully Very truly yours	(1) Mr. Vice President or Mr. Smith (2) the Vice President or the Vice President, Mr. Smith or Vice President Smith or John Smith; Vice President of the United States

GOVERNMENT OFFICIALS—LOCAL

	Address	Salutation	Complimentary close	Spoken / Introduction
alderman	The Honorable John / Amelia R. Smith, Alderman *or* Alderman John / Amelia R. Smith	Dear Mr. / Ms. / Mrs. / Miss Smith Dear Alderman Smith	Very truly yours Sincerely yours Very truly yours Sincerely yours	(1 and 2) Mr., Ms., Mrs., Miss Smith
city attorney (includes city counsel, corporation counsel)	The Honorable John / Amelia R. Smith	Dear Mr. / Ms. / Mrs. / Miss Smith	Very truly yours Sincerely yours	(1 and 2) Mr., Ms., Mrs., Miss Smith
councilman—*see* ALDERMAN				
county clerk	The Honorable John / Amelia R. Smith, Clerk of ---- County	Dear Mr. / Ms. / Mrs. / Miss Smith	Very truly yours Sincerely yours	(1 and 2) Mr., Ms., Mrs., Miss Smith
county treasurer—*see* COUNTY CLERK				
judge	The Honorable John / Amelia R. Smith, Judge of the ---- Court of ----	Dear Judge Smith	Very truly yours Sincerely yours	(1 and 2) Judge Smith
mayor	The Honorable John / Amelia R. Smith, Mayor of ----	Sir / Madam Dear Mayor Smith	Very truly yours Sincerely yours	(1) Mayor Smith (2) Mayor Smith *or* the Mayor *or* ---- Smith, Mayor of ----

Addressee	Form of Address	Salutation	Complimentary Close	(1) Oral Reference (2) Written Reference
selectman—see ALDERMAN				
GOVERNMENT OFFICIALS—*STATE*				
assemblyman—see REPRESENTATIVE, STATE				
attorney (as commonwealth's attorney, state's attorney)	The Honorable John } R. Smith Amelia } (*title*)	Dear Mr. } Ms. } Smith Mrs. } Miss }	Very truly yours Sincerely yours	(1 and 2) Mr., Ms., Mrs., Miss Smith
attorney general	The Honorable John } R. Smith Amelia } Attorney General of the State of ——	Sir Madam Dear Mr. } Attorney Madam } General	Very truly yours Sincerely yours	(1) Mr., Ms., Mrs., Miss Smith or Attorney General Smith (2) the Attorney General, Mr., Ms., Mrs., Miss Smith or the state Attorney General
clerk of a court	John } R. Smith, Esq. Amelia } Clerk of the Court of ——	Dear Mr. } Ms. } Smith Mrs. } Miss }	Very truly yours Sincerely yours	(1 and 2) Mr., Ms., Mrs., Miss Smith
delegate—see REPRESENTATIVE, STATE				
governor	The Honorable The Governor of —— or The Honorable John } R. Smith Amelia } Governor of —— or in some states	Sir Madam or Sir Madam Dear Governor Smith	Respectfully yours Very sincerely yours Respectfully yours Very sincerely yours	(1) Governor Smith or Governor (2) Governor Smith or the Governor or the Governor of —— (only used outside his or her state)

	Envelope and inside address	Salutation	Complimentary close	In conversation / introduction
governor (continued)	His } Her } Excellency, the Governor of ----	Sir Madam Dear Governor Smith	Respectfully yours Very sincerely yours	(1 and 2) same as above
governor (acting)	The Honorable John } Amelia } R. Smith Acting Governor of ----	Sir Madam Dear Mr. / Ms. / Mrs. / Miss Smith	Respectfully yours Very sincerely yours	(1 and 2) Mr., Ms., Mrs., Miss Smith
governor-elect	The Honorable John } Amelia } R. Smith Governor-elect of ----	Dear Mr. / Ms. / Mrs. / Miss Smith	Very truly yours Sincerely yours	(1) Mr., Ms., Mrs., Miss Smith (2) Mr., Ms., Mrs., Miss Smith, the Governor-elect
governor (former)	The Honorable John } Amelia } R. Smith	Dear Mr. / Ms. / Mrs. / Miss Smith	Very truly yours Sincerely yours	(1) Mr., Ms., Mrs., Miss Smith (2) John } Amelia } R. Smith, former Governor of ----
judge, state court	The Honorable John } Amelia } R. Smith Judge of the ---- Court	Dear Judge Smith	Very truly yours Sincerely yours	(1 and 2) Judge Smith

judge/justice,
state supreme court—see SUPREME COURT, STATE

Addressee	Form of Address	Salutation	Complimentary Close	(1) Oral Reference (2) Written Reference
lieutenant governor	The Honorable The Lieutenant Governor of ---- *or* The Honorable John ⎱ R. Smith Amelia ⎰ Lieutenant Governor of ----	Sir Madam Sir Madam Dear Mr. ⎱ Ms. ⎬ Smith Mrs. ⎰ Miss	Respectfully yours Respectfully yours Sincerely yours	(1) Mr., Ms., Mrs., Miss Smith (2) Lieutenant Governor Smith or the Lieutenant Governor or ---- Smith, Lieutenant Governor of ---- (only used outside his or her state) or the Lieutenant Governor of ---- (only used outside his or her state)
representative, state (includes assemblyman, delegate)	The Honorable John ⎱ R. Smith Amelia ⎰ House of Representatives (or The State Assembly or The House of Delegates)	Sir Madam Dear Mr. ⎱ Ms. ⎬ Smith Mrs. ⎰ Miss	Very truly yours Sincerely yours	(1) Mr., Ms., Mrs., Miss Smith (2) Mr., Ms., Mrs., Miss Smith or ---- Smith, the state Representative (or Assemblyman or Delegate) from ----
secretary of state	The Honorable The Secretary of State of ---- *or* The Honorable John ⎱ R. Smith Amelia ⎰ Secretary of State of ----	Sir Madam Sir Madam Dear Mr. ⎱ Madam ⎰ Secretary	Very truly yours Very truly yours Sincerely yours	(1) Mr., Ms., Mrs., Miss Smith (2) Mr., Ms., Mrs., Miss Smith or ---- Smith, Secretary of State of ----

	Address on envelope	Salutation	Complimentary close	Informal address
senate, state, president of	The Honorable John / Amelia R. Smith, President of the Senate of the State (or Commonwealth) of ----	Sir / Madam / Dear Mr. / Ms. / Mrs. / Miss Smith [Senator]	Very truly yours / Sincerely yours	(1 and 2) Senator, Mr., Ms., Mrs., Miss Smith
senator, state	The Honorable John / Amelia R. Smith, The Senate of ----	Sir / Madam / Dear Senator Smith	Very truly yours / Sincerely yours	(1) Senator Smith or Senator (2) Senator Smith or ---- Smith, the state Senator from ----
speaker, state assembly, house of delegates, or house of representatives	The Honorable John / Amelia R. Smith, Speaker of ----	Sir / Madam / Dear Mr. / Ms. / Mrs. / Miss Smith	Very truly yours / Sincerely yours	(1) Mr., Ms., Mrs., Miss Smith (2) the Speaker of the ---- or ---- Smith, Speaker of the ----
supreme court, state, associate justice	The Honorable John / Amelia R. Smith, Associate Justice of the Supreme Court of ----	Sir / Madam / Dear Justice Smith	Very truly yours / Sincerely yours	(1) Mr., Madam Justice Smith or Judge Smith (2) Mr., Madam Justice Smith or Judge Smith or ---- Smith, associate justice of the ---- Supreme Court
supreme court, state, chief justice	The Honorable John / Amelia R. Smith, Chief Justice of the Supreme Court of ----	Sir / Madam / Dear Mr. / Madam Chief Justice	Very truly yours / Sincerely yours	(1) Mr., Madam Chief Justice or Chief Justice Smith or Judge Smith (2) Chief Justice Smith or ---- Smith, Chief Justice of the ---- Supreme Court

Addressee	Form of Address	Salutation	Complimentary Close	(1) Oral Reference (2) Written Reference
supreme court, state, presiding justice	The Honorable John } R. Smith Amelia } ----- Presiding Justice ----- Division Supreme Court of -----	Sir Madam Dear Mr. } Justice Madam	Very truly yours Sincerely yours	(1) Mr., Madam Justice Smith or Judge Smith (2) Mr., Madam Justice Smith or Judge Smith or ----- Smith, Presiding Justice of -----

MILITARY RANKS—A TYPICAL BUT NOT EXHAUSTIVE LIST: TITLES APPLY TO BOTH MALE AND FEMALE MEMBERS OF THE ARMED FORCES—BOTH FULL TITLES AND ABBREVIATIONS SHOWN

Addressee	Form of Address	Salutation	Complimentary Close	(1) Oral Reference (2) Written Reference
admiral (coast guard or navy)	Admiral or ADM John R. Smith, USN	Dear Admiral Smith	Very truly yours Sincerely yours	(1 and 2) Admiral Smith
rear admiral	Rear Admiral or RADM John R. Smith, USCG	Dear Admiral Smith	Very truly yours Sincerely yours	(1 and 2) Admiral Smith
vice admiral	Vice Admiral or VADM John R. Smith, USN	Dear Admiral Smith	Very truly yours Sincerely yours	(1 and 2) Admiral Smith
airman *as* **airman basic airman airman first class**	AB AMN } John R. Smith, A1C } USAF	Dear Airman Smith Dear Airman Smith Dear Airman Smith	Sincerely yours Sincerely yours Sincerely yours	(1 and 2) Airman Smith (1 and 2) Airman Smith (1 and 2) Airman Smith
brigadier general—SEE GENERAL				
cadet U.S. Air Force Academy U.S. Military Academy	Cadet John } R. Smith Amelia } Cadet John } R. Smith Amelia }	Dear Cadet Smith Dear Cadet Smith	Sincerely yours Sincerely yours	(1 and 2) Cadet Smith (1 and 2) Cadet Smith

captain				
air force	Captain or CPT John R. Smith, USAF	Dear Captain Smith	Sincerely yours	(1 and 2) Captain Smith
army	Captain or CPT John R. Smith, USA	Dear Captain Smith	Sincerely yours	(1 and 2) Captain Smith
coast guard	Captain or CAPT John R. Smith, USCG	Dear Captain Smith	Sincerely yours	(1 and 2) Captain Smith
marine corps	Captain or Capt. John R. Smith, USMC	Dear Captain Smith	Sincerely yours	(1 and 2) Captain Smith
navy	Captain or CAPT John R. Smith, USN	Dear Captain Smith	Sincerely yours	(1 and 2) Captain Smith
colonel (air force, army)	Colonel or COL John R. Smith, USAF (or USA)	Dear Colonel Smith	Sincerely yours	(1 and 2) Colonel Smith
(marine corps)	Colonel or Col. John R. Smith, USMC	Dear Colonel Smith	Sincerely yours	(1 and 2) Colonel Smith
commander (coast guard or navy)	Commander or CDR John R. Smith, USCG (or USN)	Dear Commander Smith	Sincerely yours	(1 and 2) Commander Smith
corporal (army)	Corporal or CPL John R. Smith, USA	Dear Corporal Smith	Sincerely yours	(1 and 2) Corporal Smith
lance corporal (marine corps)	Lance Corporal or L/Cpl. John R. Smith, USMC	Dear Corporal Smith	Sincerely yours	(1 and 2) Corporal Smith
ensign (coast guard, navy)	Ensign or ENS John R. Smith, USN (or USCG)	Dear Mr. Smith or if female Dear Ensign Smith	Sincerely yours	(1) Mr. Smith; Ensign Smith (if female) (2) Ensign Smith
first lieutenant (air force, army)	First Lieutenant or 1LT John R. Smith, USAF	Dear Lieutenant Smith	Sincerely yours	(1 and 2) Lieutenant Smith
(marine corps)	First Lieutenant or 1st. Lt. John R. Smith, USMC	Dear Lieutenant Smith	Sincerely yours	(1 and 2) Lieutenant Smith

Addressee	Form of Address	Salutation	Complimentary Close	(1) Oral Reference (2) Written Reference
general (air force, army)	General or GEN John R. Smith, USAF (or USA)	Dear General Smith	Very truly yours Sincerely yours	(1 and 2) General Smith
(marine corps)	General or Gen. John R. Smith, USMC		Very truly yours Sincerely yours	(1 and 2) General Smith
brigadier general (air force, army)	Brigadier General or BG John R. Smith, USAF (or USA)	Dear General Smith	Very truly yours Sincerely yours	(1 and 2) General Smith
(marine corps)	Brigadier General or Brig. Gen. John R. Smith, USMC	Dear General Smith	Very truly yours Sincerely yours	(1 and 2) General Smith
lieutenant general (air force, army)	Lieutenant General or LTG John R. Smith, USAF (or USA)	Dear General Smith	Very truly yours Sincerely yours	(1 and 2) General Smith
(marine corps)	Lieutenant General or Lt. Gen. John R. Smith, USMC	Dear General Smith	Very truly yours Sincerely yours	(1 and 2) General Smith
major general (air force, army)	Major General or MG John R. Smith, USAF (or USA)	Dear General Smith	Very truly yours Sincerely yours	(1 and 2) General Smith
(marine corps)	Major General or Maj. Gen. John R. Smith, USMC	Dear General Smith	Very truly yours Sincerely yours	(1 and 2) General Smith
lieutenant (coast guard, navy)	Lieutenant or LT John R. Smith, USCG (or USN)	Dear Mr. Smith or if female Dear Lieutenant Smith	Sincerely yours	(1) Mr. Smith; Lieutenant Smith (if female) (2) Lieutenant Smith

lieutenant colonel (air force, army)	Lieutenant Colonel or LTC John R. Smith, USAF (or USA)	Dear Colonel Smith	Sincerely yours	(1) Colonel Smith (2) Lieutenant Colonel Smith
(marine corps)	Lieutenant Colonel or Lt. Col. John R. Smith, USMC	Dear Colonel Smith	Sincerely yours	(1) Colonel Smith (2) Lieutenant Colonel Smith
lieutenant commander (coast guard, navy)	Lieutenant Commander or LCDR John R. Smith, USCG (or USN)	Dear Commander Smith	Sincerely yours	(1) Commander Smith (2) Lieutenant Commander Smith

lieutenant, first—see FIRST LIEUTENANT

lieutenant general—see GENERAL

lieutenant junior grade (coast guard, navy)	Lieutenant (j.g.) or LTJG John R. Smith, USCG (or USN)	Dear Mr. Smith or if female Dear Lieutenant Smith	Sincerely yours	(1) Mr. Smith; Lieutenant Smith (if female) (2) Lieutenant (j.g.) Smith

lieutenant, second—see SECOND LIEUTENANT

major (air force, army)	Major or MAJ John R. Smith, USAF (or USA)	Dear Major Smith	Sincerely yours	(1 and 2) Major Smith
(marine corps)	Major or Maj. John R. Smith, USMC	Dear Major Smith	Sincerely yours	(1 and 2) Major Smith

major general—see GENERAL

midshipman (Coast Guard and Naval Academies)	Midshipman John Amelia } R. Smith	Dear Midshipman Smith	Sincerely yours	(1 and 2) Midshipman Smith

Addressee	Form of Address	Salutation	Complimentary Close	(1) Oral Reference (2) Written Reference
petty officer and chief petty officer ranks (coast guard, navy)	Petty Officer or PO John R. Smith, USN (or USCG)	Dear Mr. Smith	Sincerely yours	(1) Mr. Smith (2) Mr. Smith or Petty Officer Smith
	Chief Petty Officer or CPO John R. Smith, USN (or USCG)	Dear Mr. Smith		(1) Mr. Smith or Chief Smith or Chief Petty Officer Smith
private (army)	Private or PVT John R. Smith, USA	Dear Private Smith	Sincerely yours	(1 and 2) Private Smith
(marine corps)	Private or Pvt. John R. Smith, USMC	Dear Private Smith	Sincerely yours	(1 and 2) Private Smith
private first class (army)	Private First Class or PFC John R. Smith, USA	Dear Private Smith	Sincerely yours	(1 and 2) Private Smith
seaman (coast guard, navy)	Seaman or SMN John R. Smith, USCG (or USN)	Dear Seaman Smith	Sincerely yours	(1 and 2) Seaman Smith
seaman first class	Seaman First Class or S1C John R. Smith, USCG (or USN)	Dear Seaman Smith	Sincerely yours	(1 and 2) Seaman Smith
second lieutenant (air force, army)	Second Lieutenant or 2LT John R. Smith, USAF (or USA)	Dear Lieutenant Smith	Sincerely yours	(1 and 2) Lieutenant Smith
(marine corps)	Second Lieutenant or 2nd. Lt. John R. Smith, USMC	Dear Lieutenant Smith	Sincerely yours	(1 and 2) Lieutenant Smith
sergeant (a cross section of sergeant ranks)				

first sergeant (army) (marine corps)	First Sergeant or 1SG John R. Smith, USA First Sergeant or 1st. Sgt. John R. Smith, USMC	Dear Sergeant Smith Dear Sergeant Smith	Sincerely yours Sincerely yours	(1 and 2) Sergeant Smith (1 and 2) Sergeant Smith
gunnery sergeant (marine corps)	Gunnery Sergeant or Gy. Sgt. John R. Smith, USMC	Dear Sergeant Smith	Sincerely yours	(1 and 2) Sergeant Smith
master sergeant (air force) (army)	Master Sergeant or MSGT John R. Smith, USAF Master Sergeant or MSG John R. Smith, USA	Dear Sergeant Smith Dear Sergeant Smith	Sincerely yours Sincerely yours	(1 and 2) Sergeant Smith (1 and 2) Sergeant Smith
senior master sergeant (air force)	Senior Master Sergeant or SMSGT John R. Smith, USAF	Dear Sergeant Smith	Sincerely yours	(1 and 2) Sergeant Smith
sergeant (army, air force)	Sergeant or SGT John R. Smith, USA (or USAF)	Dear Sergeant Smith	Sincerely yours	(1 and 2) Sergeant Smith
sergeant major (army) (marine corps)	Sergeant Major or SGM John R. Smith, USA Sergeant Major or Sgt. Maj. John R. Smith, USMC	Dear Sergeant Major Smith Dear Sergeant Major Smith	Sincerely yours Sincerely yours	(1 and 2) Sergeant Major Smith (1 and 2) Sergeant Major Smith
staff sergeant (air force) (army)	Staff Sergeant or SSGT John R. Smith, USAF Staff Sergeant or SSG John R. Smith, USA	Dear Sergeant Smith Dear Sergeant Smith	Sincerely yours Sincerely yours	(1 and 2) Sergeant Smith (1 and 2) Sergeant Smith
technical sergeant (air force)	Technical Sergeant or TSGT John R. Smith, USAF	Dear Sergeant Smith	Sincerely yours	(1 and 2) Sergeant Smith

Addressee	Form of Address	Salutation	Complimentary Close	(1) Oral Reference / (2) Written Reference
specialist (army) as specialist fourth class	Specialist Fourth Class or S4 / John R. Smith, USA	Dear Specialist Smith	Sincerely yours	(1 and 2) Specialist Smith
warrant officer (army) as warrant officer W1	Warrant Officer W1 or WO1 / John R. Smith, USA	Dear Mr. Smith	Sincerely yours	(1) Mr. Smith (2) Mr. Smith or Warrant Officer Smith
chief warrant officer (army) as chief warrant officer W4	Chief Warrant Officer W4 or CWO4 / John R. Smith, USA	Dear Mr. Smith	Sincerely yours	(1) Mr. Smith (2) Mr. Smith or Chief Warrant Officer Smith
other ranks not listed	full title + full name + comma + abbreviation of branch of service	*Dear* + rank + surname	Sincerely yours	(1 and 2) rank + surname

MISCELLANEOUS PROFESSIONAL TITLES

Addressee	Form of Address	Salutation	Complimentary Close	(1) Oral Reference / (2) Written Reference
attorney	Mr. / Ms. / Mrs. / Miss { John / Amelia } R. Smith Attorney-at-Law or { John / Amelia } R. Smith, Esq.	Dear { Mr. / Ms. / Mrs. / Miss } Smith	Very truly yours	(1) Mr., Ms., Mrs., Miss Smith (2) Mr., Ms., Mrs., Miss Smith or Attorney (or Atty.) Smith
dentist	{ John / Amelia } R. Smith, D.D.S. or Dr. { John / Amelia } R. Smith	Dear Dr. Smith	Very truly yours / Sincerely yours	(1 and 2) Dr. Smith

physician	John } R. Smith, M.D. Amelia } or Dr. John } R. Smith Amelia }	Dear Dr. Smith	Very truly yours Sincerely yours	(1 and 2) Dr. Smith
veterinarian	John } R. Smith, D.V.M. Amelia } or Dr. John } R. Smith Amelia }	Dear Dr. Smith	Very truly yours Sincerely yours	(1 and 2) Dr. Smith

UNITED NATIONS OFFICIALS

representative, American (with ambassadorial rank)	The Honorable John } R. Smith Amelia } United States Permanent Representative to the United Nations (address)	Sir Madam My dear Mr. } Ambassador Madam } Dear Mr. } Ambassador Madam }	Respectfully Sincerely yours	(1) Mr., Madam Ambassador or Mr., Ms., Mrs., Miss Smith (2) Mr., Ms., Mrs., Miss Smith or the United States Representative to the United Nations or UN Representative ---- Smith
representative foreign (with ambassadorial rank)	His } Excellency Her } John } R. Smith Amelia } Representative of ---- to the United Nations (address)	Excellency My dear Mr. } Ambassador Madame } Dear Mr. } Ambassador Madame }	Respectfully Sincerely yours	(1) Mr., Madame Ambassador or Mr., Ms., Mrs., Miss Smith (2) Mr., Ms., Mrs., Miss Smith or the Representative of ---- to the United Nations or UN Representative ---- Smith

Addressee	Form of Address	Salutation	Complimentary Close	(1) Oral Reference / (2) Written Reference
secretary-general	His Excellency John R. Smith Secretary-General of the United Nations (address)	Excellency My dear Mr. Secretary-General Dear Mr. Secretary-General	Respectfully Sincerely yours	(1) Mr. Smith or Sir (2) the Secretary-General of the United Nations or UN Secretary-General Smith or The Secretary-General or Mr. Smith
undersecretary	The Honorable John } R. Smith Amelia } Undersecretary of the United Nations (address)	Sir Madam Madame My dear Mr. / Ms. / Mrs. / Miss } Smith Dear Mr. / Ms. / Mrs. / Miss } Smith	Very truly yours Sincerely yours Sincerely yours	(1) Mr., Ms., Mrs., Miss Smith (2) Mr., Ms., Mrs., Miss Smith or the Undersecretary of the United Nations or UN Undersecretary ---- Smith

Multiple Addressees

Inside Address Styling	Salutation Styling
two or more men with same surname	
Mr. Arthur W. Jones	Gentlemen
Mr. John H. Jones	
or	*or*
Messrs. A. W. and J. H. Jones	
or	Dear Messrs. Jones
The Messrs. Jones	
two or more men with different surnames	
Mr. Angus D. Langley	Gentlemen *or* Dear Mr. Langley and
Mr. Lionel P. Overton	Mr. Overton
or	
Messrs. A. D. Langley and	Dear Messrs. Langley and Overton
L. P. Overton	
or	
Messrs. Langley and Overton	
two or more married women with same surname	
Mrs. Arthur W. Jones	Mesdames
Mrs. John H. Jones	
or	*or*
Mesdames A. W. and J. H. Jones	
or	Dear Mesdames Jones
The Mesdames Jones	
two or more unmarried women with same surname	
Miss Alice H. Danvers	Ladies
Miss Margaret T. Danvers	
or	*or*
Misses Alice and Margaret Danvers	
or	Dear Misses Danvers
The Misses Danvers	
two or more women with same surname but whose marital status is unknown or irrelevant	
Ms. Alice H. Danvers	Dear Ms. Alice and Margaret Danvers
Ms. Margaret T. Danvers	
two or more married women with different surnames	
Mrs. Allen Y. Dow	Dear Mrs. Dow and Mrs. Frank
Mrs. Lawrence R. Frank	
or	*or*
Mesdames Dow and Frank	Mesdames *or* Dear Mesdames Dow
	and Frank
two or more unmarried women with different surnames	
Miss Elizabeth Dudley	Ladies *or* Dear Miss Dudley and
Miss Ann Raymond	Miss Raymond
or	*or*
Misses E. Dudley and A. Raymond	Dear Misses Dudley and Raymond
two or more women with different surnames but whose marital status is unknown or irrelevant	
Ms. Barbara Lee	Dear Ms. Lee and Ms. Key
Ms. Helen Key	

SPECIAL TITLES, DESIGNATIONS, AND ABBREVIATIONS: A GUIDE TO USAGE

Doctor If *Doctor* or its abbreviation *Dr.* is used before a person's name, academic degrees (as *D.D.S., D.V.M., M.D.,* or *Ph.D.*) are not included after the surname. The title *Doctor* may be typed out in full or abbreviated in a salutation, but it is usually abbreviated in an envelope address block and in an inside address in order to save space. When *Doctor* appears in a salutation, it must be used in conjunction with the addressee's surname:

Dear Doctor Smith   *or*   Dear Dr. Smith   *not*   Dear Doctor

If a woman holds a doctorate, her title should be used in business-related correspondence even if her husband's name is also included in the letter:

Dr. Ann R. Smith and
  Mr. James O. Smith
Dear Dr. Smith and Mr. Smith

If both husband and wife are doctors, one of the following patterns may be followed:

Dr. Ann R. Smith and
  Dr. James O. Smith
or
The Drs. Smith
or
The Doctors Smith
or
Drs. Ann R. and James O. Smith
or
Ann R. Smith, M.D.
James O. Smith, M.D.
more formal
My dear Doctors Smith
informal
Dear Drs. Smith
Dear Doctors Smith

Address patterns for two or more doctors associated in a joint practice are:

Drs. Francis X. Sullivan and
  Philip K. Ross
or
Francis X. Sullivan, M.D.
Philip K. Ross, M.D.
more formal
My dear Drs. Sullivan and Ross
informal
Dear Drs. Sullivan and Ross
Dear Doctors Sullivan and Ross
Dear Dr. Sullivan and Dr. Ross
Dear Doctor Sullivan and Doctor Ross

Esquire The abbreviation *Esq.* for *Esquire* is used in the United States after the surnames of professional persons such as architects, attorneys, and consuls, regardless of their sex. In Great Britain, it is generally used after the surnames of people who have distinguished themselves in professional, diplomatic, or social circles. For example, when addressing a letter to a high corporate officer of a British firm, one should include *Esq.* after his surname, both on the envelope and in the inside address. Under no circumstances should *Esq.* appear in a salutation. This rule applies to both American and British correspondence. If a courtesy title such as *Dr., Hon., Miss, Mr., Mrs.,* or *Ms.* is used before the addressee's name, *Esq.* is omitted. The plural of *Esq.* is *Esqs.* and is used with the surnames of multiple addressees.

Examples:

Carolyn B. West, Esq.
American Consul

Dear Ms. West

Samuel A. Sebert, Esq.
Norman D. Langfitt, Esq.
or
Sebert and Langfitt, Esqs.
or
Messrs. Sebert and Langfitt
Attorneys-at-Law

Gentlemen
Dear Mr. Sebert and Mr. Langfitt
Dear Messrs. Sebert and Langfitt

Simpson, Tyler, and Williams, Esqs.
or
Scott A. Simpson, Esq.
Annabelle W. Tyler, Esq.
David I. Williams, Esq.

Dear Ms. Tyler and Messrs. Simpson
  and Williams

British

Jonathan A. Lyons, Esq.
President

Dear Mr. Lyons

Honorable In the United States, *The Honorable* or its abbreviated form *Hon.* is used as a title of distinction (but not rank) and is accorded elected or appointed (but not career) government officials. Neither the full form nor the abbreviation is ever used by its recipient either in written signatures, letterhead, business or visiting cards, or in typed signature blocks. While it may be used in an envelope address block and in an inside address of a letter addressed to him or her, it is <u>never</u> used in a salutation. *The Honorable* should never appear before a surname standing alone: there must always be an intervening first name, an initial or initials, or a courtesy title:

The Honorable John R. Smith
The Honorable J. R. Smith
The Honorable J. Robert Smith
The Honorable Mr. Smith
The Honorable Dr. Smith

If *The Honorable* is used with a full name, a courtesy title should not be added. *The Honorable* may also precede a woman's name:

The Honorable Jane R. Smith
The Honorable Mrs. Smith

However, if the woman's full name is given, a courtesy title should not be added. When an official and his wife are being addressed, his full name should be typed out, as

The Honorable John R. Smith   *or*   The Honorable and Mrs. John R. Smith
  and Mrs. Smith   Dear Mr. and Mrs. Smith

The stylings "Hon. and Mrs. Smith" and "The Honorable and Mrs. Smith" should never be used. If, however, the official's full name is unknown, the styling is:

The Honorable Mr. Smith and Mrs. Smith

If a married woman holds the title and her husband does not, her name appears first on business-related correspondence addressed to both persons. However, if the couple is being addressed socially, the woman's title may be dropped unless she has retained her maiden name for use in personal as well as business correspondence:

business correspondence
The Honorable Harriet M. Johnson   Dear Mrs. (*or* Governor, etc.)
   and Mr. Johnson   Johnson and Mr. Johnson

social correspondence
Mr. and Mrs. Robert Y. Johnson   Dear Mr. and Mrs. Johnson

if maiden name retained:

business correspondence
The Honorable Harriet A. Mathieson   Dear Ms. Mathieson
   and Mr. Robert Y. Johnson   and Mr. Johnson

social correspondence
Ms. Harriet A. Mathieson   Dear Ms. Mathieson
Mr. Roger Y. Johnson   and Mr. Johnson

If space is limited, *The Honorable* may be typed on the first line of an address block, with the recipient's name on the next line:

The Honorable
John R. Smith
   and Mrs. Smith

When *The Honorable* occurs in a running text or in a list of names in such a text, the *T* in *The* is then lowercased:

. . . a speech by the Honorable Charles H. Patterson, the American Consul in Athens. . . .

In informal writing such as newspaper articles, the plural forms *the Honorables* or *Hons.* may be used before a list of persons accorded the distinction. However, in official or formal writing either *the Honorable Messrs.* placed before the entire list of surnames or *the Honorable* or *Hon.* repeated before each full name in the list may be used:

formal   . . . was supported in the motion by the Honorable Messrs. Clarke, Good-
                   fellow, Thomas, and Harrington.
                   . . . met with the Honorable Albert Y. Langley and the Honorable Frances P.
                   Kelley.
informal   . . . interviewed the Hons. Jacob Y. Stathis, Samuel P. Kenton, William L.
                   Williamson, and Gloria O. Yarnell—all United States Senators.

Jr. and **Sr.** The designations *Jr.* and *Sr.* may or may not be preceded by a comma, depending on office policy or writer preference; however, one styling should be selected and adhered to for the sake of uniformity:

John K. Walker Jr.
or
John K. Walker, Jr.

Jr. and *Sr.* may be used in conjunction with courtesy titles, and with academic degree abbreviations or with professional rating abbreviations, as

Mr. John K. Walker[,] Jr.
Dr. John K. Walker[,] Jr.
General John K. Walker[,] Jr.
The Honorable John K. Walker [,] Jr.
Hon. John K. Walker[,] Jr.
John K. Walker[,] Jr., Esq.
John K. Walker[,] Jr., M.D.

Formation of the possessive with either *Jr.* or *Sr.* follows this pattern:

singular possessive
John K. Walker, Jr.'s hospitality suite is open.

plural possessive
The John K. Walker, Jrs.' house is on this street.

Plural patterns for *Jr.* and *Sr.* are:

The John K. Walkers Jr. are here.
The John K. Walkers, Jr. are here.
The John K. Walker Jrs. are here.
The John K. Walker, Jrs. are here.

Madam and **Madame** The title *Madam* should be used only in salutations of highly impersonal or high-level governmental and diplomatic correspondence, unless the writer is certain that the addressee is married. The French form *Madame* is recommended for salutations in correspondence addressed to foreign diplomats and heads of state. See Forms of Address Chart for examples.

Mesdames The plural form of *Madam, Madame,* or *Mrs.* is *Mesdames,* which may be used before the names of two or more married women associated together in a professional partnership or in a business. It may appear with their names on an envelope and in an inside address, and it may appear with their names or standing alone in a salutation:

Mesdames T. V. Meade and P. A. Tate
Mesdames Meade and Tate

Dear Mesdames Meade and Tate
Mesdames

Mesdames V. T. and A. P. Stevens
The Mesdames Stevens

Dear Mesdames Stevens
Mesdames

See also the Multiple Addressees Chart.

Messrs. The plural abbreviation of *Mr.* is *Messrs.* It is used before the surnames of two or more men associated in a professional partnership or in a business. *Messrs.* may appear on an envelope, in an inside address, and in a salutation when used in conjunction with the surnames of the addressees; however, this abbreviation should never stand alone. Examples:

Messrs. Archlake, Smythe, and Dabney
Attorneys-at-Law

Dear Messrs. Archlake, Smythe, and Dabney
Gentlemen

Messrs. K. Y. and P. B. Overton
Architects

Dear Messrs. Overton
Gentlemen

Messrs. should never be used before a compound corporate name formed from two surnames:

Lord & Taylor
Woodward & Lothrup

For correct use of *Messrs.* + *The Honorable* or + *The Reverend,* see pages 78 and 82, respectively.

Misses The plural form of *Miss* is *Misses,* and it may be used before the names of two or more unmarried women who are being addressed together. It may appear on an envelope, in an inside address, and in a salutation. Like *Messrs., Misses* should never stand alone but must occur in conjunction with a name or names. Examples:

Misses Hay and Middleton
Misses D. L. Hay and H. K. Middleton
Dear Misses Hay and Middleton
Ladies
Misses Tara and Julia Smith
The Misses Smith
Dear Misses Smith
Ladies

For a complete set of examples in this category, see the Multiple Addressees Chart, page 75.

Professor If used with a surname, *Professor* should be typed out in full; however, if used with a given name and initial or a set of initials as well as a surname, it may be abbreviated to *Prof.* It is, therefore, usually abbreviated in envelope address blocks and in inside addresses, but typed out in salutations. *Professor* should not stand alone in a salutation. Examples:

Prof. Florence C. Marlowe
Department of English
Dear Professor Marlowe
or
Dear Dr. Marlowe
or
Dear Miss Marlowe
      Mrs. Marlowe
      Ms. Marlowe
but not
Dear Professor

When addressing a letter to a professor and his wife, the title is usually written out in full unless the name is unusually long:

Professor and Mrs. Lee Dow
Prof. and Mrs. Henry Talbott-Smythe
Dear Professor and Mrs. Dow
Dear Professor and Mrs. Talbott-Smythe

Letters addressed to couples of whom the wife is the professor and the husband is not may follow one of these patterns:

Professor Diana Goode and Mr. Goode	*business correspondence*
Mr. and Mrs. Lawrence F. Goode	*business or social correspondence*
Professor Diana Falls Mr. Lawrence F. Goode	*if wife has retained maiden name*

Dear Professor Goode and Mr. Goode	*business correspondence*
Dear Mr. and Mrs. Goode	*business or social correspondence*
Dear Professor (*or* Ms.) Falls and Mr. Goode	*wife having retained her maiden name*

When addressing two or more professors—male or female, whether having the same or different surnames—type *Professors* and not "Profs.":

Professors A. L. Smith and C. L. Doe
Dear Professors Smith and Doe
Dear Drs. Smith and Doe
Dear Mr. Smith and Mr. Doe
Dear Messrs. Smith and Doe
Gentlemen
Professors B. K. Johns and S. T. Yarrell
Dear Professors Johns and Yarrell
Dear Drs. Johns and Yarrell
Dear Ms. Johns and Mr. Yarrell
Professors G. A. and F. K. Cornett
The Professors Cornett

Dear Professors Cornett	*acceptable for any combination*
Dear Drs. Cornett	
Gentlemen	*if males*
Ladies *or* Mesdames	*if females*
Dear Mr. and Mrs. Cornett	*if married*
Dear Professors Cornett	
Dear Drs. Cornett	

Reverend In formal or official writing, *The* should precede *Reverend;* however, *The Reverend* is often abbreviated to *The Rev.* or just *Rev.* especially in unofficial or informal writing, and particularly in business correspondence where the problem of space on envelopes and in inside addresses is a factor. The typed-out full form *The Reverend* must be used in conjunction with the clergyman's full name:

The Reverend Philip D. Asquith
The Reverend Dr. Philip D. Asquith
The Reverend P. D. Asquith

The Reverend may appear with just a surname only if another courtesy title intervenes:

The Reverend Mr. Asquith
The Reverend Professor Asquith
The Reverend Dr. Asquith

The Reverend, The Rev., or *Rev.* should not be used in the salutation, although any one of these titles may be used on the envelope and in the inside address. In salutations, the following titles are acceptable for clergymen: *Mr.* (or *Ms., Miss, Mrs.*), *Father, Chaplain,* or *Dr.* See the Forms of Address Chart under the section entitled "Clerical and Religious Orders" for examples. The only exceptions to this rule are salutations in letters addressed to high prelates of a church (as bishops, monsignors, etc.). See the Forms of Address Chart. When addressing a letter to a clergyman and his wife, the typist should follow one of these stylings:

The Rev. and Mrs. P. D. Asquith
or
The Rev. and Mrs. Philip D. Asquith
or

The Reverend and Mrs. P. D. Asquith
or
The Reverend and Mrs. Philip D. Asquith
but never
Rev. and Mrs. Asquith
Dear Mr. (*or, if having a doctorate,* Dr.) and Mrs. Asquith

Two clergymen having the same or different surnames should not be addressed in letters as "The Reverends" or "The Revs." or "Revs." They may, however, be addressed as *The Reverend* (or *The Rev.*) *Messrs.* or *The Reverend* (or *The Rev.*) *Drs.,* or the titles *The Reverend, The Rev.,* or *Rev.* may be repeated before each clergyman's name; as

The Reverend Messrs. S. J. and D. V. Smith
The Rev. Messrs. S. J. and D. V. Smith
The Reverend Messrs. Smith
The Rev. Messrs. Smith

and, as

The Rev. S. J. Smith and
  The Rev. D. V. Smith
Rev. S. J. Smith and
  Rev. D. V. Smith

with "Gentlemen" being the correct salutation. When writing to two or more clergymen having different surnames, the following patterns are acceptable:

The Reverend Messrs. P. A. Francis
  and F. L. Beale
The Rev. Messrs. P. A. Francis
  and F. L. Beale
The Rev. P. A. Francis
The Rev. F. L. Beale
Gentlemen
Dear Mr. Francis and Mr. Beale
Dear Father Francis and Father Beale

In formal texts, "The Reverends", "The Revs.", and "Revs." are not acceptable as collective titles (as in lists of names). *The Reverend* (or *Rev.*) *Messrs.* (or *Drs.* or *Professors*) may be used, or *The Reverend* or *The Rev.* or *Rev.* may be repeated before each clergyman's name. If the term *clergymen* or the expression *the clergy* is mentioned in introducing the list, a single title *the Reverend* or *the Rev.* may be added before the list to serve all of the names. While it is true that "the Revs." is often seen in newspapers and in catalogs, this expression is still not recommended for formal, official writing. Examples:

. . . were the Reverend Messrs. Jones, Smith and Bennett, as well as. . . .
Among the clergymen present were the Reverend John G. Jones, Mr. Smith, and Dr. Doe.
Prayers were offered by the Rev. J. G. Jones, Rev. Mr. Smith, and Rev. Dr. Doe.

Second, Third These designations after surnames may be styled as Roman numerals:

II
III
IV

or as ordinals:

2nd / 2d
3rd / 3d
4th

Such a designation may or may not be separated from a surname by a comma, depending on office policy or writer preference:

Mr. Jason T. Johnson III (*or* 3rd *or* 3d)
Mr. Jason T. Johnson, III (*or* 3rd *or* 3d)

Plural patterns for such designation are:

The Samuel Z. Watsons III (*or* 3rd *or* 3d) are here.
The Samuel Z. Watson IIIs (*or* 3rds *or* 3ds) are here.

Possessive patterns are:

Samuel Z. Watson III's (*or* 3rd's *or* 3d's) house is for sale.
The Samuel Z. Watson IIIs' (*or* 3rds' *or* 3ds') house is for sale.

The following illustrates the proper order of occurrence of initials representing academic degrees, religious orders, and professional ratings that may appear after a name and that are separated from each other by commas:

religious orders (as *S.J.*)
theological degrees (as *D.D.*)
academic degrees (as *Ph.D.*)
honorary degrees (as *Litt.D.*)
professional ratings (as *C.P.A.*)

Examples:

John R. Doe, B.S., M.S., P.E.

John R. Doe, B.S., Ph.D., D.V.M.

John R. Doe, M.D., Ph.D.
Chief of Staff
———— Hospital

John R. Doe, B.A., M.A., Ph.D., Litt.D.
Professor of English

The Rev. John R. Doe, S.J., D.D., LL.D.
Chaplain
———— College

1.9

CORRESPONDENCE WITH UNITED STATES GOVERNMENT AGENCIES: Letter Format and Security Precautions

Increasing government and private industry tie-ins have made it necessary that civilian contractors be familiar with special correspondence and security procedures. While it is true that letter format and security precautions vary with the policies of each government contracting agency and with the nature of each contract, the following overview should nevertheless be an adequate orientation and point of departure for the secretary heretofore unfamiliar with these matters.

The two most basic problems are: (1) ensuring that all material regardless of its classification be marked in such a way that it will be speedily delivered to its intended addressee and that copies of it are readily retrievable in company files, and (2) ensuring that all classified material be safeguarded according to government guidelines so that unauthorized persons may not gain access to it.

CORRESPONDENCE FORMAT
Letters to government agencies should conform to the guidelines of the agency with which one's firm is working. Letters incorrectly set up and addressed may be delayed, lost, rejected, or returned—a situation that at the least may cause costly production delays, or at the most may result in loss of a contract especially if bidding is going on under a deadline.

When writing to a nonmilitary government agency, it is correct to use any one of the generally accepted business letter stylings that have been discussed in this chapter, providing that a subject line and a reference line are included. These data are necessary for proper interagency routing of the letter. Elected and appointed officials should be correctly addressed, and their forms of address may be found in this chapter in the Forms of Address Chart.

The following general principles are applicable to correspondence directed to the Department of Defense:

1. A general Modified Block Letter style with numbered paragraphs is recommended.

2. If any section of the letter is classified, the highest classification category therein must be stamped at the top and the bottom of each page. This stamp is affixed above the printed letterhead and below the last line of the message on the first sheet, and above the heading and below the last notation on a second sheet. The CLASSIFIED BY and NATIONAL SECURITY INFORMATION stamps must be affixed at the bottom of the letterhead sheet.

3. A special mailing notation, if needed, is typically typed in all-capital letters or stamped in the upper left corner of the letterhead sheet and in the upper left corner of a continuation sheet or sheets.

4. The writer's courtesy title and surname, followed by a slash, followed by the typist's initials and another slash, followed by his telephone extension (if not already included in the printed letterhead) may be typed in the upper right corner of the first sheet.

5. An inverted date (day, month, year) forms the date line, blocked flush left about three lines from the last line of the letterhead. The date may be styled as
1 January 19--
or
1 Jan -- (last 2 digits of year)
but one styling should be used consistently throughout the letter. Abbreviations for the twelve months are:

Jan	May	Sep
Feb	Jun	Oct
Mar	Jul	Nov
Apr	Aug	Dec

6. Companies contracted to the government for specific projects usually assign control numbers to files and correspondence related to the project. This number should be included in the date line block, one line below the date.

7. The next element of the letter—whether it be the SUBJECT block or the TO block (the order varies according to agency)—is typed about three lines below the last line of the date block and is blocked flush left. The SUBJECT block, shown first in this book, consists of:
line 1. contract number
line 2. name of program or project
line 3. subject of the letter + appropriate security classification expressed as a parenthetical abbreviation, as (C) = Confidential, (S) = Secret, or (TS) = Top Secret.

8. The TO block which is really the inside address, is typed about three lines below the date block or the SUBJECT block (order varies with agency policy). Its internal elements are:
   line 1. initials or name of office
   line 2. name of applicable administrator (the addressee)
   line 3. name of organization
   line 4. geographical address + ZIP Code

9. The THROUGH or VIA block (caption varies with agency policy) is typed about three lines below any other blocks that precede it. This block is used in letters that must be sent through designated channels before reaching the addressee. Each agency, office, or individual should be named and addressed as in the TO block.

10. The REFERENCE block is typed about three lines below the last typed block. It contains a list of material or previous correspondence that must be consulted before the letter can be acted on by the addressee. This information is listed alphabetically or by numerals.

Note: Regardless of the order of the items discussed above, the captions SUBJECT, TO, THROUGH, and REFERENCE should <u>not</u> be visible in the window area of a window envelope. Only the address in the TO block should be visible in such an envelope. The styling of these captions varies; they may be entirely in capitals, they may be in capitals and lowercase, or they may be abbreviated to SUBJ, THRU, etc. Use the styling recommended by the agency with which your company is dealing.

11. There is no salutation.

12. The message begins flush left, two lines below the last line of the REFERENCE block. Paragraphs are numbered consecutively and are single-spaced internally but double-spaced between each other. Subparagraphs are alphabetized, are single-spaced internally, and are double-spaced between each other:
   1. xxxxxxxxxxxxxxxxxxxxxxxxxxxxxxxxxxxxxxxxxxxxxxxxxxxxxxxxxxxxxxxxxxxxxxxxxxx
      xxxxxxxxxxxxxxxxxxxxxxxxxxxxxxxxxxxxxxxxxxxxxxxxxxxxxxxxxxxxxxxxxxxxxxxxxxx

      a. xxxxxxxxxxxxxxxxxxxxxxxxxxxxxxxxxxxxxxxxxxxxxxxxxxxxxxxxxxxxxxxxxxxxxxxxx
         xxxxxxxxxxxxxxxxxxxxxxxxxxxxxxxxxxxxxxxxxxxxxxxxxxxxxxxxxxxxxxxxxxxxxxxxx

      b. xxxxxxxxxxxxxxxxxxxxxxxxxxxxxxxxxxxxxxxxxxxxxxxxxxxxxxxxxxxxxxxxxxxxxxxxx
         xxxxxxxxxxxxxxxxxxxxxxxxxxxxxxxxxxxxxxxxxxxxxxxxxxxxxxxxxxxxxxxxxxxxxxxxx

         1. xxxxxxxxxxxxxxxxxxxxxxxxxxxxxxxxxxxxxxxxxxxxxxxxxxxxxxxxxxxxxxxxxxxxxx
            xxxxxxxxxxxxxxxxxxxxxxxxxxxxxxxxxxxxxxxxxxxxxxxxxxxxxxxxxxxxxxxxxxxxxx

         2. xxxxxxxxxxxxxxxxxxxxxxxxxxxxxxxxxxxxxxxxxxxxxxxxxxxxxxxxxxxxxxxxxxxxxx
            xxxxxxxxxxxxxxxxxxxxxxxxxxxxxxxxxxxxxxxxxxxxxxxxxxxxxxxxxxxxxxxxxxxxxx

   2. xxxxxxxxxxxxxxxxxxxxxxxxxxxxxxxxxxxxxxxxxxxxxxxxxxxxxxxxxxxxxxxxxxxxxxxxxxx
      xxxxxxxxxxxxxxxxxxxxxxxxxxxxxxxxxxxxxxxxxxxxxxxxxxxxxxxxxxxxxxxxxxxxxxxxxxx

If there is a paragraph *1*, there must be a *2*, if there is an *a*, there must be a *b*, and so on.

13. There is no complimentary close.

14. The company name is typed flush left entirely in capital letters two lines beneath the last line of the message. The writer's name is typed in capitals and lowercase at least four lines below the company name, also flush left. His title and department name, if not already appearing on the printed letterhead, may be included beneath his name in capitals and lowercase, also flush left.

15. The typist's initials if not already included in the top right corner of the first sheet may be typed flush left, two lines below the last element of the signature block.

16. Enclosures are listed and identified two lines below the typist's initials. The numeral stylings 1. or (1) may be used. The appropriate headings are *Enclosure*(s), *Encl.*, or *Enc.* for the Air Force and Navy; and *Inclosure*(s), *Inc.* for the Army. Classification categories should be noted at the beginning of each applicable enclosure description as shown in enclosure (3) below. Example:

    Enc.: (1) 3 copies of Test Procedure Report
                 WXYzz dated 1 January 19--
          (2) 1 copy of Contract AF 45(100)-1147
          (3) (C) 2/c ea. specifications mentioned
                 in paragraph 7

    Some government agencies require that enclosures be noted in a block two or three spaces below the REFERENCE block.

    If enclosures are to be mailed under separate cover, they still must be listed on the letter and their classification categories noted.

17. The carbon copy notation *cc:* or *Copy to* is typed flush left two lines below any other notations. It includes an alphabetical listing of all individuals or persons not associated with the company who will receive copies. Addresses should be included. Internal copies should contain a complete list of external and internal recipients of copies. Example:

    cc: COL John K. Walker, + address
         (w/enc. (1)-2 copies)

18. In some correspondence, an approval line may be the last typed item on the page if the contracting agency must approve the material and return it to the contractor. In this case, two copies of the letter must be enclosed in the envelope. Example:

    APPROVED:

    _____

    (addressee's title)

    date

    This material may be typed two to four lines beneath the last notation and blocked with the left margin.

19. Continuation-sheet headings are typed six lines from the top edge of the page. The message is continued four lines beneath the heading. Continuation-sheet headings should include the SUBJECT block data as well as the company control number, the appropriate date, and the page number. See the following facsimile for setup.

CLASSIFIED MATERIAL

Both the United States government and its civilian contractors are responsible for the security of sensitive material passing between them—responsibility that specifically means the safeguarding of classified material against unlawful or unauthorized dissemination, duplication, or observation. Each employee of a firm that handles or has knowledge of classified material shares responsibility for protecting it while it is in use, in storage, or in transit. The Department of Defense has established an Information Security Program to implement its security regulations. These regulations are outlined in DoD 5200.1-R *Information Security Program Regulation* for sale by the Superintendent of Documents, U.S. Government Printing Office, Washington, DC 20402.

Letter Styling for Department of Defense Correspondence

CONFIDENTIAL

CERTIFIED MAIL

Mr. Exec/tp/413-734-4444

G.&C. Merriam Company
PUBLISHERS OF MERRIAM-WEBSTER REFERENCE BOOKS

1 January 19—
76TRANS123

SUBJECT: Contract AF 45(100)-1147
          Foreign Technology Program
          Life Sciences Translation QC (C)

TO: Initials or Name of Office
          Name of Applicable Administrator
          Organization
          Geographical Address + ZIP Code

THROUGH: Applicable Channels
          and Addresses
          Listed and Blocked

REFERENCE: (a) WXYZ letter ABCD/EF dated 1 December 19—
            (b) EFGH letter IJKL/MN dated 1 November 19—

1. This is a typical format for letters directed to the Department of Defense. Styling varies with the agency or department one is writing to; thus, a format consensus is shown here.

2. In letters containing classified information, the highest classification category of any included information must be noted at the top and bottom of each page.

   a. Since the subject of this letter is supposed to be CONFIDENTIAL, it is so stamped above the letterhead and at the bottom of the page.

   b. The parenthetical abbreviation (C) for CONFIDENTIAL is typed at the end of the subject line.

   c. Appropriate classification stamps are affixed at the bottom of the first page.

3. Special mailing notations if required are typically typed in the upper left corner of the page.

CLASSIFIED BY: _____

EXEMPT FROM GENERAL DECLASSIFICATION
SCHEDULE OF EXECUTIVE ORDER 11652
EXEMPTION CATEGORY
DECLASSIFY on

CONFIDENTIAL

NATIONAL SECURITY INFORMATION
Unauthorized disclosure subject to criminal sanctions.

47 FEDERAL STREET. SPRINGFIELD. MASSACHUSETTS 01101 TELEPHONE (413)-734-3134

CONFIDENTIAL

CERTIFIED MAIL

Contract AF 45(100)-1147   1 January 19—
Foreign Technology Program   76TRANS123
Life Sciences QC (C)   Page 2

4. If the writer's name and telephone number are not on the printed letterhead,
    they may be typed with the typist's initials in the upper right corner of
    the first page.

5. The date line featuring an inverted date and the company control number are
    flush left, with the date line three lines below the letterhead.

6. The SUBJECT block, sometimes placed after the TO and/or THROUGH blocks
    depending on agency preference, contains the contract number, project name,
    and subject of the letter.

7. The TO block is really the inside address. The THROUGH or VIA block lists
    the designated channels through which the letter must pass before it reaches
    the addressee.

8. The REFERENCE block lists related material or previous correspondence that
    must be referred to before action can be taken.

9. The SUBJECT, TO, THROUGH, and REFERENCE blocks are separated by triple-
    spacing, and are internally single-spaced.

10. There is no salutation. The message, comprising numbered paragraphs and
    alphabetized subparagraphs, begins two lines below the last line in the
    REFERENCE block.

11. Continuation-sheet headings begin six lines from the top edge of the page
    and contain subject data, date, pagination, and control number. The
    classification category must be stamped at the top and bottom of each
    continuation sheet.

12. There is no complimentary close. The company name is typed all in capitals
    two lines below the last message line, followed four lines down by the
    writer's name, title, and department in capitals and lowercase.

13. Typist's initials if not shown at the top of the first page may appear two
    lines below the signature block. Enclosures should be listed numerically
    and identified, as should carbon-copy recipients. Only external distribu-
    tion lists appear on the original.

G. & C. MERRIAM COMPANY

Executive Signature
Project Manager

Enclosures (1)   (C) 3 copies of Translation
                  Printout dated 30 December 19—

           (2)   1 copy of Contract AF 44(100)-1147

CONFIDENTIAL

Classification in industrial operations is based on government security guidance. Private sector management does not make original security classification decisions or designations but does implement the decisions of the government contracting agency with respect to classified information and material developed, produced, or handled in the course of a project. Management also designates persons within the firm who will be responsible for assuring that government regulations are followed. Each system and program involving research, development, testing, and evaluation of technical information is supported by its own program security guide.

What _is_ classified information and material? The following mini-glossary adapted from Department of Defense definitions should give the secretary some insight:

classified information official information which requires, in the interests of national security, protection against unauthorized disclosure and which has been so designated

national security a collective term encompassing both the national defense and the foreign relations of the United States

information knowledge which can be communicated by any means

official information information which is owned by, produced for or by, or is subject to the control of the United States government

material any document, product, or substance on or in which information may be recorded or embodied

document any recorded information (as written or printed material, data processing cards and tapes, graphics, and sound, voice, or electronic recordings in any form) regardless of its physical form or characteristics

upgrade to determine that certain classified information requires, in the interest of national security, a higher degree of protection against unauthorized disclosure than currently provided, and to change the classification designation to reflect this higher degree

downgrade to determine that certain classified information requires, in the interest of national security, a lower degree of protection against unauthorized disclosure than currently provided, and to change the classification designation to reflect this lower degree

declassify to determine that certain classified information no longer requires, in the interest of national security, any degree of protection against unauthorized disclosure, and to remove or cancel the classification designation

The classification categories

Unclassified referring to information or material requiring, in the interests of national security, no protection against unauthorized disclosure

Confidential referring to information or material requiring protection because its unauthorized disclosure could cause damage to the national security

Secret referring to information requiring a substantial degree of protection because its unauthorized disclosure could cause serious damage (as a serious disruption of foreign relations) to the national security

Top Secret referring to information or material requiring the highest degree of protection because its unauthorized disclosure could cause exceptionally grave damage (as armed hostilities against the U.S.) to the national security

are designated on correspondence and other matter by the stamps (not less than ¼″ in height)

UNCLASSIFIED	**SECRET**
CONFIDENTIAL	**TOP SECRET**

They may also be represented before individual paragraphs, in subject lines, and in enclosure notations by the parenthetical abbreviations

(U)   (C)   (S)   (TS)

The following general marking procedures are required by the government:

1. The overall classification of a document whether or not permanently bound or any copy or reproduction thereof must be conspicuously marked or stamped at the top and bottom on the outside of the front cover (if any), on the title page (if any), on the first page, on the last page, and on the outside of the back cover (if any). Each inside page of the document will be marked or stamped top and bottom with the highest classification category applicable to the information appearing there.
2. Each section, paragraph, subparagraph, or part of a document will be marked with the applicable parenthetical classification abbreviation (TS), (S), (C), or (U) when there are several degrees of classified information therein.
3. Large components of complex documents which may be used separately should be appropriately marked. These components include: attachments and appendices to a memorandum or a letter, annexes or appendices to a plan or program, or a major part of a report.
4. Files, folders, or packets for classified documents should be conspicuously marked on both front and back covers with the highest category of classification occurring in documents they enclose.
5. Transmittal documents including endorsements and comments should carry the highest classification category applicable to the information attached to them.

Basic mailing procedures for classified documents are outlined below. For detailed information on mailing and on hand-carrying such documents, see DoD publication 5200.1–R:

1. Classified material must be enclosed in two sealed opaque envelopes before it may be mailed through the U.S. Postal Service or by means of a commercial carrier.
2. Both envelopes must contain the names and addresses of the sender and the receiver.
3. The inner envelope must contain the appropriate classification category stamp, which must not be visible through the outer envelope.
4. The classified information should be protected from the inner envelope by being folded inward, or by use of a blank cover sheet.
5. The inner envelope must contain an appropriate classified-material receipt.
6. Confidential material is sent by CERTIFIED MAIL and Secret information is sent by REGISTERED MAIL. Top Secret documents require specialized transit procedures.

Classified material is downgraded and declassified as soon as there is no longer any national-security reason for it to be classified. The Department of Defense makes these judgments. An automatic schedule of downgrading has been set up for the three categories:

TOP SECRET will be downgraded automatically to SECRET at the end of the second full calendar year in which it was originated; downgraded to CONFIDENTIAL at the end of the fourth full calendar year in which it was originated; and declassified at the end of the tenth full calendar year in which it was originated.

SECRET will be downgraded automatically to CONFIDENTIAL at the end of the second full calendar year following the year in which it was originated, and will be declassified at the end of the eighth full calendar year following the year in which it was originated.

CONFIDENTIAL will be automatically declassified at the end of the sixth full calendar year following the year it was originated.

Classified documents therefore must be conspicuously marked or stamped to indicate the intended automatic downgrading timephase. This information is typed or stamped on the first or title page of a document immediately below or adjacent to the classification stamp.

Exemptions to the General Declassification Schedule will bear the following information affixed immediately below or adjacent to the classification stamp on the first or title page:

```
CLASSIFIED BY: _____
EXEMPT FROM GENERAL DECLASSIFICATION
SCHEDULE OF EXECUTIVE ORDER 11652
EXEMPTION CATEGORY
DECLASSIFY on
```

See the letter facsimile in this section for the positioning of the above information on a confidential document.

2

A GUIDE TO EFFECTIVE BUSINESS ENGLISH

CONTENTS

2.1

INTRODUCTION

The importance of cleanly typed business correspondence is discussed in Chapter 1, as are the appropriate ways to address the recipients of business correspondence. However, the mechanics of typing attractive-looking material is only one factor contributing to effective written communication. Other equally important elements are standard grammar, correct spelling, felicitous style, and sound presentation of ideas within logically constructed sentences and paragraphs. While the physical appearance and mechanical setup of the material will impress a reader at first glance, these other factors will create even more lasting impressions as a reader studies the material carefully and reflects on its content.

Thus, all of the interrelated elements illustrated in the diagram are vital to effective communication: If the grammar is substandard, if the spelling is incorrect, if the sentence structure is contorted, if the paragraph orientation is cloudy or irrational, and if the text is riddled with padding and clichés, one can reasonably anticipate negative reader reaction. Although the writer or dictator does bear the prime re-

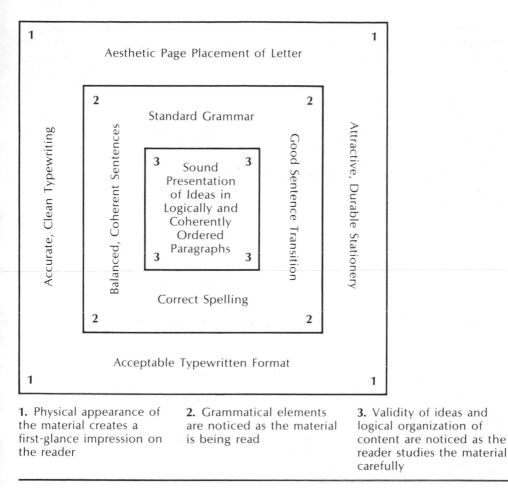

1. Physical appearance of the material creates a first-glance impression on the reader

2. Grammatical elements are noticed as the material is being read

3. Validity of ideas and logical organization of content are noticed as the reader studies the material carefully

sponsibility for his or her own grammar, diction, and usage, the secretary still should be competent enough in these areas to recognize basic grammatical and stylistic infelicities. Before typing questionable material, the secretary should research any doubtful points and then tactfully query the writer. The following sections have been prepared as a quick reference tool for just this sort of situation. Highly specialized questions may be answered by consulting a current book on English grammar (see the Appendix for a list of titles).

2.2

ABBREVIATIONS

The occurrence of abbreviations in typed or printed material is directly related to the nature of the material itself. For example, technical literature (as in the fields of aerospace, engineering, data processing, and medicine) abounds in abbreviations, but formal literary writing features relatively few such terms. By the same token, the presence or absence of abbreviations in business writing depends on the nature of the business. A secretary in a university English department and one in an electronics firm each will encounter widely different abbreviations.

Abbreviation styling (as capitalization and punctuation) is, unfortunately, inconsistent and at the same time arbitrary. No rules can be set down to cover all possible variations, exceptions, and peculiarities. Abbreviation styling depends most often on the writer's preference or the organization's policy; for example, some companies style the abbreviations for *cash on delivery* as *COD*, but others prefer *C.O.D.* It can be said, however, that some abbreviations (as *a.k.a., e.g., etc., f.o.b., i.e., No.,* and *viz.*) are backed by a strong punctuation tradition, and that others (as *GATT, LIFO, MIRV, PAYE,* and *SCAT*) that are pronounced as solid words tend to be all capitalized and unpunctuated. Styling problems can be alleviated by (1) consulting an adequate dictionary especially for capitalization guidance (2) following the guidelines of one's own organization, and (3) consulting an abbreviations dictionary for answers to highly specialized questions (see the Appendix for a list of titles).

Abbreviations are used (1) to avoid repetition of long words and phrases that may distract the reader (2) to save space and time (3) to reduce keystrokes and increase output, and (4) to reflect statistical data in limited space. When using an abbreviation that may be unfamiliar or confusing to the reader, one should give the full form first, followed by the abbreviation in parentheses, as

I shall address the American Bar Association (ABA) meeting in . . . .

followed in subsequent references by just the abbreviation, as

At this particular ABA meeting, I intend to . . . .

The chart on the following pages offers abbreviation guidelines with applicable illustrations. These guidelines are listed alphabetically by key words in boldface type.

ABBREVIATIONS

1. a or **an** before an abbreviation; *see* page 137.	
2. A.D. and **B.C.** are usually styled in printed matter as small punctuated unspaced capitals, but in typed material as punctuated unspaced capitals.	[41 B.C.] [41 B.C.] [A.D. 185 *also* 185 A.D.] [A.D. 185 *also* 185 A.D.] [fourth century A.D.] [fourth century A.D.]
3. Beginning a sentence with an abbreviation should be avoided unless the abbreviation represents a courtesy title.	[Page 22 contains . . . .] *but not* [P. 22 contains . . . .] *however* [Dr. Smith is here.] *or* [Doctor Smith is here.]
4. Capitalization of abbreviations; *see* page 98.	
5. Compass points are abbreviated when occurring after street names, and they can be unpunctuated; *however* compass points are usually typed out in full when they form essential internal elements of street names.	[2122 Fourteenth Street, NW] [192 East 49th Street]

6. **Dates** (as days and months) should not be abbreviated in running texts; months should not be abbreviated in general business-letter date lines but they may be abbreviated in government or military correspondence.

[I expect to meet with you in Chicago on Monday, June 1, 19--.]
general business-letter date line
[June 1, 19--]

military date line
[1 Jun --]

---

7. **Division of an abbreviation** either at the end of a line or between pages should be avoided.

[received his M.B.A. degree . . . .]
but not
[received his M.B.-
A. degree . . . .]

---

8. **Company names** are not abbreviated unless abbreviations comprise their official names;
and
the words *Airlines, Associates, Consultants, Corporation, Fabricators, Manufacturing,* and *Railroad* should not be abbreviated when part of proper names.

[Ginn and Company]
[The Bailey Banks and Biddle Company]
but
[Gulf + Western Industries, Inc.]
[Harwood Engineering Co., Inc.]

[Crompton & Knowles Corporation]
[Eastern Airlines]

---

9. **Footnotes** are sometimes introduced by abbreviations.

[4 Ibid.]

---

10. **Geographical and topographical names.** U.S. Postal Service abbreviations for states are all-capitalized and unpunctuated, as are the Postal Service abbreviations for streets and localities when used on envelopes addressed for automated mass handling,
and
ordinals are abbreviated in some street addresses

also
names of countries are typically abbreviated in tabular data, but are typed in full in running texts (exception: *U.S.S.R.*)
and
United States is often abbreviated when it modifies names of federal agencies, policies, or programs; when it is used as a noun, it is usually typed in full.

[Smithville, ST 56789]
addressed for automated handling
[1234 SMITH BLVD
SMITHVILLE, ST 56789]
regular address styling
[1234 Smith Blvd. (*or* Boulevard)
Smithville, ST 56789]

[147 East 31st Street]
[147 East 3d Avenue]
[147 East 3rd Avenue]

in a table [U.A.R. *or* UAR]
in a text [The United Arab Republic and the U.S.S.R. announced the trade agreement.]

[U.S. Information Agency]
[U.S. foreign policy]
but
[The United States has offered to. . . .]

---

11. **Latin words and phrases** commonly used in general writing are often abbreviated.

[etc.] [i.e.] [e.g.] [viz.]

---

12. **Latitude and longitude** are abbreviated in tabular data, but are typed in full in running texts.

in a table
[lat. 10°20′N *or* lat. 10-20N]
in a text
[from 10°20′ north latitude to 10°30′ south latitude. . . .]

13. Laws and bylaws when first quoted are typed in full; however, subsequent references to them in a text may be abbreviated.	*first reference* [Article I, Section 1] *subsequent references* [Art. I, Sec. 1]
14. Measures and weights may be abbreviated in figure + unit combinations; however, if the numeral is written out, the unit must also be written out.	[15 cu ft] *or* [15 cu.ft.] *but* [fifteen cubic feet]
15. Number when part of a set unit (as a contract number), when used in tabular data, or when used in bibliographic references may be abbreviated to *No.* (sing.) or *Nos.* (plural).	[Contract No. N-1234-76-57] [Policy No. 123-5-X] [Publ. Nos. 12 and 13]
16. Period with abbreviations; *see* PERIOD, RULE 3.	
17. Personal names should not be abbreviated; however, initials of famous persons are sometimes used in place of their full names.	[George S. Patterson] *not* [Geo. S. Patterson] *but* [J.F.K. *or* JFK]
18. Plurals of abbreviations may be formed by addition of *-s* *or* by the addition of *-'s* especially if the abbreviation is internally punctuated, except for a few such terms that are punctuated only with terminal periods, in which case the apostrophe is omitted *or* by repeating a letter of the abbreviation *or* by no suffixation.	[MLDs] [MPs] [PNs] [f.o.b.'s] *but* [Nos. 3 and 4] [Figs. A and B] [p. → pp.] [f. → ff.] [1 sec → 30 sec] [1 ml → 24 ml]
19. Possessives of abbreviations are formed in the same way as those of nouns: the singular possessive is signaled by addition of *-'s* *and* the plural possessive, by addition of *-s'*.	[the British PM's decision] [British Commonwealth PMs' decisions]
20. Saint may be abbreviated when used before the name of a saint; however, it may or may not be abbreviated when it forms part of a surname, depending on the name.	[St. Peter] *or* [Saint Peter] *but* [Ruth St. Denis] [Augustus Saint-Gaudens]
21. Scientific terms In binomial nomenclature a genus name may be abbreviated after the first reference to it is typed out.	[(first reference) *Escherichia coli*] [(subsequent references) *E. coli*]

22. **Time** When time is expressed in figures, the abbreviations that follow may be set in unspaced punctuated lowercase letters; if capitals or small capitals are used, one space should separate the letters (the writer's or organization's preference will dictate the particular style used)
and
standard measurements of time (as in tabular data) are expressed in figures and typically unpunctuated abbreviations.

[8:30 a.m. *or* 8:30 A. M. *or* 8:30 A. M.]

[10 sec] [18 min] [24 hr]
[17 yr] [52 wk] [19 mo] [100 da]

23. **Titles** The only titles that are invariably abbreviated are *Mr., Ms., Mrs.,* and *Messrs.* Other titles (except for *Doctor* which may be written out or abbreviated) are given in full form in business-letter salutations;

[Ms. Lee A. Downs]
[Messrs. Lake, Mason, and Nambeth]
[Dear Doctor Howe] *or*
[Dear Dr. Howe]
but
[Dear Professor Howe]
[Dear General Howe]
[Dear Private Howe]

but
titles may be abbreviated in envelope address blocks and in inside addresses;

[Dr. John P. Howe]
[COL John P. Howe, USA]
[GEN John P. Howe, USA]
[PVT John P. Howe, USA]

also
Honorable and *Reverend* when used with *The* are typed out, but if used without *The,* they may be abbreviated; *see also pages* 77–78; 81–82.

[The Reverend Samuel I. O'Leary]
[The Honorable Samuel I. O'Leary]
but
[Rev. Samuel I. O'Leary]
[Hon. Samuel I. O'Leary]

24. **Versus** is abbreviated as the lowercase Roman letter *v.* in legal contexts; it is either typed in full or abbreviated as lowercase Roman letters *vs.* in general contexts.

in a legal context
[*Smith* v. *Vermont*]
in a general context
[honesty versus dishonesty]
or
[honesty vs. dishonesty]

2.3

CAPITALIZATION

Capitals are used for two broad purposes in English: They mark a beginning (as of a sentence) and they signal a proper noun or adjective. The following eighty-one principles, each with a bracketed example or examples, describe the most common uses of capital letters. These principles are alphabetically ordered under the following headings:

Abbreviations
Beginnings
Proper Nouns, Pronouns, and Adjectives
    armed forces

awards
deity
epithets
geographical and topographical references
governmental, judicial, and political bodies
names of organizations
names of persons
numerical designations
particles and prefixes
personifications
pronouns
scientific terms
time periods, zones, and divisions
titles of persons
titles of printed matter
trademarks
transport

When uncertain about the capitalization of a term not shown below, the secretary should consult a dictionary such as *Webster's New Collegiate Dictionary.*

CAPITALIZATION

Abbreviations

1.	Abbreviations are capitalized if the words they represent are proper nouns or adjectives; consult a dictionary when in doubt of styling.	[98 F for *Fahrenheit*] [Nov. for *November*] [NBC for National Broadcasting Company] *but* [a.k.a. for *also known as*]
2.	Most acronyms are capitalized unless they have been assimilated into the language as parts of speech, and as such are lowercased; consult a dictionary when in doubt of styling.	[OPEC] [CREEP] [MIRV] [GATT] *but* [quasar] [laser] [radar] [sonar] [scuba] [snafu]
3.	Abbreviations of government agencies, military units, and corporate names are usually capitalized.	[CIA] [FBI] [HEW] [USIA] [USAF] [MAAG] [RCA] [ITT]
4.	Abbreviations of air force, army, coast guard, and navy ranks are all-capitalized; those of the marine corps are capitalized and lowercased; *see* FORMS OF ADDRESS.	[BG John T. Dow, USA] [LCDR Mary I. Lee, USN] [Col. S. J. Smith, USMC]
5.	Abbreviations of compass points are capitalized; punctuation styling depends on the writer's or organization's preference.	[lat. 10°20′N] [2233 Fourteenth Street, N.W. 2233 Fourteenth Street, NW. 2233 Fourteenth Street, NW]
6.	Abbreviations of academic degrees and professional ratings may be all-capitalized or capitalized and lowercased, depending on the word; consult a dictionary when in doubt of styling.	[D.D.S.] [M.B.A.] [P.E.] [C.P.A.] [Ph.D.] [Litt.D.]

Beginnings

7. The first word of a sentence, of a sentence fragment, or of a complete sentence enclosed in parentheses is capitalized;
however
the first word of a parenthetical phrase or sentence enclosed by parentheses and occurring within another sentence is lowercased.

[The meeting was postponed.]
[No! I cannot do it.]
[Will you go?]
[Prices. Nothing has gone down.
—*Audio-Visual Communications*]
[The meeting ended. (The results were not revealed.)]
but
[She studied economics under Dr. Heller (he wrote this text, you know) at the university.]

8. The first word of a direct quotation is capitalized
but
a split direct quotation tightly bound to the rest of a sentence may be lowercased at the beginning of its continued segment or segments.

[He said, "We must consider the sales problems."]
["The Administration has denied the story," the paper reports, and goes on to say that "the President feels the media are irresponsible."]

9. The first word of a direct question within a sentence or of a series of questions within a sentence may be capitalized.

[That question is this: Is man an ape or an angel?
—*Benjamin Disraeli*]
[Is there someone standing behind you? On your right? On your left?
—*Management World*]

10. The first word following a colon may be lowercased or capitalized if it introduces a complete sentence; while the former is the more usual styling, the latter is common especially when the sentence introduced by the colon is fairly lengthy and distinctly separate from the preceding clause.

[The advantage of this particular system is clear: it's inexpensive.]
[The situation is critical: This company cannot hope to recoup the fourth-quarter losses that were sustained in five operating divisions.]

11. The first words of run-in or blocked enumerations that form complete sentences are capitalized as are the first words of phrasal lists and enumerations blocked beneath running texts;

[The advantages of the task inventories are . . . as follows: 1. The technique is economical. 2. The information . . . is quantifiable.
—*Business Education World*]
[Occupations are divided into the following . . . areas:
Business, marketing, and management
Personal and public services
Health
. . . .
—*Business Education World*]

however
phrasal enumerations run-in with the introductory text are lowercased.

but
[. . . the following sequence of activities has proven . . . satisfying . . . (1) teacher demonstration; (2) performance by students; (3) diagnosis of errors. . . .
—*Business Education World*]

12. The words *Whereas* and *Resolved* are capitalized in minutes and legislation, as is the word *That* or an alternative word or expression which immediately follows either.	[Resolved, That. . . .] [Whereas, Substantial benefits. . . .] [Whereas, The Executive Committee. . . .] [Resolved by the ----, the ---- concurring, That. . . .]

13. The first letter of the first word in an outline heading is capitalized.	[I. Editorial tasks
	  II. Production responsibilities
	      A. Cost estimates
	      B. Bids]

14. The first letter of the first word in a salutation and a complimentary close is capitalized as is the first letter of each noun following SUBJECT and TO headings (as in memorandums).	[Dear Bob] [Gentlemen] [My dear Dr. Smith] [Very truly yours] [Yours very truly] [SUBJECT: Pension Plan] [TO: All Department Heads]
15. The first word of a line of poetry is conventionally capitalized.	[Yet this abundant issue seem'd to me But hope of orphans and unfather'd fruit; For summer and his pleasures wait on thee, And, thou away, the very birds are mute. . . . —William Shakespeare]

Proper Nouns, Pronouns, and Adjectives

Armed Forces

16. Branches and units of the armed forces are capitalized as are easily recognizable short forms of full branch and unit designations.	[United States Army] *and* [a contract with the Army] [Corps of Engineers] *and* [a bridge built by the Engineers]

Awards

17. Awards and prizes are capitalized.	[the Nobel Prize for Literature] [Nobel Peace Prize] [Nobel Prize winners] [Academy Award] [Oscar] [Emmy]

Deity

18. Words designating the Deity are usually capitalized; *compare* RULE 55.	[An anthropomorphic, vengeful Jehovah became a spiritual, benevolent Supreme Being. —A. R. Katz]

Epithets

19. Epithets used in place of names or titles are capitalized.	[the Big Board] [the Fleet Street boys] [No. 10 Downing Street announced . . . .] [The White House has verified . . . .]

Geographical and Topographical References

20. Divisions of the earth's surface and names of distinct areas, regions, places, or districts are capitalized, as are adjectives and some derivative nouns and verbs; consult a dictionary when in doubt.	[the Middle East] [the Middle Eastern situation] [Eastern Hemisphere] [the Great Divide] [Tropic of Cancer] [Geneva] [Texas] [Vietnam] [Vietnamization] [Vietnamize] *but* [sovietism *often* Sovietism] [sovietize *often* Sovietize]

21. Compass points are capitalized when they refer to a geographical region or when they are part of a street name, but are lowercased when they refer to simple direction.	[out West] [back East] [down South] [up North] [the South] [the Middle West] [the West Coast] [157 East 92nd Street] *but* [west of the Rockies] [traveling east on I-84] [the west coast of Florida]
22. Adjectives derived from compass points and nouns designating the inhabitants of some geographical regions are capitalized; when in doubt of the proper styling, consult a dictionary.	[a Southern accent] [a Western drawl] [members of the Eastern Establishment] [Northerners]
23. Popular names of localities are capitalized.	[the Corn and Wheat Belts] [the Gold Coast] [the Loop] [the Eastern Shore] [City of Brotherly Love] [Foggy Bottom] [the Village]
24. Topographical names are capitalized, as are generic terms (as *channel, lake, mountain*) that are essential elements of total names.	[the English Channel] [Lake Como] [the Blue Ridge Mountains] [Atlantic Ocean] [Great Barrier Reef] [Mississippi River] [Black Sea] [Bering Strait] [Strait of Gilbraltar] [Ohio Valley]
25. Generic terms occurring before topographical names are capitalized except when *the* precedes them, in which case the generic term is lowercased.	[Lakes Michigan and Superior] [Mounts Whitney and Rainier] *but* [the rivers Don and Volga] [the river Thames]
26. Plural generic terms occurring after multiple topographical names are lowercased, as are singular or plural generic terms that are used descriptively or alone.	[the Himalaya and Andes mountains] [the Don and Volga rivers] [the valley of the Ohio] [the Ohio River valley] [the river valley] [the valley]
27. Words designating global, national, regional, or local political divisions are capitalized when they are essential elements of specific names; however, they are usually lowercased when they precede a proper name or stand alone.	[the British Empire] *but* [the empire] [Oregon State] *but* [the state of Oregon] [Bedford County] *but* [the county of Bedford] [New York City] *but* [the city of New York] [Ward 1] *but* [fires in three wards]
28. Terms designating public places are capitalized when they are essential elements of specific names; however, they are lowercased when they occur after multiple names or stand alone.	[Fifth Avenue] [Brooklyn Bridge] [Empire State Building] [St. John's Church] [the Dorset Hotel] [Central Park] [Washington Square] [Bleecker Street] [Ford Theater] *but* [on the bridge] [Fifth and Park avenues] [the Dorset and the Drake hotels] [St. John's and St. Mark's churches]
29. Well-known short forms of place names are capitalized.	[Fifth Avenue → the Avenue] [Wall Street → the Street] [New York Stock Exchange → the Exchange]

Governmental, Judicial, and Political Bodies

30. The terms *administration* and *government* are capitalized when they are applicable to a particular government in power.

[The Administration announced a new oil and gas program.] [the Ford Administration] *but* [White House parties vary from one administration to another.]

31. The names of international courts are capitalized.

[the International Court of Arbitration]

32. The U.S. Supreme Court and the short forms *Supreme Court* and *Court* referring to it are capitalized.

[the Supreme Court of the United States] [the United States Supreme Court] [the U.S. Supreme Court] [the Supreme Court] [the Court]

33. Official and full names of higher courts are capitalized; however, the single designation *court* is usually lowercased when referring to them.

[the United States Court of Appeals for the Second Circuit] [the Michigan Court of Appeals] [the Virginia Supreme Court] [the Court of Queen's Bench] *but* [the federal courts] [the court of appeals ruled that . . . .] [the state supreme court] [the court]

34. Names of city and county courts are usually lowercased.

[the Lawton municipal court] [the Owensville night court] [police court] [the county court] [juvenile court]

35. The single designation *court* when specifically applicable to a judge or a presiding officer is capitalized.

[It is the opinion of this Court that. . . .] [The Court found that. . . .]

36. The term *federal* is capitalized only when it is an essential element of a name or title, when it identifies a specific government, or often when it refers to a particular principle of government.

[the Federal Bureau of Investigation] [. . . efforts made by the Federal Government. . . .] [the Federal principle of government] *but* [federal court] [federal district court] [federal agents] [federal troops]

37. Full names of legislative, deliberative, executive, and administrative bodies are capitalized as are the easily recognizable short forms of these names; however, nonspecific noun and adjective references to them are usually lowercased.

[United Nations Security Council] *and* [the Security Council] *but* [the council] [United States Congress] *and* [the Congress] *but* [congressional elections] [the Maryland Senate] *but* [the state senate] [Department of State] *and* [the State Department] *and* [State] *but* [the department]

38. The term *national* is capitalized when it precedes a capitalized word or when it forms a part of a specific name or title; however, it is lowercased when used as a descriptive word or as a noun.

[National Socialist Party] *but* [in the interests of national security] [the screening of foreign nationals]

39. The names of political parties and their adherents are capitalized, but the word *party* may or may not be capitalized, depending on the writer's or organization's preference.

[Democrats] [Republicans] [Liberals] [Tories] [the Democratic party] *or* [the Democratic Party]

Names of Organizations

40. Names of firms, corporations, organizations, and other such groups are capitalized.

[G. & C. Merriam Company] [EXXON Corporation] [Rotary International]

41. Common nouns used descriptively and occurring after two or more organization names are lowercased.

[American and Allegheny airlines] [the ITT and IBM corporations]

42. The words *company* and *corporation* are capitalized when they refer to one's own organization even when the full organization name is omitted; however, they are lowercased when they refer to another organization.

[It is contrary to the policies of our Company to. . . .] *but* [He works for a company in Delaware.] [Give me the name of your company.]

43. Words such as *group, division, department, office,* or *agency* that designate corporate units are capitalized when used with a specific name.

[The Plastics Molding and Fabrication Division is in charge of the project.] *but* [The memorandum was sent to all operating divisions.]

Names of Persons

44. The names of persons are capitalized.

[John W. Jones, Jr.]

45. Words designating peoples and their languages are capitalized.

[Canadians] [Turks] [Swedish] [Welsh] [Iroquois] [Ibo] [Vietnamese]

46. Derivatives of proper names are capitalized when used in their primary sense; consult a dictionary when in doubt of styling.

[Saudi Arabian oil interests] [Keynesian economics] [Manhattanite] [Orwellian society] *but* [manila envelope] [pasteurize] [bohemian tastes]

Numerical Designations

47. Monetary units typed in full (as in legal documents and on checks) are capitalized.

[Your fee is Two Thousand Dollars ($2,000.00), payable upon receipt of. . . .]

48. Nouns introducing a set number (as on a policy) are usually capitalized.

[Order 123] [Policy 123-4-X] [Flight 409] [Regulation 15] [Stock Certificate X12345] [Exhibit A] [Form 2E] [Catalog No. 65432]

49. Nouns used with numbers or letters to designate major reference headings (as in a literary work) are capitalized; however, minor reference headings and subheads are typically lowercased.

[Book II] [Volume V] [Division 4] [Section 3] [Article IV] [Table 5] [Figure 8] [Appendix III] [Plate 16] [Part 1] *but* [footnote 14] [page 101] [line 8] [note 10] [paragraph 6.1] [item 16] [question 21]

Particles and Prefixes

50. Particles forming initial elements of surnames may or may not be capitalized, depending on the styling of the individual name; however, if a name with a lowercase initial particle begins a sentence, the particle is capitalized.

[Du Pont] [D'Albert] [De Camp]
[de la Mare] [de Tocqueville]
[du Maurier] [Von Braun] [von Kleist]

[The novels of du Maurier are. . . .]
but
[Du Maurier's novels are. . . .]

51. Elements of hyphened compounds are capitalized in running texts if they are proper nouns or adjectives; consult a dictionary when in doubt of styling.

[East-West trade] [U.S.-U.S.S.R. détente]
[Arab-Israeli relations]
but
[a nineteenth-century poet]
[. . . said the idea was un-American.]

52. Prefixes occurring with proper nouns or adjectives are capitalized if they are essential elements of the compounds or if they begin headings or sentences; they are lowercased in other instances. NOTE: If a second element in a two-word compound modifies the first element or if both elements constitute a single word, the second element is lowercased.

[Afro-American customs] [nationalism of the Pan-Slavic variety]
[Pro-Soviet sentiments were voiced.]
but
[The pro-Soviet faction objected.]

[French-speaking peoples]
[an A-frame house]

Personifications

53. Personifications are capitalized.

[We have Mr. and Ms. Entropy among us . . . bent on breaking down civilized discourse.
         —Alan Harrington]

[The Chair recognized the Senator from. . . .]

Pronouns

54. The pronoun *I* is capitalized.

[He and I will attend the meeting.]

55. Pronouns referring to the Deity are capitalized; *compare* RULE 18.

[. . . that when God chose to save the heathen He could do it by Himself.
         —Elmer Davis]

Scientific Terms

56. Names of geological eras, periods, epochs, and strata and of prehistoric ages are capitalized, but the generic nouns which they modify are lowercased except when those generic nouns appear <u>before</u> the names of eras, periods, epochs, strata, or divisions, in which case they are capitalized.

[Silurian period] [Pleistocene epoch]
[Neolithic age]
but
[Age of Reptiles]

57. Names of planets, constellations, asteroids, stars, and groups of stars are capitalized, but *sun, earth,* and *moon* are lowercased unless they are listed with other astronomical names.

[Venus] [Big Dipper] [Sirius] [Pleiades]
but
[sun] [earth] [moon]
[unmanned space probes to the Moon and to Mars]

58. Meterological phenomena are lower-cased.	[northern lights] [aurora borealis]
59. Genera in binomial nomenclature in zoology and botany are capitalized; however, species names are lowercased.	[a cabbage butterfly (*Pieris rapae*)] [a common buttercup (*Ranunculus acris*)] [the robin (*Turdus migratorius*)] [the haddock (*Melanogrammus aeglefinus*)]
60. New Latin names of classes, families, and all groups above genera in zoology and botany are capitalized; however, their derivative nouns and adjectives are lowercased in American English.	[Gastropoda] *but* [gastropod] [Thallophyta] *but* [thallophyte]
61. Proper names forming essential elements of terms designating diseases, syndromes, signs, tests, and symptoms are capitalized.	[Parkinson's disease] [syndrome of Weber] [German measles] [Rorschach test] *but* [mumps] [measles] [herpes simplex]
62. Proprietary (i.e., brand and trade) names of drugs are capitalized, but generic names of drugs are lowercased.	[. . .was tranquilized with Thorazine.] *but* [. . .recommended chlorpromazine—a generic name for. . . .]
63. Proper names forming essential elements of scientific laws, theorems, and principles are capitalized; however, the descriptive nouns *law*, *theorem*, *theory*, and the like are lowercased.	[Boyle's law] [the Pythagorean theorem] [Planck's constant] [Einstein's theory of relativity] [the second law of thermodynamics]
Time Periods, Zones, and Divisions **64.** Names of the seasons are capitalized if personified.	[the gentle touch of Spring] *but* [The book will be published in the spring.]
65. Days of the week, months of the year, holidays, and holy days are capitalized.	[Tuesday] [July] [Independence Day] [Good Friday] [Easter]
66. Historic periods are capitalized, but latter-day periods are often lowercased.	[Christian Era] [Golden Age of Greece] [Roaring Twenties] [Augustan Age] *often* [nuclear age] [the atomic age] [space age]
67. Numerical designations of historic time periods are capitalized when they are essential elements of proper names; otherwise, they are lowercased.	[the Roaring Twenties] *but* [the seventeenth century] [the twenties]
68. Historical events and appellations referring to particular time periods or events in time are capitalized.	[the Reign of Terror] [the Cultural Revolution] [Prohibition] [the Great Depression] [the New Frontier] [the Third Reich] [the Fourth Republic]
69. Time zones are capitalized when abbreviated, but lowercased when written out.	[EST] *but* [eastern standard time]

Titles of Persons

70. Corporate titles are capitalized when referring to specific individuals; when used in general or plural contexts, they are lowercased.

[Mr. John M. Jones, Vice-president] *and* [Mr. Carl T. Yowell, Sales Manager] *but* [The sales manager called me.] [All of our district managers will be here.]

71. Specific corporate and governmental titles may be capitalized when they stand alone or when they are used in place of particular individuals' names.

[The Executive Committee approved the Treasurer's report.] [The Secretary of State gave a news conference. The Secretary said . . . .] [The Judge will respond to your request when he returns to chambers.]

72. All titles preceding names are capitalized.

[President Roosevelt] [Archbishop Makarios] [Queen Elizabeth] [Dr. Doe] [Professor Doe] [The Honorable John M. Doe] [The Very Reverend John M. Doe] [Chief Justice Warren Burger]

73. Words of family relationship preceding names are capitalized.

[Aunt Laura] *but* [His aunt, Mrs. W. P. Jones, is the beneficiary.]

Titles of Printed Matter

74. Words in the titles of printed matter are capitalized except for internal conjunctions, prepositions (especially those having less than four letters), and articles;
also
verb segments (as *be* in *to be*) in infinitives, and particles (as *off* in *take off*) in two-word verbs are capitalized.

[*Writing and Communicating in Business*] [*Before the Fall*] [an essay entitled "Truth Instead of Falsity"] [*War and Peace*]

[*What is to Be Done?*] [*Go Down, Moses*]

75. Major sections (as a preface, an introduction, or an index) of books, long articles, or reports are capitalized when they are specifically referred to within the same material.

[The Introduction explains the scope of the book.]

76. The first word following a colon in a title is capitalized.

[*CBS: Reflections in a Bloodshot Eye*] [*The Dead of Winter: A Novel of Modern Scotland*]

77. The *the* before a title of a newspaper, magazine, or journal is capitalized if considered an essential element of the title; otherwise, it is lowercased,
and
descriptive nouns following publication titles are also lowercased.

[*The Wall Street Journal*] *but* [the New York *Times*]

[*Time* magazine]

78. Constitutional amendments are capitalized when referred to by title or number, but are lowercased when used as general terms.

[I took the Fifth Amendment] *but* [states ratifying constitutional amendments]

79. Formal titles of accords, pacts, plans, policies, treaties, constitutions, and similar documents are capitalized.	[The Geneva Accords] [Kellogg-Briand Pact] [the first Five Year Plan] [New Economic Policy] [Treaty of Versailles] [the United States Constitution] [the North Carolina Constitution] *but* [gun-control legislation] [various new economic policies] [the state constitution]
Trademarks **80.** Brand names, trademarks, and service marks are capitalized.	[the IBM Selectric] [Xerox] [Wite-Out correction fluid] [Air Express] [Laundromat]
Transport **81.** The names of ships, airplanes, and often spacecraft are capitalized.	[M. V. *West Star*] [Lindbergh's *Spirit of St. Louis*] [*Apollo 13*]

2.4

ITALICIZATION

The following are usually italicized in print and underlined in typescript or manuscript:

1. foreign words and phrases that have not been naturalized in English	[*aere perennius*] [*che sarà, sarà*] [*sans peur et sans reproche*] [*ich dien*] *but* [quid pro quo] [pasta] [enfant terrible] [a priori]
2. legal citations, both in full and shortened form, except when the person involved rather than the case itself is being discussed, in which instance the reference is typed in Roman letters without underlining	[*Jones v. Massachusetts*] [the *Jones* case] [*Jones*] *but* [the Jones trial and conviction]
3. letters when used as run-in enumerations (as in printed matter)	[. . . provided examples of (*a*) typing (*b*) transcribing (*c*) formatting (*d*) graphics . . . .]
4. names of ships and airplanes and often spacecraft	[M. V. *West Star*] [Lindberg's *Spirit of St. Louis*] [*Apollo 13*]
5. New Latin scientific names of genera, species, subspecies, and varieties (but not groups of higher rank such as phyla, classes, or orders, or derivatives of any of these) in botanical and zoological names	[a thick-shelled American clam *Mercenaria mercenaria*] [a cardinal (*Richmondena cardinalis*)] *but* [looked like an amoeba] [felid]

6. **titles** of books (but not chapter titles), magazines, newspapers, plays, movies, (but not radio or TV programs), works of art, and long musical compositions (but not symphonies)

[T. S. Eliot's *The Waste Land*] [the magazine *Business Week*] [*The Wall Street Journal*] [Shakespeare's *Othello*] [the movie *Gone With the Wind*] [Gainsborough's *Blue Boy*] [Mozart's *Don Giovanni*]
but
[CBS's "Sixty Minutes"] [the Ninth Symphony] ["Strangers in the Night"] [Pushkin's "Queen of Spades"] [Robert Frost's "Dust of Snow"] [his unpublished dissertation "Problems in Cost Accounting Procedures"]

NOTE 1: Titles of essays, short stories, short poems, and unpublished works are not italicized but are enclosed by quotation marks.

NOTE 2: Plurals of such italicized titles have Roman-type inflectional endings.

[. . . had two *Business Week*s under his arm.]

7. **words, letters, and figures** when referred to as words, letters, or figures

[The word *stationery* meaning "paper" is often misspelled.] [The *g* key on my typewriter sticks.] [The first 2 and the last 0 in that ZIP code are illegible.]

2.5

NUMERALS

In modern business writing, most numerals—and especially exact numbers above *ten*—are expressed in figures. However, general usage allows all numbers below 100 to be styled as words. Therefore, if material is being prepared for publication (as in a professional journal), the writer and the typist should familiarize themselves with the particular style guidelines of the publication to which the manuscript will be submitted. The most important suggestion that can be offered is this: one should be consistent. For example, if one decides to use a figure in expressing a monetary unit, one should not use a written-out numerical designation in expressing a similar monetary unit within the same text. Since usage is divided on some points, the following alphabetically arranged guidelines sometimes show alternative stylings.

NUMERALS

1. **Compounds** When two numbers comprise one item or unit, one of the numbers (usually the first) should be expressed in words, and the other (usually the second) should be expressed in figures; if, however, the second number is the shorter, it may be expressed in words instead.

[two 7-drawer files]
but
20 ten-drawer files]

2. **Compounds adjacent to other figures** Two sets of figures (except for those in monetary units) should not be typed in direct succession in a text unless they comprise a series; *compare* MONETARY UNITS; SERIES

[By 1976, one hundred shares of stock will be . . . .]
but not
[By 1976, 100 shares of stock will be . . . .]

3. **Date lines** Figures are used to express days and years in business-letter date lines.

[January 1, 19--]

---

4. **Enumerations** Run-in and vertical enumerations are often numbered.

[felt that she should (1) accept more responsibility (2) increase her overall production (3) maintain security precautions (4) . . . .]
[. . . . responsibilities include:
  1. Taking dictation
  2. Transcribing dictated matter
  3. Typing correspondence
  4. Routing the mail]

---

5. **Exact amounts** Exact amounts are usually expressed in figures unless they begin sentences, in which case they are expressed in words.

[We have processed your order for 300 copies of *Webster's Medical Speller*. . . .]
but
[Three hundred copies of *Webster's Medical Speller* have been shipped. . . .]

---

6. **Figures** Figures are usually used to indicate policy, catalog, contract, and page numbers; street, apartment, room, or suite numbers; sizes, weights, and measures; shares, mixed amounts, percentages, and fractions.

[Policy No. 1-234-X] [page 67] [Room 1000] [Apt. 1A] [Suite 40] [1234 Smith Boulevard] [size 7] [120 lb] [9' x 12'] [17 1/4] [14,280 shares] [78.654] [10 percent *or* 10%]

---

7. **Footnotes** Unspaced superscript numerals follow footnoted text material and superscript numerals followed by one space introduce the footnotes themselves.

[. . .is a prime factor in successful management."[2]]
[[2] Ibid., p. 300.]

---

8. **Four-digit numbers** A number of four or more digits has each set of three digits separated by a comma except in set combinations such as policy, contract, check, street, room, or page numbers, which are unpunctuated; *see also* COMMA, RULE 14

[15,000 keystrokes] [assets of $12,500] [a population of 1,500,000] [4,600 words]
but
[Check 34567] [page 4589] [the year 1980] [Room 6000] [Policy No. 3344]

---

9. **Fractions** Single fractions and fractions occurring with whole numbers are expressed in words in running texts; however, fractions occurring in series and in tabulations are expressed in figures.
NOTE: When some figure fractions in a text or table are not included on the keyboard, all fractions should be made up. Do not mix made-up and keyboard fractions.

[About three fourths of the budget has been used.] [The book weighs three and one-half pounds.]
but
[item 1 . . . . . 3 1/4 lb
 item 2 . . . . . 5 1/6 lb
 item 3 . . . . . 8 1/3 lb]
[1 1/2" x 1 1/8"] *not* [1½" x 1 1/8"]

---

10. **Market quotations** are expressed in figures.

[16 bid—20 asked]

11. **Measures and weights** may be styled as figure + abbreviated unit combinations (as in tables); however, if the unit of measure or weight is typed out in full, the number is expressed in words.

[15 cu ft] *or* [15 cu.ft.]
but
[fifteen cubic feet]

12. **Monetary units** when containing both mixed and even-dollar amounts and typed in series should each contain: decimal point + 2 ciphers for the even-dollar amounts; also, the $ should be repeated before each unit. Units of less than one dollar are usually typed in running texts as: figure + *cents* (or *¢*). Monetary units of one dollar or more or of less than one dollar are usually typed in vertical tabulations as: $ + decimal + figures on the first line, followed by decimals and figures only.

[The price of the book rose from $7.95 in 1970 to $8.00 in 1971 and to $8.50 in 1972.]
but
[The bids were $80, $100, and $300.]
[$10–$20]
[The pencil costs 15 cents.]
or
[The pencil costs 15¢.]
[$16.95
  .06
$17.01]

13. **No.** *or* **#** should be avoided when a descriptive word appears before a figure, except for catalog or contract numbers, which may be so labeled.

[periscope lens 345] [page 12]
but
[Stock No. 1234]

14. **Ordinals** are expressed in words in running texts, but they may be expressed in figure and abbreviation combinations in some street addresses; *see also page* 14.

[the twentieth century] [The fifteenth applicant is in the outer office.]
but
[167 East 93rd (*or* 93d) Street]

15. **Percentages** are usually styled in running text as: figure + *percent,* but in tabulations as: figure + %.

[. . .reported 55 percent of the editing complete. . . .]
but
[completed copy editing   60%
completed proofreading 10%
completed graphics   70%]

16. **Roman numerals** (as those used in outlines) should be aligned to the right for uniformity in the appearance of the typescript that follows the numerals. Horizontal strokes should not be added to the numerals I–X, since this multiplies the numbers by 1,000.

[V.
  VI.
 VII.
VIII.
  IX.
  X.]

17. **Round numbers** and approximations are usually expressed in words, although some writers prefer to express them in figures for added emphasis. Numbers over one million are often expressed in figures + words to save keystrokes and to facilitate the reader's interpretation; *compare* EXACT AMOUNTS

[about thirty to fifty applicants]
or for added emphasis
[processed more than 3,000 citations]

[a $10 million profit] *or*
[a 10 million-dollar profit]

18. **Series** Figures are usually used to express a series of numbers that occur in a sentence even if the amounts are less than ten or are rounded off.

[We need 4 desks, 3 chairs, and 5 typewriters.] [They ordered about 15 pen sets, 7 blotters, and 9 legal pads.]

19. Short numbers Numbers expressible in one or two short words may be written in words.	[. . . interviewed two new applicants.] *but* [. . . received 24 dozen job applications.]
20. Time Time of day is expressed in words when it is followed by the contraction *o'clock* or when *o'clock* is understood; when time is followed by the abbreviations *a.m.* or *p.m.,* it is expressed in figures.	[He left for the day at four o'clock.] [He left for the day at four.] [We shall arrive at a quarter to ten.] *but* [He left for the day at 4:30 p.m.] [We shall arrive at 9:45 a.m.]
21. Weights—*see* MEASURES AND WEIGHTS	

2.6

PUNCTUATION

The English writing system uses punctuation marks to separate groups of words for meaning and emphasis; to convey an idea of the variations of pitch, volume, pauses, and intonation of speech; and to help avoid contextual ambiguity. Punctuation marks should be used sparingly: overpunctuating often needlessly comlicates a passage and also increases keystrokes. English punctuation marks, together with general rules and bracketed examples of their use, follow in alphabetical order. At the end of the section, a Punctuation-Spacination Chart will be found.

' APOSTROPHE

1. indicates the possessive case of singular and plural nouns and indefinite pronouns, as well as of surname and terminal title combinations	[Mr. Wilson's store] [Senator Ceccacci's office] [the boy's mother] [the boys' mothers] [anyone's guess] [everyone's questions] [his father-in-law's car] [their father-in-laws' cars] [John Burns' *or* Burns's insurance policy] [the Burnses' insurance policy] [Jay Adams' *or* Adams's boat] [the Adamses' boat] [a witness' *or* witness's testimony] [John K. Walker Jr.'s house] [the John K. Walker Jrs.' house]
NOTE: The use of an apostrophe + *s* with words ending in /s/ or /z/ sounds usually depends on the pronounceability of the final syllable: if the syllable is pronounced, the apostrophe + *s* is usually used; if the syllable is silent, the apostrophe is retained but an *s* is usually not appended to the word.	[Mr. Gomez's store] [Knox's products] [the class's opinion] *but* [Degas' paintings] [Moses' laws] [for righteousness' sake]
2. indicates joint possession when appended to the last noun in a sequence	[Appleton and Delaney's report] [Doyle Dane Bernbach's advertisement]

3. indicates individual possession when appended to each noun in a sequence	[Appleton's and Delaney's report] [John's, Bill's, and Tim's boats] [Benton & Bowles' and Doyle Dane Bernbach's advertisements]
4. indicates possession when appended to the final element of a compound construction	[Norfolk, Virginia's newest shopping center contains a wide variety of stores.] [XYZ Corporation's order]
5. indicates understood possession	[The book is at your bookseller's.]
6. marks omissions in contractions	[isn't] [you're] [aren't] [o'clock]
7. marks omissions of numerals	[the class of '67]
8. often forms plurals of letters, figures, or words especially when they are referred to as letters, figures, or words	[His 1's and 7's looked alike.] [She has trouble pronouncing her *the*'s.] [five YF-16's] [the 1970's] *also* [the 1970s]
9. is often used with *s* in expressions of time, measurement, and money *but* is not used with a plural noun used as a modifier	[a dollar's worth of gas] [a year's subscription] [ten cents' worth] [six weeks' vacation] *but* [earnings statement] [sales projection]
10. is used with *s* before a gerund or gerund phrase	[She objected to the editor's changing her material.]

BRACKETS

1. set off extraneous data (as editorial comments especially within quoted material)	[He wrote, "I recieved [sic] your letter."]
2. function as parentheses within parentheses	[Bowman Act (22 Stat., Ch. 4, § [or sec.] 4, p. 50)]

● COLON

1. introduces a clause or phrase that explains, illustrates, amplifies, or restates what has gone before	[The sentence was poorly constructed: it lacked both unity and coherence.]
2. directs attention to an appositive	[He had only one pleasure: eating.]
3. introduces a series	[Three countries were represented: England, France, and Belgium.]
4. introduces lengthy quoted matter set off from a running text by blocked indentation but not by quotation marks	[I quote from Part I of the market study:]

5.	separates elements in statements of time and in bibliographic and biblical references	[8:30 a.m.] [New York: Smith Publishing Company] [John 4:10]
6.	separates titles and subtitles (as of books)	[*CBS: Reflections in a Bloodshot Eye*]
7.	punctuates the salutation in a business letter featuring the mixed punctuation pattern	[Gentlemen:] [Dear Bob:] [Dear Mr. Smith:]
8.	punctuates memo and government correspondence headings, and some subject lines in general business letters	[TO:] [THROUGH:] [VIA:] [SUBJECT:] [REFERENCE:]
9.	separates writer/dictator/typist initials in the identification lines of business letters	[WAL:coc] [WAL:WEB:coc]
10.	separates carbon copy or blind carbon copy abbreviations from the initials or names of copy recipients in business letters	[cc: RWP JES] [bcc: MWK FCM]

⁹ COMMA

1.	separates main clauses joined by coordinating conjunctions (such as *and, but, for, nor, or,* and sometimes *so* and *yet*) and very short clauses not so joined NOTE: Two very brief and tightly connected clauses joined by a coordinating conjunction and two predicates also so joined may be unpunctuated.	[She knew very little about him, and he volunteered nothing.] [He wanted to see her, so she went to his office.] [She knew, she was there, she saw it.] [He had found the motive, anyone could.] *but* [We have tested the computer and we are pleased.] [He discussed several important marketing problems in great detail and followed them with an appraisal of current sales.]
2.	sets off an adverbial clause that precedes a main clause	[When she found that her friends had deserted her, she sat down and cried.] [Although the airport was shut down for an hour, I was still able to fly home that night.]
3.	sets off an introductory phrase (as a participial, infinitive, or prepositional phrase) that precedes a main clause NOTE: If a phrase or a noun clause is the ʹsubject of the sentence, it is unpunctuated.	[Having made that decision, he turned to other matters.] [To understand this situation fully, you have to be familiar with the background.] [On Monday, he left early.] *but* [To have followed your plan would have been dishonest.] [Whatever is worth doing is worth doing well.]

4.	sets off from the rest of a sentence interrupting transitional words and expressions (such as *on the contrary, on the other hand*), conjunctive adverbs (such as *consequently, furthermore, however*), and expressions that introduce an illustration or example (such as *namely, for example*)	[Your second question, on the other hand, is unanswerable.] [The market predictions, however, remain fluid.] [He expects to travel through two countries, namely, France and England.] [He believes in responsibility, i.e., corporate responsibility.]
5.	often sets off contrasting and opposing expressions within sentences NOTE: When *and, or, either . . . or,* or *neither . . . nor* join items in a pair or in a series, the series is internally unpunctuated.	[I note that he has changed his style, not his ethics.] [The cost is not $65.00, but $56.65.] [A holiday, but not a vacation day, is still open.] *but* [The cost is either $65.00 or $56.65.] [A holiday and a vacation day are still open.] [He has changed neither his style nor his ethics nor his attitude.]
6.	separates words, phrases, or clauses in series joined at the end by a coordinating conjunction NOTE: The final comma before the conjunction in a series is optional; its purpose is to clarify meaning; *compare* COMMA, RULE 13	[Men, women, and children crowded into the square.] [He was young, eager, and restless.] [It requires one to travel constantly, to have no private life, and to need no income. . . . —Sara Davidson] [The hors d'oeuvres consisted of celery, pâté, olives, onions, and mushrooms.] *but meaning could be different* [The hors d'oeuvres consisted of celery, pâté, olives, onions and mushrooms.]
7.	separates coordinate adjectives and phrases modifying the same word NOTE: Two or more tightly connected adjectives in series each of which modifies the same word or a whole phrase may not require punctuation.	[It was a bright, beautiful, sunny day.] [They prepared a thorough, organized, in-depth study of the sales figures.] *but* [The company rented office space in a new 90-story concrete and glass building.] [a 15-cu.ft. upright freezer]
8.	sets off from the rest of a sentence parenthetic elements (as nonrestrictive modifiers and nonrestrictive appositives) NOTE: The comma does not set off restrictive or essential modifiers or appositives required to give a sentence or a phrase meaning.	[Our guide, who wore a blue beret, was an experienced traveler.] [We visited Gettysburg, the site of a famous battle.] [The Manufacturing Manager, Joseph Dowd, attended the meeting.] *but* [the late astronaut Gus Grissom]
9.	introduces a direct quotation, terminates a direct quotation that is neither a question nor an exclamation, and encloses segments of a split quotation	[Jim said, "I am leaving."] ["I am leaving," Jim said.] ["I am leaving," Jim said with determination, "even if you want me to stay."]
10.	sets off words in direct address, absolute phrases, and mild interjections	[We would like to discuss your account, Mr. Baker.] [I fear the encounter, his temper being what it is.] [Ah, that's my idea of a sensible man.]

11.	separates a tag question from the rest of a sentence	[It's been a fine sales conference, hasn't it?]
12.	indicates the omission of a word or words, and especially a word or words used earlier in a sentence	[Common stocks are favored by some investors; bonds, by others.]
13.	is used to avoid ambiguity and also to emphasize a particular phrase; *compare* COMMA, RULE 6, NOTE	[To Mary, Jane was someone special.] [The more accessories on a car, the higher the price.]
14.	groups numerals into units of three in separating thousands, millions, etc.; it is generally not used with numbers of four or more digits in set combinations; *see also* NUMERALS, RULE 8	[Smithville, pop. 100,000] *but* [3600 rpm] [the year 1980] [page 1411] [1127 Smith Street] [Room 3000]
15.	punctuates the date line of a business letter, an informal letter, and the expression of dates in running texts	[January 1, 19--] [On January 1, 19--, this company reported net profits of. . . .]
16.	follows a personal-letter salutation	[Dear Bob,]
17.	follows the complimentary close of a business letter or of an informal letter featuring the mixed punctuation pattern	[Very truly yours,] [Affectionately,]
18.	sometimes separates names from corporate titles in envelope address blocks, inside addresses, and signature blocks	[Mr. John P. Dow, President SWC Corporation Smithville, ST 56789] [Very truly yours, Lee H. Cobb, Editor General Reference Books]
19.	may separate elements within some official corporate names	[Leedy Manufacturing Co., Inc.] [Manville Rubber Products, Inc.]
20.	punctuates an inverted name	[Smith, John W.]
21.	separates a surname from a following academic, honorary, religious, governmental, or military title	[John W. Smith, M.D.] [John W. Smith, Esq.] [The Reverend John W. Smith, S.J.] [General John W. Smith, USA]
22.	sets off geographical names (as that of a state or county from that of a city), items in dates, and addresses from the rest of a running text	[Shreveport, Louisiana, is the site of a large air base.] [On December 7, 1941, Pearl Harbor was attacked.] [Mail your check to: XYZ Corporation, 1234 Smith Boulevard, Smithville, ST 56789.]

■■■■■■   **DASH**

1. usually marks an abrupt change or break in the continuity of a sentence	[When in 1960 the stockpile was sold off—indeed, dumped as surplus —natural-rubber sales were hard hit. —Barry Commoner]
2. is sometimes used in place of other punctuation (as the comma) when special emphasis is required (as in advertising)	[Mail your subscription—now!]
3. introduces a summary statement that follows a series of words or phrases	[Oil, steel, and wheat—these are the sinews of industrialization.]
4. often precedes the attribution of a quotation	[The next question was . . . how many administrative secretaries to a zone. —Samuel T. Rose]
5. may occur inside quotation marks if considered part of the quoted matter	["I'm just not going to—" and then he broke off very abruptly.]
6. may be used with the exclamation point or the question mark	[The faces of the crash victims—how bloody!—were shown on TV.] [Your question—was it on our proposed merger?—just can't be answered.]

● ● ● **ELLIPSIS** *or* **SUSPENSION POINTS** ● ● ● ●

1. indicates by three periods the omission of one or more words within a quoted passage	[The figures are accumulated for a month . . . and then the department's percentage of effectiveness is calculated. —Joyce B. Jewell]
2. indicates by four periods (the last of which represents a period) the omission of one or more sentences within a quoted passage or the omission of a word or words at the end of a sentence	[That recovering the manuscripts would be worth almost any effort is without question. . . . The monetary value of a body of Shakespeare's manuscripts would be almost incalculable. —Charlton Ogburn] [It will take scholars years to determine conclusively the origins, the history, and, most importantly, the significance of the finds. . . . —Robert Morse]
3. is used as a stylistic device especially in advertising copy to catch and hold the reader's attention	[An indispensable survival manual for job seekers . . . must reading for personnel managers. . . . —*Publishers Weekly*]
4. indicates halting speech or an unfinished sentence in dialogue	["I'd like to . . . that is . . . if you don't mind. . . ." He faltered and then stopped speaking.]

5. may be used as leaders (as in tables of contents)when spaced and extended for some length across a page
NOTE: leaders should be in perfect alignment vertically and should end precisely at the same point.

[Punctuation . . . . page 1
Capitalization . . . . page 10]

6. usually indicates omission of one or more lines of poetry when extended the length of a line

[Thus driven
By the bright shadow of that
                    lovely dream,
. . . .
He fled.
                    —Percy Bysshe Shelley]

● EXCLAMATION POINT

1. ends an emphatic phrase or sentence   [Mail your subscription—now!]

2. terminates an emphatic interjection   [Encore!]

▬ HYPHEN

1. marks division at the end of a line concluding with a syllable of a word that is to be carried over to the next line
[mill-
stone]
[pas-
sion]

2. is used between some prefix and root combinations, such as
prefix + proper name;   [pre-Renaissance art]
some prefixes ending with vowels + root;   [re-ink] *but* [reissue]
sometimes prefix + word beginning often with the same vowel;   [co-opted] *but* [cooperate]
stressed prefix + root word, especially when this combination is similar to a different word   [re-cover a sofa] *but* [recover from an illness]

3. is used in some compounds, especially those containing prepositions; consult a dictionary when in doubt of styling
[president-elect] [attorney-at-law]
[air-conditioned his house]
but
[bought an air conditioner]

4. is often used between elements of a compound modifier in attributive position in order to avoid ambiguity
[He is a small-business man.]
but
[He is a man who owns a small business.]

5. suspends the first part of a hyphened compound when joined with another hyphened compound in attributive position
[a six- or eight-cylinder engine]
but
[an engine of six or eight cylinders]

6. is used in expressing written-out numbers between 21 and 99

[forty-one]
[one hundred twenty-eight]

---

7. is used between the numerator and the denominator in writing out fractions especially when they are used as modifiers; however, fractions used as nouns are usually styled as open compounds

[a two-thirds majority of the stockholders]
but
[used two thirds of the stationery]

---

8. serves as an arbitrary equivalent of the phrase "(up) to and including" when used between numbers and dates

[pages 40–98] [the decade 1960–1970]

---

9. is used in the compounding of two or more capitalized names
but
is not used when a single capitalized name is in attributive position

[caught a New York-Chicago flight]
[U.S.-U.S.S.R. détente]
but
[a New York garbage strike]
[Middle East exports]

( ) PARENTHESES

1. set off supplementary, parenthetic, or explanatory material when the interruption is more marked than that usually indicated by commas and when the inclusion of such material does not essentially alter the meaning of the sentence; *see also* CAPITALIZATION, RULE 7

[Three old typewriters (all broken) will be scrapped.] [He is hoping (as we all are) that the economy will turn around.] [We appreciate your nice remarks (especially your reference to our New York salesman).]

---

2. enclose Arabic numerals confirming a typed-out number in a general text or in a legal document

[Delivery will be made in thirty (30) days.] [The fee for your services is Two Thousand Dollars ($2,000.00), payable. . . .]

---

3. may enclose numbers or letters separating and heading individual elements or items in a series

[We must set forth (1) our long-term goals, (2) our immediate objectives, and (3) the means at our disposal.]

---

4. enclose abbreviations synonymous with typed-out forms and occurring after those forms

[. . . whose chief products are polyethylene and polyvinyl chloride (PVC) bottles and containers. . . .
                    —Ethyl Corporation
                    Annual Report]

---

5. indicate alternate terms and omissions (as in form letters)

[Please sign the enclosed form(s) and return. . . .] [On (date) we mailed you. . . .]

---

6. are used as follows with other punctuation:
a. If the parenthetic expression is an independent sentence standing alone at the end of another sentence, its first word is capitalized and a period is typed <u>inside</u> the last parenthesis.

[The discussion was held in the boardroom. (The results are still confidential.)]

b. Parenthetic material within a sentence may be internally punctuated by a question mark, a period after an abbreviation only, an exclamation point, or a set of quotation marks.

[Years ago, someone (who?) told me. . . .] [The conference was held in Vancouver (that's in B.C.).] [Sales this year have been better (knock on wood!), but. . . .] [He was depressed ("I must resign") and refused to promise anything.]

c. No punctuation mark should be placed directly before parenthetic material in a sentence; if a break is required, the punctuation should be placed after the final parenthesis.

[I'll get back to you tomorrow (Monday), when I have more details.]

● PERIOD

1.	terminates sentences or sentence fragments that are neither interrogative nor exclamatory	[Take dictation.] [She took dictation.] [She asked whether he wanted her to take dictation.]
2.	often terminates polite requests especially in business correspondence	[Will you please return these forms as soon as possible.]
3.	punctuates some abbreviations and some contractions, as	[f.o.b.] [a.k.a.] [sec'y.] [Ass'n.]
	a. courtesy titles and honorifics backed by a strong tradition of punctuation	[Mr.] [Mrs.] [Ms.] [Dr.] [Prof.] [Rev.] [Hon.] [Esq.] [Jr.] [Sr.] [Ph.D.] [Litt.D.]
	b. some abbreviations (as of measure) especially when absence of punctuation could cause misreading	[98.6° F.] *also* [98.6° F] [p. 20] [Paper, 521 ff.] [18 in.] [No. 2 pencils] [fig. 15]
	c. abbreviations of Latin words and phrases commonly used in texts	[etc.] [i.e.] [e.g.] [c. *or* ca. *or* circ.] [q.v.] [viz.]
	d. abbreviations of Latin phrases used in footnotes	[Ibid.] [Op. cit.] [Loc. cit.]
	e. compass points NOTE: Punctuation styling varies.	[1400 Sixteenth Street, N.W.] *or* [1400 Sixteenth Street, NW.] *or* [1400 Sixteenth Street, NW]
	f. some geographical-name abbreviations NOTE: Punctuation styling varies.	[U.S.-U.S.S.R. détente] *or* [US-USSR détente] *but not* [U.S.-USSR détente] *and not* [US-U.S.S.R. détente]
	g. abbreviated elements of some official corporate names	[Dowden, Hutchinson & Ross, Inc.]
4.	is used with an individual's initials	[Mr. W. A. Morton]

5. is used after Roman numerals in enumerations and outlines but not with Roman numerals used as part of a title	[I. Objectives] *but* [Queen Elizabeth II]
6. is often used after Arabic numerals in enumerations whose numerals stand alone	[Required skills are: 1. Shorthand 2. Typing 3. Transcription]

? QUESTION MARK

1. terminates a direct question	[Who signed the memo?] ["Who signed the memo?" he asked.]
2. punctuates each element of an interrogative series that is neither numbered nor lettered; however, only one such mark punctuates a numbered or lettered interrogative series	[Can you give us a reasonable forecast? back up your predictions? compare them with last-quarter earnings?] *but* [Can you (1) give us a reasonable forecast (2) back up your predictions (3) supply enough figures (4) compare them with last-quarter earnings?]
3. indicates the writer's ignorance or uncertainty	[John Jones, the President (?) of that company said. . . .] [Omar Khayyám, Persian poet (?–?1123)]

66   99 QUOTATION MARKS, DOUBLE

1. enclose direct quotations in conventional usage	[He said, "I am leaving."] *but* [He said that he was leaving.]
2. enclose fragments of quoted matter when reproduced exactly as originally stated	[The agreement makes it quite clear that he "will be paid only upon receipt of an acceptable manuscript."]
3. enclose words or phrases borrowed from others, words used in a special way, and often a word of marked informality when it is introduced into formal writing	[As the leader of a gang of "droogs," he is altogether frightening, as is this film. —Liz Smith] [He called himself "emperor," but he was just a cheap tinhorn dictator.] [He was arrested for smuggling "smack."]
4. enclose titles of reports, catalogs, short poems, short stories, articles, lectures, chapters of books, songs, short musical compositions, and radio and TV programs; *compare* ITALICIZATION, RULE 6	[the report "College Graduates and Their Employers"] [the catalog "Automotive Parts and Accessories"] [Robert Frost's "Dust of Snow"] [Pushkin's "Queen of Spades"] [The third chapter of *Treasure Island* is entitled "The Black Spot."] ["America the Beautiful"] [Ravel's "Bolero"] [NBC's "Today Show"]

5. are used with other punctuation marks in the following ways:

the period and the comma fall <u>within</u> the quotation marks

[He was arrested for smuggling "smack."] ["I am leaving," he said.] [His camera was described as "waterproof," but "moisture-resistant" would have been a better description.]

the semicolon falls <u>outside</u> the quotation marks

[He spoke of his "little cottage in the country"; he might have called it a mansion.]

the dash, question mark, and the exclamation point fall <u>within</u> the quotation marks when they refer to the quoted matter only; they fall <u>outside</u> when they refer to the whole sentence

[He asked, "When did you leave?"] [What is the meaning of "the open door"?] [The sergeant shouted, "Halt!"] [Save us from his "mercy"!]

6. are <u>not</u> used with quoted material comprising more than three typed lines and only one paragraph: such material is blocked and single-spaced internally but double-spaced top and bottom to set it off from the rest of the text

[An article entitled "The Secretary in the Management Function" on page 9 of the December, 1975, issue of *The Secretary* makes this point:

Good supervision comes from good planning before trying to meet goals, knowing the work and duties of each subordinate, carefully assigning the work, communicating both orally and through written facilities, and evaluating the work and correcting the deviations.

This, then, summarizes the major aspects of secretarial supervision.]

7. are used with long quoted matter comprising more than three typed lines and having two or more paragraphs: double quotation marks are typed at the beginning of each paragraph and at the end of the final paragraph

[*U.S. News & World Report* offers these economic predictions:

"Recession, marked by sharp cutbacks in jobs and output, will continue into spring.

"Economic activity will then show little change—and no real improvement—for about three months, with one possible exception: Home building may experience a little recovery before summer.

"After the middle of the year, a broad upturn in business will develop, very sluggish at first, but gaining speed by the end of the year."

This material is included in an article entitled "Uphill Road for Business" on page 13 of the February 17, 1975, issue of the magazine.]

' ' QUOTATION MARKS, SINGLE

1. enclose a quotation within a quotation in conventional English

[The witness said, "I distinctly heard him say, 'Don't be late,' and then I heard the door close."]

2. are sometimes used in place of double quotation marks especially in British usage NOTE: When both single and double quotation marks occur at the end of a sentence, the period typically falls <u>within</u> both sets of marks.	[The witness said, 'I distinctly heard him say, "Don't be late," and then I heard the door close.'] [The witness said, "I distinctly heard him say, 'Don't be late.'"]

•

⟩ SEMICOLON

1. links main clauses not joined by coordinating conjunctions	[Some people are good managers in their willingness to accept responsibility and delegate authority with wisdom; others do not measure up.]
2. links main clauses joined by conjunctive adverbs (as *consequently, furthermore, however*)	[Speeding is illegal and dangerous; furthermore, it is uneconomical in view of current gasoline prices.]
3. links clauses which themselves contain commas even when such clauses are linked by coordinating conjunctions; see *page 132 for a list of coordinating conjunctions*	[Thus our search was for people who could think in very fundamental ways, who could buttress their views with careful analysis; people who were able to hang in during deliberations. . . . —Frank Newman]
4. often occurs before phrases or abbreviations (as *for example, for instance, that is, that is to say, namely, e.g.,* or *i.e.*) that introduce expansions or series	[We are pleased with your performance; for example, the large number of sales calls, the sizable orders. . . .]

 VIRGULE

1. separates alternatives	[. . . designs intended for high-heat and/or high-speed applications. —F. S. Badger, Jr.]
2. separates successive divisions (as months or years) of an extended period	[the fiscal year 1975/76]
3. often represents *per* in numeral + abbreviation combinations	[9 ft/sec] [20 km/hr] [4000 bbl/da] [200 gal/min]
4. often is an arbitrary punctuation mark within an abbreviation	[B/L] [L/C] [C/D]
5. serves as a dividing line between run-in lines of poetry in quotations	[Say, sages, what's the charm on earth/ Can turn death's dart aside? —Robert Burns]

PUNCTUATION–SPACINATION SUMMARY

Position	Example
Degree of Spacination No Space	
1. between any word and the punctuation immediately following it	[Here is the car.] [Is the car here?] [Here is the car!] [The car is here, isn't it?] [The car is here; however, I don't need it now.] [The car is here: now, do I get in, or not?] [The car is here. . . .]
2. between quotation marks and the quoted matter	["I am leaving," he said.] [He said, "I am leaving."]
3. between parentheses and the words or figures they enclose	[He is (should I say it?) just a bit peculiar.] [(1)]
4. between brackets and the words or figures they enclose	[had recieved [sic] the gift]
5. between initials comprising punctuated or unpunctuated abbreviations	[f.o.b.] [A.D.] [i.e.] [p.m.] [GATT] [MIRV] [CREEP] [PhD or Ph.D.]
6. between elements in figure + abbreviation or other word combinations when they are in attributive position	[a 200-hp engine] [a $15-million project]
7. between ellipses in leaders except for initial and terminal ellipsis points which are preceded & followed by one space, respectively; *compare* ONE SPACE, RULE 13	[Item 1 .... page 1]
8. between elements of hyphened compounds	[to air-condition a room] [$10–$20] [United States-Canadian tariffs]
9. before or after an apostrophe within or attached to a word	[isn't] [o'clock] [the boys' story]
10. on either side of a dash	[If she understands the contract—and I'm sure she does—we'll have no trouble.]
11. between words, letters, or figures separated by a virgule	[1976/77] [and/or]
12. between figures and symbols	[$12.95] [75%] [90°F] [7.654] [8¢] [$.08]
13. within units expressing time of day	[9:30 a.m.] [9:30 p.m.]
14. in identification lines, and in carbon copy notations indicating only one recipient designated by initials	[FCM:hol] [MWK:FCM:hol] [cc:FCM] [bcc:MWK]
15. between footnoted textual material and the footnote symbol or number	[. . . is a prime factor in successful management"*] *or* [. . . is a prime factor in successful management."1]
Degree of Spacination One Space	
1. after a comma	[The car is here, isn't it?] [Scarsdale, New York] [January 1, 19—]

Position	Example
Degree of Spacination One Space	
2. after a semicolon	[The car is here; however, I don't need it now.]
3. after a period following an initial	[Mr. H. C. Matthews]
4. before and after *x* meaning "by" or "times"	[a 3 x 5 card] [3 x 5 = 15]
5. after a suspended hyphen	[the long- and short-term results]
6. on each side of a hyphen in the Simplified Letter signature block	[SAMUEL T. LEE - SENIOR EDITOR]
7. on each side of a hyphen in some street addresses	[2135 - 71st Street, NW]
8. between a question mark and the first letter of the next word in a series question	[Are you coming today? tomorrow? the day after?]
9. between Postal Service state abbreviations and ZIP Codes	[Smithville, ST 56789]

10. after the heading cc that is unpunctuated in letters following the open punctuation pattern and that introduces a list of names	[cc Mr. Slaughter
	    Mr. Tate
	    Mr. Watson]

11. between a final quotation mark and the rest of a sentence	["I am leaving," he said.]
12. in a footnote entry between the superscript figure and the first letter of the first word following it	[[1] Albert H. Marckwardt, *American English* (New York: Oxford University Press, 1958), p. 94.]
13. between ellipses in leaders except for initial and terminal ellipsis points which are preceded and followed by at least two spaces, respectively (this styling is optional); *compare* NO SPACE, RULE 7	[Item 1 . . . . . page 1]
Degree of Spacination Two Spaces	
1. after a period ending a sentence	[Here is the car. Do you want to get in?]
2. after a question mark or an exclamation point ending a sentence	[Get out of here! Well, what are you waiting for? I've said enough.]
3. after a colon in running texts, in bibliographic references, in publication titles, and in letter or memorandum headings	[The car is here: Now, do I get in, or not?] [New York: Macmillan, 1976] [*Typewriting: A Guide*] [SUBJECT: Project X]
4. after a carbon copy notation punctuated with a colon + a full name	[cc: Mr. Johnson]

5. after a figure + a period that introduces an item in an enumeration	[The following skills are essential:
	    1. typing
	    2. shorthand]

2.7

WORD DIVISION

In the United States more time and energy have been spent worrying about the division of words at the end of a printed or typed line than the subject merits. The very fact that widely used and respected dictionaries published by different houses indicate different points at which to divide many words is evidence enough that there is no absolute right or wrong, and that for numerous words there are acceptable end-of-line division alternatives. The best policy to follow in individual instances is to consult an adequate dictionary whose main entries indicate points of division. End-of-line division is not based solely upon pronunciation, and in any case there is great variety in pronunciation throughout the English-speaking world. The question of end-of-line division occurs only in written contexts, and it is perhaps unreasonable to expect the spoken form of the language to dictate a consistent set of principles for an essentially mechanical problem.

Common sense suggests some guidelines which will help to minimize the time spent consulting a dictionary. For instance, the division of a single letter at the beginning or end of a word should be avoided. On the one hand, in typed material a single letter hanging onto the end of a line with a hyphen may be dropped to the next line without leaving unsightly right-hand margins, and in printed material the space required for two characters (the letter and the hyphen) is, in most circumstances, easily filled. On the other hand, if there is room for a hyphen at the end of a line, there is room for the last letter of a word in its place. Thus, *ablaze* and *oleo* should not be divided, for such divisions as

a-	*o-*	*ole-*
blaze	*leo*	*o*

would detract from rather than add to the appearance of the page.

Compounds containing one or more hyphens will cause a reader less trouble if divided after the hyphen. For the words *bumper-to-bumper, smoking-room,* and *vice-president* the divisions

bumper-	*bumper-to-*	*smoking-*	*vice-*
to-bumper	*bumper*	*room*	*president*

are less obtrusive than such divisions as

bum-	*bumper-to-bum-*	*smok-*	*vice-pres-*
per-to-bumper	*per*	*ing-room*	*ident*

although there are no "rules" against the latter set of examples, and such divisions may occasionally prove necessary especially in narrow columns.

Similarly, closed compounds are best divided between component elements; thus, the divisions

every-	*may-*	*speaker-*
one	*flower*	*phone*

appear more natural and will cause the reader less trouble than

ev-	*mayflow-*	*speak-*
eryone	*er*	*erphone*

though divisions such as the ones above may be required in exceptional circumstances.

For words that are not compound, it is best to consult a dictionary or a guide to word division, and in order to maintain greatest consistency it is preferable always to consult the same source. Another general principle is to avoid end-of-line division altogether whenever possible, especially in successive lines.

There are, in addition, some specific instances in which one should avoid end-of-line division if at all possible. These are as follows:

1. The last word in a paragraph should not be divided.
2. The last word on a page (as of a business letter or a memorandum) should not be divided.
3. Items joined by *and/or* and the coordinating conjunction *and/or* itself should not be divided.
4. Proper names, courtesy titles, and following titles (as *Esq.*) should not be divided either on envelopes, in inside addresses, or in running texts:

correct	*incorrect*
. . . to	. . . to Mr.
Mr. J. R. Smith.	J. R. Smith.

The one exception to this rule is the separation of long honorary titles from names especially in envelope address blocks and in inside addresses where space is often limited:

correct	*incorrect*
The Honorable	The Honorable John
John R. Smith	R. Smith

5. If dates must be divided (as in running texts), the division should occur only between the day and the year:

correct	*incorrect*
. . . arrived on	. . . arrived on Jan-
January 1, 19--.	uary 1, 19--.

correct	*incorrect*
. . . arrived on January 1,	. . . arrived on January
19--.	1, 19--.

6. Set units (as of time and measure) as well as single monetary units should not be divided:

correct	*incorrect*
. . . at 10:00 a.m.	. . . at 10:00
	a.m.

correct	*incorrect*
. . . had a temperature of 98.6°F.	. . . had a temperature of 98.6°
	F.

correct	*incorrect*
. . . a fee of $4,900.50.	. . . a fee of $4,900.-
	50.

7. Abbreviations should not be divided:

correct	*incorrect*
. . . received the M.B.A.	. . . received the M.B.-
from Harvard.	A. from Harvard.

8. Compound geographic designations (as city + state combinations) should not be divided:

correct	*incorrect*
. . . to St. Paul, Minnesota.	. . . to St.
	Paul, Minnesota.

2.8

COMPONENTS OF DISCOURSE

The word *discourse* is defined in *Webster's New Collegiate Dictionary* as "formal and orderly and usually extended expression of thought. . . ." Thus, no guide to effective communication can ignore the fundamental components of discourse: the word, the phrase, the clause, the sentence, and the paragraph. Each of these increasingly complex units contributes to the expression of a writer's points, ideas, and concepts.

The word, of course, is the simplest component of discourse. Words have been traditionally classified into eight parts of speech. This classification system is determined chiefly by a word's inflectional features, its general grammatical functions, and its positioning within a sentence. On the following pages, the parts of speech—the adjective, adverb, conjunction, interjection, noun, preposition, pronoun, and verb—are alphabetically listed and briefly discussed. Each part of speech is introduced by an applicable definition from *Webster's New Collegiate Dictionary*. The phrase, the clause, the sentence, and the paragraph are discussed later in this section.

PARTS OF SPEECH

Adjective	²**adjective** *n* **:** a word belonging to one of the major form classes in any of numerous languages and typically serving as a modifier of a noun to denote a quality of the thing named, to indicate its quantity or extent, or to specify a thing as distinct from something else

The main structural feature of an adjective is its ability to indicate degrees of comparison (positive, comparative, superlative) by addition of the suffixal endings *-er/-est* to the base word (*clean, cleaner, cleanest*), by addition of *more/most* or *less/least* before the base word (*meaningful, more meaningful, most meaningful; less meaningful, least meaningful*), or by use of irregular forms (*bad, worse, worst*). Some adjectives are compared in two ways (as *smoother, smoothest/more smooth, most smooth*), while still others (as *prior, optimum,* or *maximum*), called "absolute adjectives," are ordinarily not compared since they are felt to represent ultimate or highest conditions.

Adjectives may occur in the following positions within sentences:

1. preceding the nouns they modify, as
   the *black* hat
   a *dark brown* coat
2. following the nouns they modify, as
   an executive *par excellence*
   I painted my room *blue.*
3. following the verb *to be* in predicate-adjective position, as
   The hat is *black.*
   and following other linking (or "sense") verbs in predicate-adjective position, as
   He seems *intelligent.*
   The food tastes *stale.*
   I feel *queasy.*
4. following some transitive verbs used in the passive voice, as
   The room was painted *blue.*
   The passengers were found *dead* at the crash site.

Adjectives may describe something or represent a quality, kind, or condition (a *sick* man); they may point out or indicate something (*these* men); or they may convey the force of questions (*Whose* office is this?). Some adjectives (as *Orwellian, Churchillian, Keynesian,* and others) are called "proper adjectives." They are derived from proper nouns, take their meanings from what characterizes the nouns, and are capitalized.

The following are general points of adjective usage:

Absolute adjectives   Some adjectives (as *prior, maximum, optimum, minimum, first,* and the like) ordinarily admit no comparison because they represent ultimate conditions. However, printed usage indicates that many writers do compare and qualify some of these words in order to show connotations and shades of meaning that they feel are less than absolute. The word *unique* is a case in point:

. . . we were fairly *unique*. . . .
        —J. D. Salinger

. . . a rather *unique* concept. . . .
        —E. Ohmer Milton

. . . some of the more *unique* and
colorful customs. . . .
        —Ernest Osborne

. . . the most *unique* human faculty. . . .
        —Robert Plank

The more we study him, the less
unique he seems. . . .
        —James Joyce

While many examples may be found of qualification and/or comparison of *unique,* it is difficult to find printed evidence showing comparison of a word like *optimum.* When one is in doubt about the inflection of such an adjective, one should consult a dictionary.

Coordinate adjectives   Adjectives that share equal relationships to the nouns they modify are called coordinate adjectives and are separated from each other by commas:

a *concise, coherent, intelligent* essay

However, in the following locution containing the set phrase *short story*

a *concise, coherent* short story

the adjectives *concise* and *coherent* are neither parallel nor equal in function or relationship with *short* which is an essential element of the total compound *short story.* The test to use before inserting commas is to insert *and* between questionable adjectives, and then to decide whether the sentence still makes sense. Whereas *and* could fit between *coherent* and *intelligent* in the first example, it could not work between *coherent* and *short* in the second example.

Adjective/noun agreement   The number (singular or plural) of a demonstrative adjective (*this, that, these, those*) should agree with that of the noun it modifies:

these kinds of typewriters	*not*	these kind of typewriters
those sorts of jobs	*not*	those sort of jobs
this type of person	*not*	these type of people

Double comparisons   Double comparisons should be avoided since they are considered nonstandard:

the easiest
or
the most easy   solution   *not*   the most easiest solution

an easier
or
a more easy   method   *not*   a more easier method

Incomplete or understood comparisons   Some comparisons are left incomplete because the context clearly implies the comparison; hence, the expressions

Get *better* buys here!
We have *lower* prices.

These are commonly used especially in advertising. It should be understood, however, that the use of incomplete comparisons is often considered careless or illogical especially in formal writing.

Adverb

¹**ad•verb. . .** *n* **. . . :** a word belonging to one of the major form classes in any of numerous languages, typically serving as a modifier of a verb, an adjective, another adverb, a preposition, a phrase, a clause, or a sentence, and expressing some relation of manner or quality, place, time, degree, number, cause, opposition, affirmation, or denial

---

An adverb admits three degrees of comparison (positive, comparative, superlative) ordinarily by addition of *more/most* or *less/least* before the base word (*quickly, more quickly, most quickly*). However, a few adverbs (such as *fast, slow, loud, soft, early, late,* and *quick*) may be compared in two ways: by the method described above, or by the addition of the suffixal endings *-er/-est* to the base word (*quick, quicker, quickest*).

Adverbs may occur in the following positions within sentences:

1. before the subject, as
   Then he announced his resignation.
2. after the subject, as
   He *then* announced his resignation.
3. before the predicate, as
   He praised the committee's work and *then* announced his resignation.
4. at the end of the predicate, as
   He announced his resignation *then*.
5. in various other positions (as before adjectives or other adverbs), as
   He also made an *equally* important announcement—that of his resignation.
   He adjourned the meeting *very* abruptly.

Adverbs answer the following questions: "when?" (Please reply *at once*), "how long?" (She wants to live here *forever*), "where?" (I work *there*), "in what direction?" (Move the lever *upward*), "how?" (The staff moved *expeditiously* on the project), and "how much?" or "to what degree?" (It is *rather* hot).

Adverbs modify verbs, adjectives, or other adverbs, as

He studied the balance sheet *carefully*.
He gave the balance sheet *very* careful study.
He studied the balance sheet *very* carefully.

and may also serve as clause joiners or sentence connectors, as

clause joiner
You may share our car pool; *however*, please be ready at 7:00 a.m.
sentence connector
He thoroughly enjoyed the symposium. *Indeed*, he was fascinated by the presentations.

In addition, adverbs may be essential elements of two-word verb collocations commonly having separate entry in dictionaries, such as

He looked *over* the figures.
He looked the figures *over*.

The waiter took the tray *away*.
The waiter took *away* the tray.

See also page 133 for a discussion of conjunctive adverbs, words like *however* in the example on page 129 that are adverbs functioning as conjunctions in sentences. The following are general points of adverb usage:

Placement within a sentence   Adverbs are generally positioned as close as possible to the words they modify if such a position will not result in misinterpretation by the reader:

unclear
The project that he hoped his staff would support completely disappointed him.

Does the writer mean "complete staff support" or "complete disappointment"? Thus, the adverb may be moved to another position or the sentence may be recast, depending on intended meaning:

clear
The project that he hoped his staff would completely support had disappointed him.
or
He was completely disappointed in the project that he had hoped his staff would support.

Emphasis   Adverbs (such as *just* and *only*) are often used to emphasize certain other words. Thus, a writer should be aware of the various reader reactions that may result from the positioning of an adverb in a sentence:

strong connotation of curtness
He just nodded to me as he passed.
but
emphasis on timing of the action
He nodded to me *just* as he passed.

In some positions and contexts these adverbs can be ambiguous:

I will only tell it to you.

Does the writer mean that he will only tell it, not put it in writing, or does he mean that he will tell no one else? If the latter interpretation is intended, a slight shift of position would remove the uncertainty, as

I will tell it only to you.

Adverbs vs. adjectives: examples of misuse
a. Adverbs but not adjectives modify action verbs:
not   He answered very harsh.
but   He answered very harshly.

b. Complements referring to the subject of a sentence and occurring after linking verbs conventionally take adjectives but not adverbs:
questionable   I feel badly.
                    The letter sounded strongly.
acceptable   I feel bad.
                    The letter sounded strong.
but
acceptable   He looks good these days.
                    He looks well these days.

In the last two examples, either *good* or *well* is acceptable, because both words may be adjectives or adverbs, and here they are functioning as adjectives in the sense of "being healthy."

c. Adverbs but not adjectives modify adjectives and other adverbs:

not   She seemed dreadful tired.
but   She seemed dreadfully tired.

Double negatives   A combination of two negative adverbs (as *not* + *hardly, never, scarcely,* and the like) used to express a single negative idea is considered substandard:

not   We cannot see scarcely any reason why we should adopt this book.
but   We can see scarcely any reason why we should adopt this book.

    We can't ⎫
      cannot ⎬ see any reason why we should adopt this book.

Conjunction

con•junc•tion . . . . *n* . . . **4** : an uninflected linguistic form that joins together sentences, clauses, phrases, or words : CONNECTIVE

Conjunctions exhibit no characteristic inflectional or suffixal features. They may occur in numerous positions within sentences; however, they ordinarily do not appear in final position unless the sentence is elliptical. Three major types of conjunctions are listed and illustrated according to their functions in the table on page 132.

    A comma is traditionally used <u>before</u> a coordinating conjunction linking coordinate clauses especially when these clauses are lengthy or when the writer desires to emphasize their distinctness from one another:

The economy is in serious condition, and it shows few signs of improvement.
Shall we consider this person's application, or shall we consider that one's?
We do not discriminate between men and women, but we do have high professional standards and qualifications that the successful applicant must meet.

    In addition to the three main types of conjunctions in the table on page 132, the English language has transitional adverbs and adverbial phrases called "conjunctive adverbs" that express relationships between two units of discourse (as two independent clauses, two complete sentences, or two or more paragraphs), and that function as conjunctions even though they are customarily classified as adverbs. The table on page 133 groups and illustrates conjunctive adverbs according to their functions.

    Occurrence of a comma fault especially with conjunctive adverbs indicates that the writer has not realized that a comma alone will not suffice to join two sentences, and that a semicolon is required. The punctuation pattern with conjunctive adverbs is usually as follows:

    clause + semicolon + conjunctive adverb + comma + clause
The following two sentences illustrate a typical comma fault and a rewrite that removes the error:

comma fault	*rewrite*
The company had flexible hours, however its employees were expected to abide by the hours they had selected for arrival and departure.	The company had flexible hours; however, its employees were expected to abide by the hours they had selected for arrival and departure.

Three Major Types of Conjunctions and their Functions

Type of Conjunction	Function	Example
coordinating conjunctions link words, phrases, dependent clauses, and complete sentences	*and* joins elements and sentences	[He ordered pencils, pens, *and* erasers.]
	but, yet exclude or contrast	[He is a brilliant *but* arrogant man.]
	or, nor offer alternatives	[You can wait here *or* go.]
	for offers reason or grounds	[The report is poor, *for* its data are inaccurate.]
	so offers a reason	[Her diction is good, *so* every word is clear.]
subordinating conjunctions introduce dependent clauses	*because, since* express cause	[*Because* she is smart, she is doing well in her job.]
	although, if, unless express condition	[Don't call *unless* you have the information.]
	as, as though, however express manner	[He looks *as though* he is ill.] [We'll do it *however* you tell us to.]
	in order that, so that express result	[She routes the mail early *so that* they can read it.]
	after, before, once, since, till, until, when, whenever, while express time	[He kept meetings to a minimum *when* he was president.]
	where, wherever express place or circumstance	[I don't know *where* he has gone.] [He tries to help out *wherever* it is possible.]
	whether expresses alternative conditions or possibilities	[It was hard to decide *whether* I should go or stay.]
	that introduces several kinds of subordinate clauses including those used as noun equivalents (as a subject or an object of a verb, or a predicate nominative)	[Yesterday I learned *that* he has been sick for over a week.]
correlative conjunctions work in pairs to link alternatives or equal elements	*either . . . or, neither . . . nor,* and *whether . . . or* link alternatives	[*Either* you go *or* you stay.] [He had *neither* looks *nor* wit.]
	both . . . and and *not only . . . but also* link equal elements	[*Both* typist *and* writer should understand style.] [*Not only* was there inflation, *but* there was *also* unemployment.]

Conjunctive Adverbs Grouped According to Meaning and Function

Conjunctive Adverbs	Functions	Examples
also, besides, further-more, in addition, in fact, moreover, too	express addition	[This employee deserves a substantial raise; *furthermore,* she should be promoted.]
indeed, that is [to say], *to be sure*	add emphasis	[He is brilliant; *indeed,* he is a genius.]
anyway, however, nevertheless, on the contrary, on the one hand/on the other hand	express contrast or discrimination	[The major responsibility lies with top management; *nevertheless,* line officers should be competent in decision-making.] [*On the one hand,* we must consider the editorial function; *on the other hand,* manufacturing procedures and costs.]
e.g., for example, for instance, i.e., namely, that is	introduce illustrations or elaborations	[Losses were due to several negative factors; *namely,* inflation, competition, and restrictive government regulation.] [He is highly competitive—*i.e.,* he goes straight for a rival's jugular vein.]
accordingly, as a result, consequently, hence, therefore, thus, so	express or introduce conclusions or results	[This division had an outstanding year; *as a result,* operating income increased 131% to a record $30.1 million.] [Government overregulation in that country reached a prohibitive level in the last quarter. *Thus,* we are phasing out all of our operations there.]
first, second, further on, later, then, in conclusion, finally	orient elements of discourse as to time or space	[*First,* we can say that the account is long overdue; *second,* that we must consider consulting our attorneys if you do not meet your obligation.] [The road is straight here; *further on,* it is winding.]

The following are general points of conjunction usage:
Conjunctions as meaning clarifiers   Properly used conjunctions ensure order and coherence in writing since they often serve to pinpoint shades of meaning, place special emphasis where required, and set general tone within sentences and paragraphs. Improperly used conjunctions may result in choppy, often cloudy writing, and in incoherent orientation of ideas. Therefore, the purpose of a conjunction is totally defeated if it creates ambiguities rather than makes things clear. The often misused conjunction-phrase *as well as* is an example:

ambiguous
Jean typed the report *as well as* Joan.
(Does the writer mean that both women
typed the report together, or that both
women typed the report equally well?)

clear
Jean typed the report just *as well as* Joan
did.
Jean and Joan typed the report equally well.
or
Both Jean and Joan typed the report.
Jean typed the report; so did Joan.
Jean typed the report, and so did Joan.

Coordinating conjunctions: proper use   These terms should link equal elements
of discourse—e.g., adjectives with other adjectives, nouns with other nouns, participles with other participles, clauses with other equal-ranking clauses, and so on.
Combining unequal elements may result in unbalanced sentences:

unbalanced
Having become disgusted *and* because he
was tired, he left the party.

balanced
Because he was tired *and* disgusted, he left
the party.
or
He left the party because he had become
tired *and* disgusted.
or
Having become tired *and* disgusted, he left
the party.

Coordinating conjunctions should not be used to string together excessively long
series of elements, regardless of their equality.

strung-out
We have sustained enormous losses in this
division, and we have realized practically
no profits even though the sales figures
indicate last-quarter gains and we are therefore reorganizing the entire management
structure as well as paring down personnel.

tightened
Since this division has sustained enormous
losses and has realized only insignificant
profits even with its last-quarter sales gains,
we are totally reorganizing its management.
We are also cutting its personnel.

Choice of just the right coordinating conjunction for a particular verbal situation
is important: the right word will pinpoint the writer's true meaning and intent, and
will highlight the most relevant idea or point of the sentence. The following three
sentences exhibit increasingly stronger degrees of contrast through the use of
different conjunctions:

neutral   He works hard *and* doesn't progress.
more contrast   He works hard *but* doesn't progress.
stronger contrast   He works hard, yet he doesn't progress.

The coordinating conjunction *and/or* linking two elements of a compound subject often poses a problem as to the number (singular or plural) of the verb that
follows. A subject comprising singular nouns connected by *and/or* may be considered singular or plural, depending on the meaning of the sentence:

singular
All loss and/or damage *is* to be the responsibility of the sender. [one or the other and
possibly both]

plural
John R. Jones and/or Robert B. Flint *are*
hereby *appointed* as the executors of my
estate. [both executors are to act, or either
of them is to act if the other dies or is
incapacitated]

Subordinating conjunctions: proper use   Subordinating conjunctions introduce
dependent clauses, and also deemphasize less important ideas in favor of more

important ideas. Which clause is made independent and which clause is made subordinate has great influence in determining the effectiveness of a sentence. Notice how differently these two versions strike the reader:

When the building burst into flames, we were just coming out of the door.

Just as we were coming out of the door, the building burst into flames.

The writer must take care that the point he or she wishes to emphasize is in the independent clause and that the points of less importance are subordinated.

Faulty clause subordination can render a sentence impotent. Compare the following examples:

faulty subordination	*improved*
Because the government of that country has nationalized our refineries, and since overregulation of prices had already become a critical problem, we decided to withdraw all our operations when the situation became intolerable.	Since that country's government has over-regulated prices and has nationalized our refineries, we have decided to withdraw our operations altogether.

Correlative conjunctions: proper use These pairs of words also join equal elements of discourse. They should be placed as close as possible to the elements they join:

misplaced	*repositioned*
Either I must send a telex *or* make a long-distance call.	I must *either* send a telex *or* make a long-distance call.

The negative counterpart of *either . . . or* is *neither . . . nor*. The conjunction *or* should not be substituted for *nor* because its substitution will destroy the negative parallelism. However, *or* may occur in combination with *no*. Examples:

He received *neither* a promotion *nor* a raise.

He received *no* promotion *or* raise.

Interjection

in·ter·jec·tion . . . *n* . . . **3 a :** an ejaculatory word (as *Wonderful*) or form of speech (as *ah*) **b :** a cry or inarticulate utterance (as *ouch*) expressing an emotion

---

Interjections exhibit no characteristic features or forms. As independent elements not having close grammatical connections with the rest of a sentence, interjections may often stand alone.

Interjections may be stressed or ejaculatory words, phrases, or even short sentences, as

Absurd!

Quickly!

Right on!

Get out!

or they may be so-called "sound" words (such as those representing shouts, hisses, etc.):

Ouch! That hurts.

Shh! The meeting has begun.

Psst! Come over here.

Ah, that's my idea of a terrific deal.

Oh, you're really wrong there.

---

	noun . . . *n* . . . **1** : a word that is the name of a subject of discourse (as a person, animal, plant, place, thing, substance, quality, idea, action, or state) and that in languages with grammatical number, case, and gender is inflected for number and case but has inherent gender **2** : a word except a pronoun used in a sentence as subject or object of a verb, as object of a preposition, as the predicate after a copula, or as a name in an absolute construction
Noun	

Nouns exhibit these characteristic features: they are inflected for possession, they have number (singular, plural), they are often preceded by determiners (as *a, an, the; this, that, these, those; all, every,* and other such qualifiers; *one, two, three,* and other such numerical quantifiers; *his, her, their,* and other such pronominal adjectives), a few of them still have gender (as the masculine *host,* the feminine *hostess),* and many of them are formed by suffixation (as with the suffixes *-ance, -ist, -ness,* and *-tion*).

The only noun case indicated by inflection is the possessive which is normally formed by addition of *-'s* (singular) or *-s'* (plural) to the base word. (See Apostrophe, pages 111–112, for other examples.)

Number is usually indicated by addition of *-s* or *-es* to the base word, although some nouns (as those of foreign origin) have irregular plurals:

regular plurals

dog→dogs	grass→grasses
race→races	dish→dishes
guy→guys	buzz→buzzes
monarch→monarchs	branch→branches

irregular and zero plurals

army→armies
ox→oxen
foot→feet
phenomenon→phenomena
libretto→librettos *or* libretti
curriculum→curricula *also* curriculums
memorandum→memorandums *or* memoranda
alga→algae
corpus delicti→corpora delicti
sergeant major→sergeants major *or* sergeant majors
sheep→sheep
encephalitis→encephalitides
pediculosis→pediculoses

When in doubt of a plural spelling, the secretary should consult a dictionary. Nouns may be subgrouped according to type and function within a sentence as shown in the table on page 138.

Nouns may be used as follows in sentences:

1. as subjects
   The *office* was quiet.
2. as direct objects
   He locked the *office*.

3. as objects of prepositions
    The file is in the *office.*
4. as indirect objects
    He gave his *wife* a ring.
5. as retained objects
    His wife was given a *ring.*
6. as predicate nominatives
    Mr. Dow is the *president.*
7. as subjective complements
    Mr. Dow was announced *president.*
8. as objective complements
    They made Mr. Dow *president.*
9. as appositives
    Mr. Dow, the *president,* wrote that memorandum.
10. in direct address
    Mr. Dow, may I present Mr. Lee?

Compound nouns   Since English is not a static and unchanging entity, it experiences continuous style fluctuations because of preferences of its users. The styling (open, closed, or hyphened) variations of noun and other compounds reflect changing usage. No rigid rules can be set down to cover every possible variation or combination, nor can an all-inclusive list of compounds be given here. The secretary should consult a dictionary when in doubt of the styling of a compound.

Use of indefinite articles with nouns   The use of a and an is not settled in all situations. In the examples below, some words or abbreviations beginning with a vowel letter nevertheless have a consonant as the first <u>sound</u> (as *one, union,* or *US*). Conversely, the names of some consonants begin with a vowel <u>sound</u> (as *F, H, L, M, N, R, S,* and X).

a

a. Before a word (or abbreviation) beginning with a consonant <u>sound</u>, a is usually spoken and written: *a BA degree, a COD package, a door, a hat, a human, a one, a union, a US senator.*

b. Before *h-* in an unstressed (unaccented) or lightly stressed (lightly accented) first syllable, a is more frequently written, although an is more usual in speech whether or not the *h-* is actually pronounced. Either one certainly may be considered acceptable in speech or writing: *a historian—an historian, a heroic attempt—an heroic attempt, a hilarious performance—an hilarious performance.*

c. Before a word beginning with a vowel <u>sound</u>, a is occasionally used in speech: *a hour, a inquiry, a obligation.* (In some parts of the United States this may be more common than in others.)

an

a. Before a word beginning with a vowel <u>sound</u>, an is usually spoken and written: *an icicle, an FCC report, an hour, an honor, an MIT professor, an nth degree polynomial, an orange, an Rh factor, an SAT, an unknown.*

b. Before *h-* in an unstressed or lightly stressed syllable, an is more usually spoken whether or not the *h-* is pronounced, while a is more frequently written. Either may be considered acceptable in speech or writing. (See the examples above at point b.)

c. Sometimes an is spoken and written before a word beginning with a vowel in its spelling even though the first <u>sound</u> is a consonant: *an European city, an unique occurrence, such an one.* This is less frequent today than in the past and it is more common in Britain than in the United States.

d. Occasionally an is used in speech and writing before a stressed syllable beginning with *h-* in which the *h-* is pronounced: *an huntress, an heritage.* This is regularly the practice of the King James Version of the Old Testament.

Nouns Subgrouped According to Type and Function

Type of Noun	Function	Example
common nouns	identify general classes of things	[valley] [college] [company] [author]
proper nouns	identify particular members of classes of things, and are capitalized	[the Ohio Valley] [Amherst College] [The Macmillan Company] [Shakespeare]
abstract nouns	name qualities and ideas that do not have physical substance or configuration	[good] [evil] [honesty] [dishonesty] [science] [philosophy] [ruthlessness] [compassion]
concrete nouns	name animate and inanimate objects	[desk] [typewriter] [chair] [building] [floor] [ceiling] [finger] [stomach]
mass nouns	identify things that are not ordinarily thought of in terms of numbered elements; they are usually singular in form, although in a few contexts the plural is appropriate especially when *types* of items within a class are being differentiated	[paper] [fruit] [water] [rice] [cotton] [Paper is costly today.] [Fruit is healthful.] [Water was scarce there.] [Rice grows in the Deep South.] [Cotton is raised in South Carolina.] *but* [Not all cottons have the same texture.]
count nouns	identify things considered as separate units that can be enumerated or counted NOTE: Many nouns have both count and non-count senses.	[paper clip] [peach] [desk] [chair] [five hundred paper clips] [many peaches] [two desks and various types of chairs] [Their firm manufactures the cloth for our book covers.] *but* [She used two cloths to polish the silver.]
collective nouns	identify things that can be construed either in terms of number or collectively; collective nouns are singular in form but are sometimes or always plural in construction	[The family was proud of her.] [The committee have been debating among themselves for an hour.] *but* [The group has decided.] [The mob was running wild.] [That audience was impolite.]

	prep·o·si·tion . . . *n* . . . : a linguistic form that combines with a noun, pronoun, or noun equivalent to form a phrase that typically has an adverbial, adjectival, or substantival relation to some other word
Preposition	

Prepositions are not characterized by inflection, number, case, gender, or identifying suffixes. Rather, they are identified chiefly by their positioning within sentences and by their grammatical functions.

Prepositions may occur in the following positions:

1. before nouns or pronouns
   below the desk
   beside them
2. after adjectives
   antagonistic *to*
   insufficient *in*
   symbolic *of*
3. after the verbal elements of idiomatically fixed verb + preposition combinations
   take *for*
   get *after*
   come *across*

Prepositions may be simple, i.e., composed of only one element (as *of, on, out, from, near, against,* or *without*); or they may be compound, i.e., composed of more than one element (as *according to, by means of,* or *in spite of*). Prepositions are chiefly used to link nouns, pronouns, or noun equivalents to the rest of a sentence:

He expected continued softness *in* the economy.
He sat down *beside* her.

Prepositions may also be used to express the possessive:

one fourth *of* the employees
the top drawer *of* my desk

The following are general points of preposition usage:

Prepositions and conjunctions: confusion between the two The words *after, before, but, for,* and *since* may function as either prepositions or conjunctions. Their positions within sentences clarify whether they are conjunctions or prepositions:

preposition	I have nothing left *but* hope. (*but* = "except for")
conjunction	I was a bit concerned *but* not panicky. (*but* links 2 adjectives)
preposition	The device conserves fuel *for* residual heating. (*for* + noun)
conjunction	The device conserves fuel, *for* it is battery-powered. (*for* links 2 clauses)

Implied or understood prepositions If two words combine idiomatically with the same preposition, that preposition need not be repeated after both of them:

We were antagonistic [to] and opposed *to* the whole idea.
but
We are interested *in* and anxious *for* raises.

Prepositions terminating sentences   There is no reason why a preposition cannot end a sentence, especially when it is an essential element of an idiomatically fixed verb phrase:

One cannot look back on industrialization without being shocked by many of its manifestations, by many of the things we put up *with.*
> —August Heckscher

Vietnam was incredibly mismanaged. It was easier to get into than to get out *of.*
> —Nancy Kissinger

Use of *between* and *among*   The preposition *between* is ordinarily followed by words representing two persons or things:

between you and me
détente *between* the United States and the Soviet Union

and *among* is ordinarily followed by words representing more than two persons or things:

among the three of us
among various nations

However, *between* sometimes may be used to express an interrelationship between more than two things when those things are being considered individually rather than collectively:

. . . travels regularly *between* New York, Baltimore, and Washington.

Pronoun

pro•noun . . . *n* . . . **:** a word belonging to one of the major form classes in any of a great many languages that is used as a substitute for a noun or noun equivalent, takes noun constructions, and refers to persons or things named or understood in the context

---

Pronouns exhibit all or some of the following characteristic features: case (nominative, possessive, objective), number (singular, plural), person (first, second, third person), and gender (masculine, feminine, neuter). Pronouns may be grouped according to major types and functions, as shown in the table on the next page. The following paragraphs discuss points of pronoun usage.

Personal pronouns   A personal pronoun agrees in person, number, and gender with the word it refers to; however, the case of a pronoun is determined by its function within a sentence:

Everybody had *his* own office.
Everybody was given an office to *himself.*
Each employee was given an office to *himself.*
You and *I* thought the meeting was useful.
Just between *you* and *me,* the meeting was useful but far too lengthy.
My assistant and *I* attended the seminar.
The vice-president told my assistant and *me* to attend the seminar.

The nominative case (as in the locutions "It is I" and "This is she") after the verb *to be* is considered standard English and is preferred by strict grammarians; however, the objective case (as in the locution "It's me") also may be used without criticism especially in spoken English.

  When a personal pronoun occurs in a construction introduced by *than* or *as,*

Types and Functions of Pronouns

Type of Pronoun	Function	Example
personal pronouns (such as *I, we, you, he, she, it, they*)	refer to beings and objects and reflect the person and gender of those antecedents	[Put the book on the table and close *it*.] [Put the baby in *his* crib and cover *him* up.]
reflexive pronouns (such as *myself, ourselves, yourself, yourselves, himself, herself, itself, themselves*)	express reflexive action on the subject of a sentence or add extra emphasis to the subject	[He hurt *himself*.] [They asked *themselves* if they were being honest.] [I *myself* am not afraid.]
indefinite pronouns (*all, another, any, anybody, anyone, anything, both, each, each one, either, everybody, everyone, everything, few, many, much, neither, nobody, none, no one, one, other, several, some, somebody, someone, something*)	are indistinguishable by gender, are chiefly used as third-person references, and do not distinguish gender	[*All* of the people are here.] [*All* of them are here.] [Has *anyone* arrived?] [*Somebody* has called.] [Does *everyone* have his paper?] [*Nobody* has answered.] [A *few* have offered their suggestions.]
reciprocal pronouns	indicate interaction	[They do not quarrel with *one another*.] [Be nice to *each other*.]
demonstrative pronouns (*this, that, these, those*)	point things out	[*This* is your seat.] [*That* is mine.] [*These* belong to her.] [*Those* are strong words.]
relative pronouns (*who, whom, which, what, that, whose*) or combinations with -ever (as *whoever, whosever, whichever, whatever*)	introduce clauses acting as nouns or as modifiers	[The thrust of this memorandum is *that* there will be no cost overruns.] [I'll do *what* you want.] [I'll do *whatever* you want.]
interrogative pronouns (as *who, which, what, whoever, whichever, whatever*)	phrase direct questions	[*Who* is there?] [*What* is his title?] [His title is *what*?] [*Whom* did the article pan?] [*Whatever* is the matter?]

it should be in the nominative case:

He received a bigger bonus than *she* [did].
She has as much seniority as *I* [do].

The suffixes *-self* and *-selves* combine only with the possessive case of the first- and second-person pronouns (*myself, ourselves, yourself, yourselves*) and with the objective case of the third-person pronouns (*himself, herself, itself, themselves*). Other combinations (as "hisself" and "theirselves") are considered nonstandard and should not be used.

When one uses the pronoun *I* with other pronouns or with other peoples' names, *I* should be last in the series:

Mrs. Smith and *I* were trained together.

He and *I* were attending the meeting.

The memorandum was directed to Ms. Montgomery and *me*.

Some companies prefer that writers use *we* and not *I* when speaking for their companies in business correspondence. *I* is more often used when a writer is referring only to himself or herself. The following example illustrates use of both within one sentence:

We [i.e., the writer speaks for the company] have reviewed the manuscript that you sent to *me* [i.e., the manuscript was sent only to the writer] on June 1, but *we* [a corporate or group decision] feel that it is too specialized a work to be marketable by *our* Company.

While the personal pronouns *it, you,* and *they* are often used as indefinite pronouns in spoken English, they can be vague or even redundant in some contexts and therefore should be avoided in precise writing:

vague	*explicit*
They said at the seminar that the economy would experience a third-quarter upturn. (The question is: Who exactly is *they*?)	The economists on the panel at the seminar predicted a third-quarter economic upturn.

redundant	*lean*
In the graph *it* says that production fell off by 50%.	The graph indicates a 50% production drop.

Notwithstanding recent concern about sexism in language, the personal pronoun *he* and the indefinite pronoun *one* are still the standard substitutes for antecedents whose genders are mixed or irrelevant:

Each employee should check *his* W-2 form.

Present the letter to the executive for *his* approval.

If *one* really wants to succeed, *one* can.

Indefinite pronouns: agreement   Agreement in number between indefinite pronouns and verbs is sometimes a problem especially in contexts where the actual number of individuals represented by the pronoun is unclear. In some instances, there is also a conflict between written and spoken usage.

The following indefinite pronouns are clearly singular, and as such take singular verbs:

another	*much*	*other*
anything	*nobody*	*someone*
each one	*no one*	*something*
everything	*one*	

And these are clearly plural:

both
few
many
several

But depending on whether they are used with mass or count nouns, the following may be either singular or plural:

all
any
each
none
some

with mass noun	*All* of the *property is* entailed.
with count noun	*All* of our *bases are* covered.

The following are singular in form, and as such logically take singular verbs; however, because of their plural connotations, informal speech has established the use of plural pronoun references to them:

anybody
anyone
everybody
everyone
somebody

The following citations illustrate usage variants involving indefinite pronouns:

Anyone who tries to discuss the problem . . . is at once met with the suggestion that *he* is unaware . . . .
                    —Wendell L. Willkie
but
. . . it may be difficult for *anyone* to find *their* path through . . . a sort of maze.
                    —Ford Madox Ford
. . . a small Mid-Western town where *everybody* knows you!
                    —William A. Tyson, Jr.
Everybody drives just where *they* want to.
                    —F. Scott Fitzgerald
Everybody has a right to describe *their* own party machine as *they* choose.
                    —Winston Churchill
Everybody fights for *their* own team . . . .
                    —Stuart Symington
I was calling *everybody* by *their* first names.
                    —Marshall McLuhan
and
Everyone from the time *he* is first conscious of *himself* until *he* dies, is continually comparing *himself* with others . . . .
                    —William J. Reilly
Somebody is always putting down a table of specifications for the good salesman.
                    —*Printers' Ink*
but
Now that *everyone* goes to the Mediterranean for *their* holidays . . . .
                    —*Times Literary Supplement*
. . . the minute *somebody* opens *their* mouth. . . . .
                    —Robert A. Hall, Jr.

The question of number in pronoun phrases such as *each* + *of* + noun(s) or other pronoun(s), *none* + *of* + noun(s) or other pronoun(s), *either/neither* + *of* + noun(s) or other pronoun(s), and *some* + *of* + noun(s) or other pronoun(s), depends on the number of the headword. For example, when *either* means "one of two or more" or "any one of more than two," it is usually singular in construction and thus takes a singular verb. However, when *of* after *either* is followed by a plural, the verb that follows the whole phrase is often plural. This decision is really a matter of writer preference:

Either of the two pronunciations *is* standard.
Either of these pronunciations *is/are* standard.
or
Either of the two *is* satisfactory.
Either of them *are* satisfactory.

The word *none* involves similar variations:

. . . *none* [i.e., *not any*] of them *were* intellectually absorbing . . . .
>—Winthrop Sargeant

None [i.e., *not any*] of those statements *are* particularly disputable . . . .
>—Tom Wicker

but

. . . *none* [i.e., *not one*] of our scholars *has* written a monograph on him . . . .
>—Norman Douglas

. . . *none* [i.e., *not one*] *is* identifiably more expert in foreign than domestic affairs, or vice versa.
>—Tom Wicker

The indefinite pronoun *any* when used in comparisons   The indefinite pronoun *any* is conventionally followed by *other(s)* or *else* when it forms part of a comparison of two individuals in the same class. Examples:

not   He is a better researcher than any in his field.
      (Is he a better researcher than all others including himself?)

but   He is a better researcher than any others in his field.
      He is a better researcher than anyone else in his field.

not   Boston is more interesting than any city in the U.S.

but   Boston is more interesting than any other city in the U.S.

Demonstrative pronouns   One problem involving demonstrative pronouns occurs when a demonstrative introduces a sentence referring to an idea or ideas contained in a previous sentence or sentences. One should be sure that the reference is definite and not cloudy:

a cloudy sentence
The heir's illness, the influence of a faith healer at court, massive military setbacks, general strikes, mass outbreaks of typhus, and failed crops contributed to the revolution. *This* influenced the course of history.
The question is: What exactly influenced the course of history? All of these factors, some of them, or the last one mentioned?

an explicit sentence
None of the participants in the incident kept records of what they said or did. *That* is quite unfortunate, and it should be a lesson to us.

When demonstrative pronouns are used with the words *kind, sort,* and *type* + *of* + nouns, they should agree in number with both nouns:

not   We want these kind of pencils.

but   We want *this kind* of *pencil.*   *or*   We want *these kinds* of *pencils.*

Relative pronouns   While a relative pronoun itself does not exhibit number, gender, or person, it does determine the number, gender, and person of the relative-clause elements that follow it because of its implicit agreement with its antecedent:

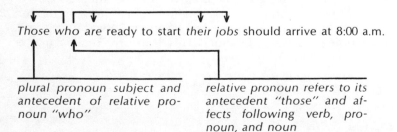

Those who are ready to start *their jobs* should arrive at 8:00 a.m.

| plural pronoun subject and antecedent of relative pronoun "who" | relative pronoun refers to its antecedent "those" and affects following verb, pronoun, and noun |

When the antecedent of a relative pronoun is compound (as two noun subjects, one of which is singular and the other plural), the number of the verb may vary according to the writer's preference. If a plural noun antecedent is closer to the verb, the writer may choose a plural verb. Examples:

He's one of those executives who *worry* a lot.
or
He's an executive who *worries* a lot.

The relative pronoun *who* typically refers to persons and some animals; *which,* to things and animals; and *that,* to both beings and things:

a man *who* sought success

. . . a hummingbird *who* came to the bushes in front must have got very slim pickings.
—Edmund Wilson

a book *which* sold well
a dog *which* barked loudly
a book *that* sold well
a dog *that* barked loudly
a man *that* we can trust

Relative pronouns can sometimes be omitted for the sake of brevity:

The man *whom* I was talking to is the president.
or
The man I was talking to is the president.

The relative pronoun *what* may be substituted for the longer and more awkward phrases "that which," "that of which," or "the thing which" in some sentences:

stiff   He was blamed for *that which* he could not have known.

easier   He was blamed for *what* he could not have known.

The problem of when to use *who* or *whom* has been blown out of proportion. The situation is very simple: standard written English makes a distinction between the nominative and objective cases of these pronouns when they are used as relatives or interrogatives, as

Who is she?
Who does she think she is, anyway?
She thinks she is the one *who* ought to be promoted.
She's the one individual *who* I think should be promoted.
Give me a list of the ones *who* you think should be promoted.
but
Whom are you referring to?
To *whom* are you referring?
He's a man *whom* everyone should know.
He's a man with *whom* everyone should be acquainted.

In speech, however, case distinctions and boundaries often become blurred, with the result that spoken English favors *who* as a general substitute for all uses of *whom* except in set phrases as "*To whom* it may concern." *Who,* then, may be used without criticism as the subject of the clause it introduces, as

I serve *who* I like.
                                                            .
    —*Irish Digest*

and *who* may be used as the object of a verb in a clause that it introduces, as

. . . old peasants . . . *who,* if isolated from their surroundings, one would expect to see in a village church. . . .
    —John Berger

Then I would have him select *who* he thought would make the best . . . candidate.
    —Joseph Napolitan

Who is used less frequently, however, as the object of a preceding or following preposition in the clause that it introduces:

. . . of *who* I know nothing.
—Raymond Paton

Who are you going to listen to, anyway. . . .
—*National Review*

The relative pronoun *whoever* likewise lends itself without criticism to flexible grammatical relationships:

. . . sells eggs to *whoever* has the money to buy. . . .
—J. R. Chamberlain

Whoever he picks has to have the stature of a collaborator, not a subordinate. . . .
—*Time*

or

. . . so that she could help *whomever* she married. . . .
—Lillian Ross

. . . *whomever* this alleged autobiography . . . is about, it is a real life. . . .
—*Springfield* (Mass.) *City Library Bulletin*

Verb

verb . . . *n* . . . : a word that characteristically is the grammatical center of a predicate and expresses an act, occurrence, or mode of being, that in various languages is inflected for agreement with the subject, for tense, for voice, for mood, or for aspect, and that typically has rather full descriptive meaning and characterizing quality but is sometimes nearly devoid of these esp. when used as an auxiliary or copula

---

Verbs exhibit the following characteristic features: inflection (*help, helps, helping, helped*), person (first, second, third person), number (singular, plural), tense (present, past, future), aspect (time relations other than the simple present, past, and future), voice (active, passive), mood (indicative, subjunctive, imperative), and suffixation (as by the typical suffixal markers *-ate, -en, -ify,* and *-ize*).

Regular verbs have four inflected forms signaled by the suffixes *-s* or *-es, -ed,* and *-ing*. The verb *help* as shown in the first sentence above is regular. Most irregular verbs have four or five forms, as

bring	*see*
brings	*sees*
bringing	*seeing*
brought	*saw*
	seen

but some, like *can, ought, put,* and *spread,* have fewer forms, as

can	*ought*	*put*	*spread*
could		*puts*	*spreads*
		putting	*spreading*

and one, the verb *be,* has eight:

be	*being*
is	*was*
am	*were*
are	*been*

When one is uncertain about a particular inflected form, one should consult a dictionary that indicates not only the inflections of irregular verbs but also those inflections resulting in changes in base-word spelling, as

blame; blamed; blaming
spy; spied; spying
picnic; picnicked; picnicking

in addition to variant inflected forms, as

bias; biased or *biassed; biasing* or *biassing*
counsel; counseled or *counselled; counseling* or *counselling*
diagram; diagramed or *diagrammed; diagraming* or *diagramming*
travel; traveled or *travelled; traveling* or *travelling*

all of which may be found at their applicable entries in *Webster's New Collegiate Dictionary.*

There are, however, a few rules that will aid one in ascertaining the proper spelling patterns of certain verb forms. These are as follows:

1. Verbs ending in a silent -e generally retain the -e before consonant suffixes (as -s) but drop the -e before vowel suffixes (as -ed and -ing):

   arrange; arranges; arranged; arranging
   hope; hopes; hoped; hoping
   require; requires; required; requiring
   shape; shapes; shaped; shaping

   Other such verbs are: *agree, arrive, conceive, grieve, imagine,* and *value.*

   NOTE: A few verbs ending in a silent -e retain the -e even before vowel suffixes in order to avoid confusion with other words:

   dye; dyes; dyed; dyeing (vs. *dying*)
   singe; singes; singed; singeing (vs. *singing*)

2. Monosyllabic verbs ending in a single consonant preceded by a single vowel double the final consonant before vowel suffixes (as -ed and -ing):

   brag; bragged; bragging
   grip; gripped; gripping
   pin; pinned; pinning

3. Polysyllabic verbs ending in a single consonant preceded by a single vowel and having an accented last syllable double the final consonant before vowel suffixes (as -ed and -ing):

   commit; committed; committing
   control; controlled; controlling
   occur; occurred; occurring
   omit; omitted; omitting

   NOTE: The final consonant of such verbs is not doubled when

   a. two vowels occur before the final consonant, as

      daub; daubed; daubing
      spoil; spoiled; spoiling

   b. two consonants form the ending, as

      help; helped; helping
      lurk; lurked; lurking
      peck; pecked; pecking

4. Verbs ending in -y preceded by a consonant regularly change the -y to -i before all suffixes except those beginning with -i (as -ing):

   carry; carried; carrying
   marry; married; marrying
   study; studied; studying

   NOTE: If the final -y is preceded by a vowel, it remains unchanged in suffixation, as

delay; delayed; delaying
enjoy; enjoyed; enjoying
obey; obeyed; obeying

5. Verbs ending in *-c* add a *-k* when a suffix beginning with *-e* or *-i* is appended, as

   mimic; mimics; mimicked; mimicking
   panic; panics; panicked; panicking
   traffic; traffics; trafficked; trafficking

   And words derived from this type of verb also add a *k* when such suffixes are added to them, as

   panicky
   trafficker

English verbs exhibit their two simple tenses by use of two single-word grammatical forms:

simple present = *do*
simple past = *did*

The future is expressed by *shall / will* + verb infinitive:

I *shall do* it.
He *will do* it.

or by use of the present or progressive forms in a revealing context, as

I *leave* shortly for New York. (present)
I *am leaving* shortly for New York. (progressive)

Aspect is a property that allows verbs to indicate time relations other than the simple present, past, or future tenses. Aspect covers these relationships:

action occurring in the past and continuing to the present	has seen	*present perfect tense*
action completed at a past time or before the immediate past	had seen	*past perfect tense*
action that will have been completed by a future time	will have seen	*future perfect tense*
action occurring now	is seeing	*progressive*

In contexts that require it, the perfective and the progressive aspects can be combined to yield special verb forms, as

had been seeing

Voice enables a verb to indicate whether the subject of a sentence is acting (he *loves* = active voice) or whether the subject is being acted upon (he *is loved* = passive voice).

Mood indicates manner of expression. The indicative mood states a fact or asks a question (He *is* here. *Is* he here?). The subjunctive mood expresses condition contrary to fact (I wish that he *were* here). The imperative mood expresses a command or request (*Come* here. Please *come* here).

Verbs may be used transitively; that is, they may act upon direct objects, as

She *contributed* money.

or they may be used intransitively; that is, they may not have direct objects to act upon, as

She *contributed* generously.

There is another group of words derived from verbs and called *verbals* that deserve added discussion. The members of this group—the gerund, the participle, and the infinitive—exhibit some but not all of the characteristic features of their parent verbs.

A gerund is an -*ing* verb form, but it functions mainly as a noun. It has both the active (*seeing*) and the passive (*being seen*) voices. In addition to voice, a gerund's verbal characteristics are as follows: it conveys the notion of a verb—i.e., action of some sort; it can take an object; and it can be modified by an adverb. Examples:

Typing tabular *data daily* is a boring task.

gerund   noun object   adverb

He liked *driving cars fast.*

gerund   noun object   adverb

Nouns and pronouns occurring before gerunds are expressed by the possessive:

Her typing is good.
She is trying to improve *her typing.*
We objected to *their telling* the story all over town.
We saw the *boy's whipping.* (i.e., the boy being whipped)
We expected the *senator's coming.* (i.e., his arrival)

Participles, on the other hand, function as adjectives and may occur alone (a *broken typewriter*) or in phrases that modify other words (*Having broken the typewriter, she gave up for the day*). Participles have active and passive forms like gerunds. Examples:

active-voice participial phrase modifying "he"
Having failed to pass the examination, he was forced to repeat the course.

passive-voice participial phrase modifying "he"
Having been failed by his instructor, he was forced to repeat the course.

Participles, unlike gerunds, are not preceded by possessive nouns or pronouns:

We saw the *boy whipping* his dog. (i.e., we saw the boy doing the whipping)
We saw the *senator coming.* (i.e., we saw him arrive)

Infinitives may exhibit active (*to do*) and passive (*to be done*) voices and they may indicate aspect (*to be doing, to have done, to have been doing, to have been done*).

Infinitives may take complements and may be modified by adverbs. In addition, they can function as nouns, adjectives, and adverbs in sentences. Examples:

noun use
To be known is to be castigated.
(subject)   (subjective complement)
He tried everything except *to bypass his superior.*
(object of preposition *except*)

adjectival use
They had found a way *to increase profits* greatly.
(modifies the noun *way*)

adverbial use
He was too furious *to speak.*
(modifies *furious*)

Although *to* is the characteristic marker of an infinitive, it is not always stated but may be understood:

He helped [to] complete the marketing report.

The following are general points of verb and verbal usage:

Sequence of tenses   If the main verb in a sentence is in the present tense, any other tense or compound verb form may follow it in subsequent clauses, as

I *realize* that you *are leaving.*
I *realize* that you *left.*
I *realize* that you *were leaving.*
I *realize* that you *have been leaving.*
I *realize* that you *had left.*
I *realize* that you *had been leaving.*
I *realize* that you *will be leaving.*
I *realize* that you *will leave.*
I *realize* that you *will have been leaving.*
I *realize* that you *can be leaving.*
I *realize* that you *may be leaving.*
I *realize* that you *must be leaving.*

If the main verb is in the past tense, that tense imposes time restrictions on any subsequent verbs in the sentence, thus excluding use of the present tense, as

I *realized* that you *were leaving.*
I *realized* that you *left.*
I *realized* that you *had left.*
I *realized* that you *had been leaving.*
I *realized* that you *would be leaving.*
I *realized* that you *could be leaving.*
I *realized* that you *might be leaving.*
I *realized* that you *would leave.*

If the main verb is in the future tense, it imposes time restrictions on subsequent verbs in the sentence, thus excluding the possibility of using the simple past tense, as

He *will see* you because he *is going* to the meeting too.
He *will see* you because he *will be going* to the meeting too.
He *will see* you because he *will go* to the meeting too.
He *will see* you because he *has been going* to the meetings too.
He *will see* you because he *will have been going* to the meetings too.

In general, most writers try to maintain an order of tenses throughout their sentences that is consistent with natural or real time, e.g., present tense = present-time matters, past tense = past matters, and future tense = matters that will take place in the future. However, there are two outstanding exceptions to these principles:

a.   If one is discussing the contents of printed or published material, one conventionally uses the present tense, as

In *Etiquette,* Emily Post *discusses* forms of address.

This analysis *gives* market projections for the next two years.

In his latest position paper on the Middle East, the Secretary of State *writes* that . . . .

b.   If one wishes to add the connotation of immediacy to a particular sentence, one may use the present tense instead of the future, as

I *leave* for Tel Aviv tonight.

c.   The sequence of tenses in sentences which express contrary-to-fact conditions is a special problem frequently encountered in writing. The examples below show the sequence correctly maintained:

If he *were* on time, we *would leave* now.

If he *had been* (not *would have been*) on time, we *would have left* an hour ago.

Subject-verb agreement   Verbs agree in number and in person with their grammatical subjects. At times, however, the grammatical subject may be singular in form, but the thought it carries—i.e., the logical subject—may have plural connotations. Here are some general guidelines:

a.   Plural and compound subjects take plural verbs even if the subject is inverted. Examples:

Music, theater, and painting *are* grouped under the heading "fine arts."

Both dogs and cats *were* tested for the virus.

b.   Compound subjects or plural subjects conveying a unitary idea take singular verbs in American English. Examples:

Lord & Taylor *has* stores in the New York area.

Five hundred dollars *is* a stiff price for a coat.

c.   Compound subjects expressing mathematical relationships may be either singular or plural. Examples:

One plus one *makes* (or *make*) two.

Six from eight *leaves* (or *leave*) two.

d.   Singular subjects joined by *or* or *nor* take singular verbs; plural subjects so joined take plural verbs. Examples:

A freshman or sophomore *is* eligible for the scholarship.

Neither freshmen nor sophomores *are* eligible for the scholarship.

If one subject is singular and the other plural, the verb usually agrees with the number of the subject that is closer to it. Examples:

Either the secretaries or the supervisor *has* to do the job.

Either the supervisor or the secretaries *have* to do the job.

e.   Singular subjects introduced by *many a, such a, every, each,* or *no* take singular verbs, even when several such subjects are joined by *and:*

Many an executive *has* gone to the top in that division.

No supervisor and no assembler *is* excused from the time check.

Every chair, table, and desk *has* to be accounted for.

f.   The agreement of the verb with its grammatical subject ordinarily should not be skewed by an intervening phrase even if the phrase contains plural elements. Examples:

One of my reasons for resigning *involves* purely personal considerations.

The president of the company, as well as members of his staff, *has* arrived.

He, not any of the proxy voters, *has* to be present.

g.   The verb *to be* agrees with its grammatical subject, and not with its complement:

His mania *was* fast cars and beautiful women.

Military skirmishes between China and the Soviet Union *is* an interesting field for study.

In addition, the verb *to be* introduced by the word *there* must agree in number with the subject following it. Examples:

There *are* many complications here.
There *is* no reason to worry about him.

NOTE: For discussion of verb agreement with indefinite-pronoun subjects, see pages 142–144. For discussion of verb number as affected by a compound subject whose elements are joined by *and/or,* see page 134.

Linking and *sense* verbs   Linking verbs (as the various forms of *to be*) and the so-called "sense" verbs (as *feel, look, taste, smell,* as well as particular senses of *appear, become, continue, grow, prove, remain, seem, stand,* and *turn*) connect subjects with predicate nouns or adjectives. The latter group often cause confusion, in that adverbs are mistakenly used in place of adjectives after these verbs. Examples:

He *is* a vice-president.
He *became* vice-president.
The temperature *continues* cold.
The future *looks* prosperous.
I *feel* awful.
This perfume *smells* nice.
The meat *tastes* good.
He *remains* healthy.

Split infinitives   The writer who consciously avoids splitting infinitives regardless of resultant awkwardness or changes in meaning is as immature in his or her position as the writer who consciously splits all infinitives as a sort of rebellion against convention. Actually, the use of split infinitives is no rebellion at all, because this construction has long been employed by a wide variety of distinguished English writers—Wycliffe, Byron, Coleridge, Browning (at least 23 times, according to one scholarly source), and Spenser—to name a few. Indeed, the split infinitive can be a useful device for the writer who wishes to delineate a shade of meaning or direct special emphasis to a word or group of words—emphasis that cannot be achieved with an undivided infinitive construction. For example, in the locution

to *thoroughly* complete the physical examination

the position of the adverb as close as possible to the verbal element of the whole infinitive phrase strengthens the effect of the adverb on the verbal element—a situation that is not necessarily true in the following reworded locutions:

to complete *thoroughly* the physical examination
thoroughly to complete the physical examination
to complete the physical examination *thoroughly*

In other instances, the position of the adverb may actually modify or change the entire meaning, as

original	*recast with new meanings*
. . . arrived in New York to *unexpectedly* find it in print.	. . . arrived in New York *unexpectedly* to find it in print.
—Harrison Smith	. . . arrived in New York to find it in print *unexpectedly.*

The main point is this: If the writer wishes to stress the verbal element of an infinitive or wishes to express a thought that is more clearly and easily shown with *to* + adverb + infinitive, such split infinitives are acceptable. However, very long adverbial modifiers such as

He wanted to *completely and without mercy* defeat his competitor.

are clumsy and should be avoided or recast, as

He wanted to defeat his competitor *completely and without mercy.*

Dangling participles and infinitives   Careful writers avoid danglers (as participles or infinitives occurring in a sentence without having a normally expected syntactic relation to the rest of the sentence) that may create confusion for the reader or seem ludicrous. Examples: '

dangling   Walking through the door, her coat was caught.
recast   While walking through the door, she caught her coat.
       Walking through the door, she caught her coat.
       She caught her coat while walking through the door.
dangling   Caught in the act, his excuses were unconvincing.
recast   Caught in the act, he could not make his excuses convincing.
dangling   Having been told that he was incompetent and dishonest, the executive fired the man.
recast   Having told the man that he was incompetent and dishonest, the executive fired him.
       Having been told by his superior that he was incompetent and dishonest, the man was fired.

Participial use should not be confused with prepositional use especially with words like *concerning, considering, providing, regarding, respecting, touching,* etc., as illustrated below:

prepositional usage
Concerning your complaint, we can tell you. . . .
Considering all the implications, you have made a dangerous decision.
Touching the matter at hand, we can say that. . . .

Having examined the eight parts of speech individually in order to pinpoint their respective characteristics and functions, we now view their performance in the broader environments of the phrase, the clause, and the sentence.

PHRASES
A phrase is a brief expression that consists of two or more grammatically related words and that may contain either a noun or a finite verb (i.e., a verb that shows grammatical person and number) but not both, and that often functions as a particular part of speech within a clause or a sentence. The table on page 154 lists and describes seven basic types of phrases.

CLAUSES
A clause is a group of words containing both a subject and a predicate and functioning as an element of a compound or a complex sentence (see pages 156–161 for discussion of sentences). The two general types of clauses are:

independent   *It is hot,* and *I feel faint.*
dependent   *Because it is hot,* I feel faint.

Like phrases, clauses can perform as particular parts of speech within a total sentence environment.

   Clauses that modify may also be described as restrictive or nonrestrictive. Whether a clause is restrictive or nonrestrictive has direct bearing on sentence punctuation.

Types of Phrases

Type of Phrase	Description	Example
noun phrase	consists of a noun and its modifiers	[*The concrete building* is huge.]
verb phrase	consists of a finite verb and any other terms that modify it or that complete its meaning	[She *will have arrived too late* for you to talk to her.]
gerund phrase	is a nonfinite verbal phrase that functions as a noun	[*Sitting on a patient's bed* is bad hospital etiquette.]
participial phrase	is a nonfinite verbal phrase that functions as an adjective	[*Listening all the time in great concentration,* he lined up his options.]
infinitive phrase	is a nonfinite verbal phrase that may function as a noun, an adjective, or an adverb	[*To do that* will be stupid.] [This was a performance *to remember.*] [It would be highly improper *to bypass your superior.*]
prepositional phrase	consists of a preposition and its object(s) and may function as a noun, an adjective, or an adverb	[Here is the desk *with the extra file drawer.*] [He now walked *without a limp.*] [*Out of here* is where I'd like to be!]
absolute phrase	is also called a nominative absolute, consists of a noun + a predicate form (as a participle), and acts independently within a sentence without modifying a particular element of the sentence	[He stalked out, *his eyes staring straight ahead.*]

Restrictive clauses are the so-called "bound" modifiers. They are absolutely essential to the meaning of the word or words they modify, they cannot be omitted without the meaning of the sentences being radically changed, and they are unpunctuated. Examples:

Women who aren't competitive should not aspire to high corporate office.

no punctuation   *restrictive clause*   *no punctuation*

In this example, the restrictive clause limits the classification of women, and as such is essential to the total meaning of the sentence. If, on the other hand, the restrictive clause is omitted as shown below, the classification of women is now not limited at all, and the sentence conveys an entirely different notion:

Women should not aspire to high corporate office.

Basic Types of Clauses with Part-of-speech Functions

Type of Clause	Description	Example
noun clause	fills a noun slot in a sentence and thus can be a subject, an object, or a complement	[*Whoever is qualified* should apply.] [I do not know *what his field is.*] [Route that journal to *whichever department you wish.*] [The trouble is *that she has no ambition.*]
adjective clause	modifies a noun or pronoun and typically follows the word it modifies	[His administrative assistant, *who was also a speech writer,* was overworked.] [I can't see the reason *why you're uptight.*] [He is a man *who will succeed.*] [Anybody *who opts for a career like that* is crazy.]
adverb clause	modifies a verb, an adjective, or another adverb and typically follows the word it modifies	[They made a valiant effort, *although the risks were great.*] [I'm certain *that he is guilty.*] [We accomplished less *than we did before.*]

Nonrestrictive clauses are the so-called "free" modifiers: They are not inextricably bound to the word or words they modify but instead convey additional information about them, they may be omitted altogether without the meaning of the sentence being radically changed, and they are set off by commas. Examples:

Our guide, who wore a green beret, was an experienced traveler.

↑ | ↑

comma   *nonrestrictive*   *comma*
clause

Obviously, the guide's attire is not essential to his experience as a traveler. Removal of the nonrestrictive clause does not affect the meaning of the sentence:

Our guide was an experienced traveler.

The following are basic points of clause usage:

Elliptical clauses Some clause elements may be omitted if the context makes clear the understood elements:

I remember the first time [that] we met. .
This typewriter is better than that [typewriter is].
When [she is] on the job, she is always competent and alert.

Clause placement In order to achieve maximum clarity and to avoid the possibility that the reader will misinterpret what he reads, one should place a modifying clause as close as possible to the word or words it modifies. If intervening words cloud the overall meaning of the sentence, one must recast it. Examples:

cloudy   A memorandum is a piece of business writing, less formal than a letter, which serves as a means of interoffice communication.

The question is: Does the letter or the memorandum serve as a means of interoffice communication?

recast   A memorandum, less formal than a letter, is a means of interoffice communication.

Tagged-on *which* clauses   Tagging on a "which" clause that refers to the total idea of a sentence is a usage fault that should be avoided by careful writers. Examples:

tagged-on
The company is retooling, which I personally think is a wise move.

recast
The company's decision to retool is a wise move in my opinion.
or
I believe that the company's decision to retool is wise.

SENTENCES

A sentence is a grammatically self-contained unit that consists of a word or a group of syntactically related words and that expresses a statement (declarative sentence), asks a question (interrogative sentence), expresses a request or command (imperative sentence), or expresses an exclamation (exclamatory sentence). A sentence typically contains both a subject and a predicate, begins with a capital letter, and ends with a punctuation mark. The following table illustrates the three main types of sentences classified by their grammatical structure.

Sentences Classified by their Grammatical Structure

Description	Example
simple sentence is a complete grammatical unit having one subject and one predicate, either or both of which may be compound	[*Paper* is costly.] [*Bond* and *tissue* are costly.] [*Bond* and *tissue* are costly and are sometimes scarce.]
compound sentence comprises two or more independent clauses	[*I could arrange to arrive late, or I could simply send a proxy.*] [*This commute takes at least forty minutes by car,* but *we can make it in twenty by train.*] [*A few of the executives had Ph.D.'s, even more of them had B.A.'s,* but *the majority of them had both B.A.'s and M.B.A.'s.*]
complex sentence combines one independent clause with one or more dependent clauses (dependent clauses are italicized in examples)	[The executive committee meeting began *when the board chairman and the president walked in.*] [*Although the czar made some reforms,* his changes came so late that they could not preserve him in power.]

How to construct sentences   The following paragraphs outline general guidelines for the construction of grammatically sound sentences.

One should maintain sentence coordination by use of connectives linking phrases and clauses of equal rank. Examples:

faulty coordination with improper use of "and"
I was sitting in on a meeting, and he stood up and started a long rambling discourse on a new pollution-control device.

recast with one clause subordinated
I sat in on a meeting during which he stood up and rambled on about a new pollution-control device.

or—recast into two sentences
I sat in on that meeting. He stood up and rambled on about a new pollution-control device.

faulty coordination with improper use of "and"
This company employs a full-time research staff and was founded in 1945.

recast with one clause subordinated
This company, which employs a full-time research staff, was founded in 1945.

or—recast with one clause reworded into a phrase
Established in 1945, this company employs a full-time research staff.

One should also maintain parallel, balanced sentence elements in order to achieve good sentence structure. Examples illustrating this particular point are as follows:

unparallel
The report gives market statistics, but he does not list his sources for these figures.

parallel
The report gives market statistics, but it does not list the sources for these figures.

unparallel
We are glad to have you as our client, and please call us whenever you need help.

parallel
We are glad to have you as our client and we hope that you will call on us whenever you need help.

or recast into two sentences
We are glad to have you as our client. Please do call on us whenever you need help.

Loose linkages of sentence elements such as those caused by excessive use of *and* should be avoided by careful writers. Some examples of this type of faulty coordination are shown below:

faulty coordination/excessive use of "and"
This company is a Class 1 motor freight common carrier of general commodities and it operates over 10,000 tractors, trailers, and city delivery trucks through 200 terminals, and serves 40 states and the District of Columbia.

recast into three shorter, more effective sentences
This company is a Class 1 motor freight common carrier of general commodities. It operates over 10,000 tractors, trailers, and city delivery trucks through 200 terminals. The company serves 40 states and the District of Columbia.

In constructing one's sentences effectively, one should choose the conjunction that best expresses the intended meaning. Examples:

not
The economy was soft *and* we lost a lot of business.

but
We lost a lot of business *because* the economy was soft.
The economy was soft, *so* we lost a lot of business.

or recast to
The soft economy has cost us a lot of business.

Good writers avoid unnecessary grammatical shifts that interrupt the reader's train of thought and needlessly complicate the material. Some unnecessary grammatical shifts are shown below, and improvements are also illustrated:

unnecessary shifts in verb voice
Any information you *can give* us *will be* greatly *appreciated* and we *assure* you that discretion *will be exercised* in its use.

rephrased (note the italicized all-active verb voice)
We *will appreciate* any information that you *can give* us. We *assure* you that we *will use* it with discretion.

unnecessary shifts in person
One can use either erasers or correcting fluid to remove typographical errors; however, *you* should make certain that *your* corrections are clean.

rephrased (note that the italicized pronouns are consistent)
One can use either erasers or correcting fluid to eradicate errors; however, *one* should make certain that *one's* corrections are clean.
or
You can use either erasers or correcting fluid to eradicate errors; however, *you* should make certain that *your* corrections are clean.

unnecessary shift from phrase to clause
Because of the current parts shortage and *we are experiencing a strike,* we cannot fill any orders now.

rephrased
Because of a parts shortage and a strike, we cannot fill any orders now.
or
Because we are hampered by a parts shortage and we are experiencing a strike, we cannot fill any orders now.

Always keeping in mind the reader's reaction, the writer should strive for a rational ordering of sentence elements. Closely related elements, for example, should be placed as close together as possible for the sake of maximum clarity. Examples:

not
We would appreciate your sending us the instructions on manuscript copy editing by mail or cable.
but
We would appreciate your sending us by mail or by cable the manuscript copy-editing instructions.
or
We would appreciate your mailing or cabling us the manuscript copy-editing instructions.
or
We would appreciate it if you would mail or cable us the manuscript copy-editing instructions.

One should ensure that one's sentences form complete, independent grammatical units containing both a subject and a predicate, unless the material is dialogue or specialized copy where fragmentation may be used for particular reasons (as to reflect speech or to attract the reader's attention). Examples:

poor
During the last three years, our calculator sales soared. While our conventional office machine sales fell off.
better
During the last three years, our calculator sales soared, but our conventional office machine sales fell off.

or, with different emphasis
While our conventional office machine sales fell off during the last three years, our calculator sales soared.
sentences fragmented for special effects
    (dialogue)
"Have you hand grenades?"
"Plenty."
"How many rounds per rifle?"
"Plenty."
"How many?"
"One hundred fifty. More maybe."
                              —Ernest Hemingway
    (advertising)
See it now. The car for the Seventies . . .
A car you'll want to own.

Sentence length   Sentence length is directly related to the writer's purpose: there is no magic number of words that guarantees a good sentence. For example, an executive covering broad and yet complex topics (as in a long memorandum) may choose concise, succinct sentences for the sake of clarity, impact, fast dictation, and reading. On the other hand, a writer wishing to elicit the reader's reflection upon what is being said may employ longer, more involved sentences. Still another writer may juxtapose long and short sentences to emphasize an important point. The longer sentences may build up to a climactic and forceful short sentence.

Sentence strategy   Stylistically, there are two basic types of sentences—the periodic and the cumulative or loose. The periodic sentence is structured so that its main idea or its thrust is suspended until the very end, thereby drawing the reader's eye and mind along to an emphatic conclusion:

buildup —
| While the Commission would wish to give licensees every encouragement to experiment on their own initiative with new and different means of providing access to their stations for the discussion of important public issues, it cannot justify the imposition of a specific right of access — *thrust* by government fiat.

                              —*Television/Radio Age*

The cumulative sentence, on the other hand, is structured so that its main thought or its thrust appears first, followed by other phrases or clauses expanding on or supporting it:

main point —| The solution must be finely honed, lest strategists err too much on the side of sophistication only to find that — *supporting* U.S. military forces can be defeated by overwhelming mass. *phrase*

                              —William C. Moore

The final phrase in a cumulative sentence theoretically could be deleted without skewing or destroying the essential meaning of the total sentence. A cumulative sentence is therefore more loosely structured than a periodic sentence.

    A writer may employ yet another strategy to focus the reader's attention on a problem or an issue. This device is the rhetorical question—a question that requires no specific response from the reader but often merely sets up the introduction of the writer's own views. In some instances, a rhetorical question works as a topic sentence in a paragraph; in other instances, a whole series of rhetorical questions may spotlight pertinent issues for the reader's consideration. The following excerpts illustrate rhetorical questions in action:

rhetorical question as *a topic sentence*	Why all the mystery about factoring? It has a lot to do with the concentration of this service in the textile business for the past hundred years. Because of this, many businessmen
author answers question *posed earlier*	have had little contact with the service, and worse, have succumbed to the mythology surrounding factoring. —William R. Gruttemeyer
series of rhetorical *questions focus on* *specific issues*	Will automatic vtr's [video tape recorders] be hooked to computers? Is this the next step in automation? What comes next in tape libraries? When will it all happen? —*Television/Radio Age*

A writer uses either coordination or subordination or a mixture of both to create different stylistic effects. As shown in the subsection on clauses, coordination links independent sentences and sentence elements by means of coordinating conjunctions, while subordination transforms elements into dependent structures by means of subordinating conjunctions. While coordination tends to promote rather loose sentence structure which can become a fault, subordination tends to tighten the structure and to focus attention on a main clause. Examples of these two strategies are shown below:

coordination
During the balance of 1976, this Company expects to issue $100,000,000 of long-term debt and equity securities *and* may guarantee up to $200,000,000 of new corporate bonds.
subordination
While this Company expects to issue $100,000,000 of long-term debt and equity securities during the balance of 1976, it may also guarantee up to $200,000,000 of new corporate bonds.

A reversal of customary or expected sentence order is yet another effective stylistic strategy, when used sparingly, because it injects a dash of freshness, unexpectedness, and originality into the prose. Examples:

customary or expected order
I find that these realities are indisputable: the economy has taken a drastic downturn, costs on all fronts have soared, and jobs are at a premium.
reversal
That the economy has taken a drastic downturn; that costs on all fronts have soared; that jobs are at a premium—these are the realities that I find indisputable.

Interrupting the normal flow of discourse by inserting comments is a strategy that some writers employ to call attention to an aside, to emphasize a word or phrase, to render special effects (as forcefulness), or to make the prose a little more informal. Since too many interrupting elements may distract the reader and disrupt his train of thought, they should be used with discretion. The following are typical interrupted sentences:

an aside	His evidence, if reliable, could send our client to prison.
emphasis	These companies—ours as well as theirs—must show more profits.
forcefulness	This, gentlemen, is the prime reason for your cost overruns. I trust it will not happen again?

While interruption breaks up the flow of discourse, parallelism and balance work together toward maintaining an even rhythmic flow of thoughts. Parallelism means a similarity in the grammatical construction of adjacent phrases and clauses that are equivalent, complementary, or antithetical in meaning. Examples:

These ecological problems are of crucial concern *to* scientists, *to* businessmen, *to* government officials, and *to* all citizens.

Our attorneys have argued *that* the trademark is ours, *that* our rights have been violated, and *that* appropriate compensation is required.

He was respected not only *for his intelligence* but also *for his integrity.*

Balance is the juxtaposition and equipoise of two or more syntactically parallel constructions (as phrases and clauses) that contain similar, contrasting, or opposing ideas:

To err is human; to forgive, divine.
—Alexander Pope

Ask not what your country can do for you—ask what you can do for your country.
—John F. Kennedy

And finally, a series can be an effective way to emphasize a thought and to establish a definite rhythmic prose pattern:

The thing that interested me . . . about New York . . . was the . . . contrast it showed between the dull and the shrewd, the strong and the weak, the rich and the poor, the wise and the ignorant. . . .
—Theodore Dreiser

PARAGRAPHS
The underlying structure of any written communication—be it a memorandum, a letter, or a report—must be controlled by the writer if the material is to be clear, coherent, logical in orientation, and effective. Since good paragraphing is a means to this end, it is essential that the writer be facile when using techniques of paragraph development and transition between paragraphs. While the writer is responsible for the paragraphing system, the secretary still should be able to recognize various kinds of paragraphs and their functions as well as the potential problems that often arise in structuring a logical paragraph system. In this way, the secretary can assist the writer, especially by pointing out possible discrepancies that might result in misinterpretation by the reader or that might detract from the total effect of the communication.

A paragraph is a subdivision in writing that consists of one or more sentences, that deals with one or more ideas, or that quotes a speaker or a source. The first line of a paragraph is indented in reports, studies, articles, theses, and books. However, the first line of a paragraph in business letters and memorandums may or may not be indented, depending on the style being followed. See Chapter 1, section 1.7, for business-letter styling.

Uses of paragraphs   Paragraphs should not be considered as isolated entities that are self-contained and mechanically lined up without transitions or interrelationship of ideas. Rather, paragraphs should be viewed as components of larger groups or blocks that are tightly interlinked and that interact in the sequential development of a major idea or cluster of ideas. The overall coherence of a communication depends on this interaction.

For example, one writer may be able to express his point in a succinct, one-sentence paragraph, while another may require several sentences to make his point. Writers' concepts of paragraphing also differ. For instance, some writers think of paragraphs as a means of dividing their material into logical segments with each unit developing one particular point in depth and in detail. Others view paragraphs as a means of emphasizing particular points or adding variety to long passages.

Writers use paragraphs in the following ways:

1. To support a generalization with facts or examples
2. To give a reason or reasons
3. To define something
4. To classify—i.e., to present something as a member of a particular class and then to explain the characteristics of that class
5. To delineate (as facts) or to list (as details) usually in support of a proposition
6. To set forth points of comparison and contrast, or pros and cons
7. To describe (as a situation or a thing)
8. To limit, expand, elaborate, or restate (as an idea)
9. To narrate (as an anecdote or story)
10. To paraphrase or to quote (an individual or a source)
11. To analyze or summarize (as a situation)
12. To summarize (as findings)

There are two general types of paragraphs: the expository—a unit of facts, details, or ideas brought together to explain or describe; and the argumentative—a unit of facts, details, or ideas brought together to persuade or convince. A writer may use or modify one or both of these prototypes, depending on the major thrust.

Paragraph development and strategy   Depending on the writer's intentions, paragraph development may take any of these directions:

1. The paragraph may move from the general to the specific.
2. The paragraph may move from the specific to the general.
3. The paragraph may exhibit an alternating order of comparison and contrast.
4. The paragraph may chronicle events in a set temporal order—e.g., from the beginning to the end, or from the end to the beginning.
5. The paragraph may describe something (as a group of objects) in a set spatial order—e.g., the items being described may be looked at from near-to-far, or vice versa.
6. The paragraph may follow a climactic sequence with the least important facts or examples described first followed by a buildup of tension leading to the most important facts or examples then followed by a gradual easing of tension. Other material can be so ordered for effectiveness; for example, facts or issues that are easy to comprehend or accept may be set forth first and followed by those that are more difficult to comprehend or accept. In this way the easier material makes the reader receptive and prepares him to comprehend or accept the more difficult points.
7. Anticlimactic order is also useful when the writer's intent is to persuade the reader. With this strategy, the writer sets forth the most persuasive arguments first so that the reader, having then been influenced in a positive way by that persuasion, moves along with the rest of the argument with a growing feeling of assent.

Keys to effective paragraphing   The following material outlines some ways of building effective paragraphs within a text.

A topic sentence—a key sentence to which the other sentences in the paragraph are related—may be placed either at the beginning or at the end of a paragraph. A lead-in topic sentence should present the main idea in the paragraph, and should set the initial tone of the material that follows. A terminal topic sentence should be an analysis, a conclusion, or a summation of what has gone before it.

Single-sentence paragraphs can be used to achieve easy transition from a preceding to a subsequent paragraph (especially when those are long and complex), if it repeats an important word or phrase from the preceding paragraph, if it contains a pronoun reference to a key individual mentioned in a preceding paragraph, or if it is introduced by an appropriate conjunction or conjunctive adverb that tightly connects the paragraphs.

Since the very first paragraph sets initial tone, introduces the subject or topic under discussion, and leads into the main thrust of a communication, it should be worded so as to immediately attract the reader's attention and arouse interest. These openings can be effective:

a. a succinct statement of purpose or point of view
b. a concise definition (as of a problem)
c. a lucid statement of a key issue or fact

But these openings can blunt the rest of the material:

a. an apology for the material to be presented
b. a querulous complaint or a defensive posture
c. a rehash of ancient history (as a word-for-word recap of previous correspondence from the individual to whom one is writing)
d. a presentation of self-evident facts
e. a group of sentences rendered limp and meaningless because of clichés

The last paragraph ties together all of the ideas and points that have been set forth earlier and reemphasizes the main thrust of the communication. These can be effective endings:

a. a setting forth of the most important conclusion or conclusions drawn from the preceding discussion
b. a final analysis of the main problem or problems under discussion
c. a lucid summary of the individual points brought up earlier
d. a final, clear statement of opinion or position
e. concrete suggestions or solutions if applicable
f. specific questions asked of the reader if applicable

But the following endings can decrease the effectiveness of a communication:

a. apologies for a poor presentation
b. qualifying remarks that blunt or negate incisive points made earlier
c. insertion of minor details or afterthoughts
d. a meaningless closing couched in clichés

The following are tests of good paragraphs:

1. Does the paragraph have a clear purpose? Is its utility evident, or is it there just to fill up space?
2. Does the paragraph clarify rather than cloud the writer's ideas?
3. Is the paragraph adequately developed, or does it merely raise other questions that the writer does not attempt to answer? If a position is being taken, does the writer include supporting information and statistics that are essential to its defense?
4. Are the length and wording of all the paragraphs sufficiently varied, or does the writer employ the same types of locutions again and again?
5. Is the sentence structure coherent?
6. Is each paragraph unified? Do all the sentences really <u>belong</u> there; or does the writer digress into areas that would have been better covered in another paragraph or that could have been omitted altogether?
7. Are the paragraphs coherent so that one sentence leads clearly and logically to another? Is easy, clear transition among the paragraphs effected by a wise selection of transitional words and phrases which indicate idea relationships and signal the direction in which the author's prose is moving?
8. Does one paragraph simply restate in other terms what has been said before?

The following essay, reproduced from page 11 of the 1974 *Annual Report* of Pacific Power & Light Company, is an example of effective paragraphing.

Our Source of Coal . . . and Pride

This is the story of your company's attempt to reconcile the energy demands of America's civilization with the necessity of preserving her great beauty, a story of Pacific's mining operation at Glenrock, Wyoming.

Energy shortage is among the most critical problems facing our country. America needs more domestic energy supply, but some don't want to mine coal, construct coal-fired plants, or use nuclear technology. People may dream of solar and geothermal energy, but without utilizing the resources and technology available to us today, exotic energy supplies in meaningful quantities will remain only a dream.

Coal, which our nation has in great supply, is one of the prime answers to this country's energy problems for the next quarter century. Under the prairielands of the Northern Great Plains lie billions of tons of coal with an energy equivalent greater than Saudi Arabia's oil reserves. Much of this coal is found in thick seams that lie close to the earth's surface, seams that can easily and economically be surface mined. This mining method maximizes the efficient use of this resource by recovering a much greater percentage than is possible by underground methods. There is virtually no waste. Safety factors are an important benefit. Surface miners have substantially less frequency and severity of accidents than underground miners. This is human conservation, an often ignored aspect of ecology. In addition to achieving a high level of productivity, safety is always at the top of corporate priorities.

The mining process begins with scrapers lifting off the layer of topsoil and piling it aside for respreading later. Then draglines remove the subsoil that covers the coal seam. After the coal is broken up with explosives, it is loaded into trucks and carried to a railhead. Now comes a technically difficult and most controversial part of the mining operation—reclamation. Bulldozers recontour the subsoil to the existing lay of the land. Scrapers then replace the original topsoil. This **reclaimed** portion is then mulched with small grained straw, seeded with special perennial grasses, and fertilized with nitrogen.

paragraph block 1
paragraph 1 functions as a topic sentence for the entire essay

paragraph 2 topic sentence sets forth a fact and occurs first in that paragraph

subsequent sentences support and expand topic sentence

paragraph block 2
paragraph 3 topic sentence offers a solution to the problem posed in paragraph 2

subsequent sentences explain in depth the solution offered in the topic sentence

last two sentences summarize and make pertinent points

*paragraph 4 is **descriptive:** it lists in temporal order the steps in a process*

paragraph transition is achieved by the repetition of key words in paragraphs 4, 5, 6, and 7

Our **reclamation** processes have undergone many years of research and experimentation so that **reclaimed** areas now exceed the native terrain in productivity. Nature herself can prove this. The number of animals which can feed in any given area is regulated by nature balance. On our 550 **reclaimed** acres of the Wyoming plains, the herds of deer and antelope are increasing markedly, positive proof that the productivity of the land has also increased.

The whole cycle of surface mining, from the time the topsoil is removed to the final seeding, takes about 2½ years and costs about $2,000 per acre. Though the surface acre may be valued at only $30, we proportion the **reclamation** cost to the value of the coal mined. The final bill will amount to about 5 cents a ton. Our commitment to **reclamation** is total. If ever the value of the coal will not support **reclamation** costs, the land will not be disturbed.

The myth that corporations are pro-pollution, relentlessly exploiting the earth, must be disclaimed. Many are often at the forefront in the struggle to preserve the environment, and preserve the land entrusted to them. Pacific has been **reclaiming** Wyoming land since 1965, four years before it became state law. There were many technical problems, but most of them are solved now. There may be more problems, but the recognition of that fact is the best assurance that we will overcome them. The responsibility to serve necessitates the obligation to keep trying.

An environmentalist is one who has learned to live in harmony with his surroundings, not be controlled by them. As the advance of society must not be made at the expense of nature, so the preservation of nature must not be achieved at the destruction of society. They must coexist, and in man's technology, ever alert and ever advancing, lies our only answer.

If man would strive for knowledge and understanding, reason, not emotion, must be the guidepost. Performance, not talk, must be the touchstone. We believe our performance speaks clearly. Pacific Power is uncovering one of nature's great resources, is supplying one of America's vital needs, and is revitalizing part of the prairie-lands of Wyoming. Both man and nature are benefiting from our recovery of necessary fossil fuel. That's our story . . . our source of pride.

paragraph block 3

last sentence of paragraph 5 contains support for preceding arguments

paragraph 6 is **expository:** *it gives facts and figures*

paragraph block 4
paragraph 7 is **argumentative:** *it begins with its major point of argument in its topic sentence, followed in subsequent sentences by supporting arguments, and supporting figures and facts*

paragraph 8 begins with a definition to which the rest of the arguments continuing from paragraph 7 are keyed

paragraph 9 offers general solutions to problems discussed throughout the essay; the tone is intentionally upbeat

last sentence neatly ties in with the title, thus exemplifying coherence

2.9

TONE IN WRITING

The tone of a communication is usually set in the first paragraph and is ordinarily maintained throughout the subsequent paragraphs to the end. Of course, tone depends on a number of factors:

1. the underlying reason or reasons why something (as a memorandum or a letter) is being written in the first place
2. the personal attitude of the writer toward his reader and his subject matter.
3. the content (as general vs. technical) of the material itself

Thus, a communication may be formal or informal, neutral or biased, friendly or critical, or it may reflect any number of other feelings and attitudes.

THE IMPORTANCE OF TONE IN COMMUNICATIONS

The effect of the tone of a communication on its reader cannot be overemphasized. A letter, for example, may feature excellent layout, clean typewriting, attractive stationery, good sentence structure, correct spelling, and easy transition from one paragraph to another. It may contain complete, logically presented data. Yet, if the tone of the letter is needlessly abrupt or indeed rude, the effect of the material on the reader will be negative, of course. Reader responses should therefore be kept in mind at all times. Some principles relevant to tone in general business communications are outlined and discussed briefly in the following paragraphs. For further examples of varying tone in business letters, the reader may consult *Webster's Secretarial Handbook.*

A communication should be reader-oriented. When one is intent on setting forth one's own objectives, especially under pressure, one often unfortunately forgets the reader's point of view and possible responses. Compare the following two approaches:

abrupt
We have read with interest your article on HDPE pipe in the October 12 issue of *Plastics*. Since our marketing division is preparing a multiclient study on plastic pipe applications, we will need offprints of the following papers you have written on this subject: . . . .

polite
We have read with interest your article on HDPE pipe in the October 12 issue of *Plastics*. Our marketing division is preparing a multiclient study on plastic pipe applications—a study that will not be complete without reference to your outstanding research. We'd therefore be pleased if you'd send us offprints of the following papers you've written on the subject: . . . .

The writer should not assume <u>automatically</u> that the reader has the same degree of familiarity with the matter to be discussed as he has. He should consciously pitch his presentation at an appropriate level, neither writing down to experts nor writing over the heads of nonexperts.

Use of the personal pronoun *you* can personalize a communication and thus make the reader feel more involved in the discussion. Compare the following pairs of examples:

impersonal
The enclosed brochure outlining this Company's services may be of interest.
This Company is gratified when its clients offer useful suggestions.

personal
We've enclosed a brochure outlining our services, which we hope will interest you.
We appreciate your taking the time to offer such a useful suggestion.

In the same way, the personal pronouns *I* and *we* should not be consciously avoided in favor of passive or impersonal constructions that, when overused, can depersonalize a communication. Examples:

impersonal	*personal*
Reference is made to your May 1 letter received by this office yesterday.	We are referring to your May 1 letter which we received yesterday.
Enclosed is the requested material.	We're enclosing the material you requested.
It is the understanding of this writer that the contract is in final negotiation stages.	I understand that the contract is in final negotiation stages.

Common courtesy and tactfulness can be exercised without resort to obsequiousness. Considerate writers use polite expressions whenever possible.

2.10

ACHIEVEMENT OF A MORE ORIGINAL WRITING STYLE

The effectiveness and overall output of communications can be markedly increased if one avoids the padding and clichés that can blunt what otherwise might be incisive writing. These expressions, sometimes called *business static,* have become fixtures in the vocabularies of far too many writers. Some of the locutions (as "enclosed please find") are best avoided because they are stale. Others (as "aforesaid"), while common to legal documents, are stiff and awkward in general business contexts. Still others (as "beg to respond") have an antique ring. And then there are some expressions (as "forward on") that are redundant, and others (as "acknowledge receipt of") that are overlong.

Unfortunately, these verbal tics seem to occur most often in conspicuous areas of a text: either at the very beginning where initial tone is being set or at the very end where summations are being made, or at the beginnings and ends of individual sentences and paragraphs where particular ideas and points are being set forth. Needless to say, a busy reader can become quite annoyed when he or she must wade through superfluous or hackneyed expressions to get at the gist of a communication.

While this section does not presume to prescribe word choice, it does attempt to spotlight ways to shave away verbal fat so that the main ideas and points in a piece of writing will stand out. The following alphabetically ordered mini-glossary is a representative list of expressions better avoided by writers who seek more clarity, brevity, and originality in their business communications.

abeyance
hold in abeyance

stilted   We are holding our final decision in abeyance....

easier   We are deferring / delaying / holding up } our final decision....

above
While use of this word as a noun ("see the above"), an adjective ("the above figure shows"), and an adverb ("see above") is indeed acceptable, its overuse within one document can distract a reader. Alternative expressions are:

See the figure on page --.
See the figure at the top of the page.
This (that) figure shows. . . .
See the material illustrated earlier.

above-mentioned
is overlong and is often overworked within a single document.

longer   The above-mentioned policy. . . .

shorter   This (That) policy. . . .

acknowledge receipt of
requires 22 keystrokes, but the alternative expression *have received* is a 13-stroke synonym. Why not use the shorter of the two?

longer	We acknowledge receipt of your check. . . .
shorter	We have ⎱ received your We've ⎰ check. . . .

advise
has been overworked when meaning "to inform." Since "to inform" can be expressed by either of the shorter verbs *say* or *tell,* why not use one of them?

longer	We regret to advise you that the book is out of stock.
shorter	We must tell you that the book is out of stock. Unfortunately, the book is out of stock. We're sorry to say that the book is out of stock.

advised and informed
is redundant, since the two conjoined words simply repeat each other.

redundant	He has been advised and informed of our position. We have advised and informed him of our position.
lean	He has been told of our position. We have told him of our position. We have outlined our position to him. He knows our position.

affix (one's) **signature to**
is padding, and can be reduced to *sign.*

padded	Please affix your signature to the enclosed documents.
lean	Please sign these documents. Please sign the enclosed documents.

aforementioned/aforesaid
are commonly used in legal documents but sound verbose and pointlessly pompous in general business contexts. The same idea may usually be conveyed by one of the demonstrative adjectives (*this, that, these, those*).

verbose	The aforementioned company. . . .
natural	This (that) company. . . . *or* The company in question. . . . The company (we) mentioned earlier. . . .
verbose	. . . must reach a decision regarding the aforesaid dispute.
natural	. . . must make a decision about this (that) dispute.

amplify to a maximum
may be pared down to *maximize.*

padded	. . . expect all salesmen to amplify to a maximum their sales calls next month.
lean	. . . expect all salesmen to maximize their next month's sales calls.

—*compare* REDUCE TO A MINIMUM

and etc.
is redundant, because *etc.* is the abbreviation of the Latin *et cetera* meaning "and the rest." Omit the *and.*

not	. . . carbon packs, onionskin, bond, and etc.
but	. . . carbon packs, onionskin, bond, etc.

as per
has been overworked when meaning "as," "in accordance with," and "following." It is a tired and formulaic way to begin a letter, paragraph, or sentence.

overworked	As per your request of. . . . As per our telephone conversation of. . . . As per our agreement. . . .
more natural	As you requested. . . . According to your request. . . . In accordance with your request. . . . As a follow-up to our telephone conversation. . . . In accordance with our telephone conversation. . . . As we agreed. . . . In accordance with our agreement. . . . According to our agreement. . . .

as regards
can also be expressed by the terms *concerning* or *regarding*.

stiff   As regards your complaint. . . .

easier   Concerning your complaint. . . .
          or
          Let's talk about your complaint.

as stated above
can be more naturally expressed as:
As we (I) have said. . . .

assuring you that
is an outmoded participial-phrase ending to a business letter that should not be used.

outmoded   Assuring you that your cooperation will be appreciated, I remain
                  Sincerely yours

current   I will appreciate your cooperation.
                  Sincerely yours

as to
has been as overworked as the phrase *as per*. Here are some alternatives for *as to:*
regarding
concerning
about
of

overworked   As to your second question. . . .

fresher   Regarding your second question. . . .

              Coming to your second question. . . .
              or
              Now for your second question.

              Let's look at your second question.

overworked   We have no means of judging as to the wisdom of that decision.

fresher   We cannot (can't) judge the wisdom of that decision.

—compare AS PER

at about
is meaningless because *at* is explicit but *about* is indefinite. Thus, when conjoined, they cancel each other's meaning.

meaningless   I'll get back to you at about 9:30 a.m. tomorrow.

explicit   I'll get back to you at 9:30 a.m. tomorrow.
              or
              I'll get back to you about 9:30 a.m. tomorrow.

at all times
may be shortened to *always*.

longer   We shall be glad to meet with you at all times.

shorter   We'll always be glad to meet with you.

at an early date
is both long and vague. If the writer means "immediately," or "by (*date*)," he should say as much; if he means "when convenient," he should specify it.

at once and by return mail
when conjoined are repetitious: either *at once* or *immediately* will suffice.

repetitive   Please send us your check at once and by return mail.

succinct   Please send us your check at once (*or* immediately).

—see *also* RETURN MAIL

attached hereto/herewith
is quite impersonal and may be expressed in a more personal way as:
Attached is/are
We are attaching
We have attached
You'll see attached
—compare ENCLOSED HEREWITH

at this point in time/at this time
may be shortened to
now
presently
at (the) present

at this writing
may be shortened to *now*

at your earliest convenience
manages to convey nothing in 28 keystrokes; however, the alternative *as soon as you can* requires only 18 strokes and states the case explicitly. Still other expressions, as
now
immediately
by (*date*)
within (*number of days*)
may also be used, depending on context.

basic fundamentals
is redundant. One of the following may be substituted:
the basics
the fundamentals

beg
beg to acknowledge
beg to advise
beg to state
and other such *beg* combinations sound antique. The following may be used instead:
We acknowledge. . . .
We've received. . . .
Thank you for. . . .
We're pleased to tell you. . . .
We can say that. . . .
We can tell you that. . . .

brought to our notice
is overlong and may be recast to:
We note . . . .
We notice . . . .
We see . . . .

contents carefully noted
contributes little or no information and should be omitted.

not	Yours of the 1st. received and contents carefully noted.
but	We've read carefully your June 1 letter.
	We've read your June 1 letter.
	The instructions in your June 1 letter have been followed.
	We've read your June 1 letter and have followed its instructions.

dated
is unnecessary when used in locutions like "your letter dated June 1." The word may be omitted:
your June 1 letter
your letter of June 1

deem (it)
is a stiff way of saying *think* or *believe*.

stiff	We deem it advisable that you . . . .
easier	We think you ought to . . . .
	We think it advisable that you . . . .

demand and insist
when conjoined are redundant; however, the use of just one of the following at a time will suffice: *demand* or *insist* or *require*

despite the fact that
may be pared down to *although* or *though*

due to
due to the fact that
are both stiff and may be reduced to:
because (of)
since

duly
is meaningless in expressions like
Your order has been duly forwarded.
and thus should be omitted:
Your order has been forwarded.
We've forwarded your order.

earnest endeavor
is cloying when used in this type of sentence:
It will be our earnest endeavor to serve our customers . . . .
It should be replaced with more direct, straightforward phrasing:
We'll (or We shall) try to serve our customers . . . .

enclosed herewith/enclosed please find
are impersonal and stilted expressions better worded as:
We enclose . . . .
We are enclosing . . . .
We have enclosed . . . .
Enclosed is/are . . . .
—compare ATTACHED HERETO/HEREWITH

endeavor
is an eight-letter verb that can be replaced by the three-letter verb *try,* which is synonymous and not pompous.
pompous and longer
We shall endeavor to . . . .
direct and shorter
We'll (or We shall) try to . . . .
or
We'll make a real effort to . . . .
We'll make every effort to . . . .
We'll do everything we can to . . . .
We'll do our best to . . . .

esteemed
is effusive when used in a sentence like
We welcome your esteemed favor of June 9.
and therefore should not be used. The sentence may be recast to:
Thank you for your June 9 letter.

favor
should never be used in the sense of a letter, an order, a check, or other such item.

not   your favor of April 14

but   your April 14 letter

for the purpose of
may be more succinctly worded as *for.*

padded   . . . necessary for purposes of accounting.

lean   . . . necessary for accounting.

forward on
is redundant, since *forward* alone conveys the meaning adequately.

redundant   We have forwarded your complaint on to the proper authorities.

explicit   We have forwarded your complaint to the proper authorities.

hand (one) **herewith**
as in the locution
We are handing you herewith an invoice for . . . .
is an inflated way of saying
We're (*or* We are) enclosing
Enclosed is/are

have before me
is superfluous. Obviously, the writer has previous correspondence at hand when responding to a letter.

not   I have before me your letter of June 1 . . . .

but   In reply ⎫
response ⎬ to your June 1
answer ⎭ letter . . . .

hereto
—*see* ATTACHED HERETO/HEREWITH

herewith
—*see* ATTACHED HERETO/HEREWITH
ENCLOSED HEREWITH/ENCLOSED PLEASE FIND

hoping for the favor (or to hear)
and other such participial-phrase endings for business letters are now outmoded and should be omitted. Instead of
Hoping for the favor of a reply,
I remain
one of these alternatives may be selected:
I (We) look forward to hearing from you.
I (We) look forward to your reply.
May I (we) hear from you soon?

I am/I remain
as in the expression
Looking forward to a speedy reply from you, I am (*or* remain)
should never be used as lead-ins to complimentary closes; however, the writer might choose one of the following expressions:
I (We) look forward to your immediate reply.
I (We) are looking forward to a reply from you soon.
May I (we) please have an immediate reply?
Will you please reply soon?

immediately and at once
when conjoined are redundant; however, each element of the expression may be used separately, as
May we hear from you immediately (*or* at once)?

incumbent
it is incumbent upon (one)
is more easily expressed as
I/we must . . . .
You must . . . .
He/she/they must . . . .

in re
should be avoided in general business letters, although it is often used in legal documents. Adequate substitutes are:
regarding
concerning
in regard to
about

stiff   In re our telephone conversation of . . . .

easier   Concerning our telephone conversation of . . . .

institute the necessary inquiries
is overlong and overformal, and may be reworded as follows:
We shall inquire . . . .
We'll find out . . . .
We are inquiring . . . .

in the amount of
is a long way to say *for.*

longer   . . . are sending you a check in the amount of $50.95.

shorter   . . . are sending you a check for $50.95.

. . . are sending you a $50.95 check.

in the course of
may be more concisely expressed by *during*
or *while*.

longer   In the course of the negotia-
            tions . . . .

shorter   During the negotiations . . . .
            While we were negoti-
            ating. . . .

in the event that
may be more concisely expressed by *if* or
in case.

longer   In the event that you cannot
            meet with me next week, we
            shall . . . .

shorter   If you cannot meet with me next
            week, we shall . . . .

in view of the fact that
may be shortened to *because* (*of*) or *since.*

longer   In view of the fact that he is now
            president of . . . .
            He was terminated in view of the
            fact that he had been negligent.

shorter   Since he is now president of . . . .
            He was terminated because of
            negligence.

it is incumbent upon
—see INCUMBENT

it is within (one's) **power**
—see POWER

line
is a vague substitute for one of the following
more explicit terms:

merchandise
line of goods (*or* merchandise)
goods
product(s)
service(s)
system(s)

meet with (one's) **approval**
is a stiff phrase more easily expressed as:
is (are) acceptable
I (we) accept (*or* approve)

stiff   If the plan meets with Mr. Doe's
            approval . . . .

easier   If the plan is acceptable to
            Mr. Doe . . . .
            If Mr. Doe accepts (*or* approves)
            the plan . . . .

note
we note that
you will note that
often constitute padding and thus should
be dropped.

padded   We note that your prospectus
            states . . . .
            You will note that the amount
            in the fourth column . . . .

lean   Your prospectus states . . . .
            The amount in the fourth col-
            umn . . . .

Or, if a word of this type is required, a more
natural substitute is *see:*
We see that you have paid the bill in full.

oblige
is archaic in the following locution:
Please reply to this letter and oblige.
The sentence should be recast to read:
Please reply to this letter immediately.

of recent date
—see RECENT DATE

of the opinion that
is a stiff way of saying:
We think (*or* believe) that . . . .
Our opinion is that . . . .
Our position is that . . . .

our Mr., Ms., Miss, Mrs. + (surname)
is best omitted.

not   Our Mr. Lee will call on you next
            Tuesday.

but   Our sales representative, Mr. Lee,
            will call on you next Tuesday.
            Mr. Lee, our sales representative,
            will call on you next Tuesday.

party
while idiomatic in legal documents, is
nevertheless awkward in general business
contexts when the meaning is "individual"
or "person."

awkward   We understand that you are
            the party who called earlier.

smoother   We understand that you are
            the person (*or* individual *or*
            one) who called earlier.

pending receipt of
while used in legal documents is, in general
contexts, a stiff way of saying "until we
receive."

stiff	We are holding your order, pending receipt of your check.
easier	We'll ship your order as soon as we receive your check.

permit me to remain
is outmoded and should not be used as part of the last sentence in a business letter.

place an order for
takes 18 keystrokes, but the verb *order* takes only 5 strokes. Why not try the shorter of the two?

position
be in a position to
The locutions

We are not in a position to
We are now in a position to

are unnecessarily long and may be recast to the shorter and more personal phrases
We cannot/can't
We are unable/aren't able
We can
We are now able

power
it is (not) **within** (one's) **power to**
is a lengthy way of saying

We can (*or* are able to)
We cannot/can't
We are unable to

longer	It is not within our power to back such an expensive project.
	It is now within our power to help you.
shorter	We cannot back such an expensive project.
	We can help you now.

prepared to offer
is a set phrase that can be reworded in a number of more original ways as shown below.

set	We are prepared to offer you the following discounts: . . . .
varied	We can offer you these discounts: . . . .
	Our discount schedule is: . . . .
	We're ready to offer you these discounts: . . . .
	We offer the following discounts: . . . .
	The discounts we're now offering are:

prior to
is a stiff way to say *before*.

stiff	Prior to receipt of your letter of July 1, we . . . .
easier	Before we received your July 1 letter, we . . . .
	Before receipt of your July 1 letter, we . . . .
	Before receiving your July 1 letter, we . . . .

—*compare* SUBSEQUENT TO

pursuant to
is a stiff phrase that unfortunately occurs in the very beginnings of many follow-up letters and memorandums. It should be reworded to read:

In accordance with
According to
Following up (*or* As a follow-up to)

stiff	Pursuant to our telephone conversation of June 1, let me say that . . . .
easier	Following up our June 1 telephone conversation, I can say that . . . .

reason is because
is ungrammatical, because the noun *reason* + the verb *is* call for a following noun clause and not an adverbial clause introduced by *because*.

The reason is:
The reason is that
This is the reason:
Because (*or* since)

receipt
—*see* PENDING RECEIPT OF

receipt is acknowledged
is an unnecessarily impersonal passive construction more concisely expressed as

We received
We have received
We've received

recent date
of recent date
is an unwieldy way to indicate an undated letter; the alternatives

your recent letter
your undated letter

are smoother. If the letter is dated, it is best to repeat the exact date.

reduce to a minimum
may be pared down to *minimize*.

wordy	This product reduces to a minimum the air pollution in work areas.
succinct	This product minimizes air pollution in work areas.

—*compare* AMPLIFY TO A MAXIMUM

refer back to
is a phrase in which *back* is redundant because the word element *re-* means "back."

redundant	We must refer back to last year's figures before we can answer your inquiry.
lean	We must refer to last year's figures before we can answer your inquiry.

refuse and decline
when conjoined are redundant; however, the use of one but not both will suffice: *refuse* or *decline*

redundant	We must refuse and decline any further dealings with your company.
lean	We must refuse any further dealings . . . . or
	We must decline to have any further dealings . . . .

—*compare* DEMAND AND INSIST

reiterate again
the adverb *again* is redundant, since the verb *reiterate* carries the total meaning by itself.

redundant	Let me reiterate our policy again.
succinct	Let me reiterate ⎫
	restate ⎬ our
	repeat ⎭ policy.
	May I reiterate ⎫
	restate ⎬ our
	repeat ⎭ policy?
	or
	Let me state our policy again.
	May I state our policy again?

return mail
by return mail
is a hackneyed and meaningless way of saying
immediately

promptly
at once
by (*explicit date*)

hackneyed	Please send us your check by return mail.
fresher	Won't you mail (us) your check immediately?
	Please send us your check at once.
	We'd like to have your check by (*date*).

said
is idiomatic in legal documents; however, it sounds stiff in general business contexts.

stiff	. . . a discussion of said matters.
easier	. . . a discussion of those (these) matters.

same
is an awkward substitute for the pronoun *it* or *them,* or for the applicable noun.

awkward	We have your check and we thank you for same.
	Your July 2 order has been received and same has been shipped.
easier	Thank you for your check which arrived yesterday.
	Your July 2 order has been received and shipped.

sells at a price of
is a 19-keystroke phrase more concisely expressed as:
costs
sells for
is priced at

separate cover
under separate cover
is a tired, overlong, vague phrase. If a specific mailing method (as SPECIAL DELIVERY) is not to be indicated, the adverb *separately* should be substituted.

hackneyed	We are mailing you our 1976 Annual Report under separate cover.
fresher	We're sending you separately our 1976 *Annual Report*.

subsequent to
is longer than its synonyms *after* or *following.* Why not opt for fewer keystrokes?

longer	Subsequent to the interview, she . . . .
shorter	After the interview, she . . . .

—compare PRIOR TO

take the liberty
is overlong and sounds somewhat obsequious.

longer	We are taking the liberty of sending you free samples of. . . .
shorter	We are sending you free samples of. . . .

thanking you in advance
is an outmoded participial-phrase ending that should not be used in modern business letters. A writer who uses this phrase is also cavalier enough to presume that his request will be honored.

not	Thanking you in advance for your help, I am
	Sincerely yours
but	Your help (or assistance) will be appreciated.
	I'll appreciate your help.
	Any help you may give me will be greatly appreciated.
	I'll appreciate any help you may give.
	If you can help me, I'll appreciate it.
	I'll be grateful for your help.
	Won't you help me?

therefor/therein/thereon
are commonly used in legal documents, but sound stiff in general business contexts.

stiff	The order is enclosed herewith with payment therefor.
	The safe is in a secure area with the blueprints kept therein.
	Enclosed please find Forms X, Y, and Z; please affix your signature thereon.
easier	We're enclosing a check with our order.
	The blueprints are kept in the safe which is located in a secure area.
	Please sign Forms X, Y, and Z which we have enclosed.

trusting you will
is an outmoded participial-phrase ending that should not be used in business letters.

A writer who uses this phrase is also cavalier enough to presume that his request will be honored.

not	Trusting that you will inform me of your decision soon, I am
	Sincerely yours
but	I hope that you'll give me your decision soon.
	Will you please give me your decision soon?
	Won't you give me your decision soon?

under date of
is an awkward locution that should be omitted.

not	. . . your letter under date of December 31. . . .
but	. . . your December 31 letter. . . .
	. . . your letter of December 31. . . .

—compare DATED

under separate cover
—see SEPARATE COVER

(the) undersigned
is awkward and impersonal.

awkward	Please return these photographs to the undersigned.
	The undersigned believes that. . . .
easier	Please return these photographs to me.
	I believe that. . . .

up to the present writing
is padding and should be omitted.

padded	Up to the present writing, we do not seem to have received. . . .
lean	We have not yet received. . . .
	As of now we have not received. . . .
	We still have not received. . . .
	We haven't received. . . .

valued
is redundant when used after the verb *appreciate* which carries the idea itself.

redundant	We appreciate your valued order of. . . .
lean	We appreciate your order of. . . .
	Your order is, of course, appreciated. . . .

APPENDIX: Suggestions for Further Reading

Accounting

Carson, Alexander B., et al. *Accounting Essentials for Career Secretaries.* Cincinnati: South-Western Publishing Co., 1972.

Palmer, Brock and Archer Binnion. *College Accounting for Secretaries.* New York: McGraw-Hill, 1971.

−see also CALCULATORS AND ELECTRONIC DATA PROCESSING

Administration

Anderson, Ruth I., et al. *The Administrative Secretary.* New York: McGraw-Hill, 1976.

Hanna, J. Marshall, et al. *Secretarial Procedures and Administration.* Cincinnati: South-Western Publishing Co., 1973.

Place, Irene, et al. *Office Management.* Scranton, PA: Canfield Press/Division of Harper & Row, 1974.

Neuner, John J., et al. *Administative Office Management.* Cincinnati: South-Western Publishing Co., 1972.

Winter, Elmer L. *The Successful Manager/Secretary Team.* West Nyack, NY: Parker Publishing Co., 1975.

Business Communication

Aurner, Robert R. and Morris P. Wolf. *Effective Communication in Business.* Cincinnati: South-Western Publishing Co., 1971.

Brock, Luther A. *How to Communicate by Letter and Memo.* New York: McGraw-Hill, 1974.

Murphy, Herta A. and Charles E. Peck. *Effective Business Communication.* New York: McGraw-Hill, 1972.

Poe, Roy W. and Rosemary T. Fruehling. *Business Communication: A Problem-Solving Approach.* New York: McGraw-Hill, 1973.

Reid, James M., Jr. and Robert M. Wendlinger. *Effective Letters: A Program for Self-Instruction.* New York: McGraw-Hill, 1973.

Sigband, Norman B. *Communication for Management and Business.* Glenview, IL: Scott, Foresman and Co., 1976.

Stewart, Marie M., et al. *College English and Communication.* New York: McGraw-Hill, 1975.

−see also ENGLISH GRAMMAR

Calculators and Electronic Data Processing

Awad, Elias M. *Business Data Processing.* Englewood Cliffs, NJ: Prentice-Hall, 1974.

Carter, Juanita E. and Darrock F. Young. *Calculating Machines: A Ten-Key Approach.* Boston: Houghton Mifflin, 1975.

Laird, Eleanor. *Data Processing Secretary's Complete Handbook.* Englewood Cliffs, NJ: Prentice-Hall, 1973.

McCready, Richard R. *Solving Business Problems with Calculators.* Belmont, CA: Wadsworth Publishing Co., 1972.

Robichaud, B. *Understanding Modern Business Data Processing.* New York: McGraw-Hill, 1966.

Dictionaries and Other Reference Books

Arpan, Jeffrey S. and David A. Ricks. *A Directory of Foreign Manufacturers in the United States.* Atlanta, GA: Georgia State University Business Publications, 1976.

Crowley, Ellen T. and Robert C. Thomas. *Acronyms and Initialisms Dictionary.* Detroit: Gale Research Co., 1973.

Peegh, Eric. *A Dictionary of Acronyms and Abbreviations.* Hamden, CT and London: Archon Books and Clive Bingley, 1969.

Rybicki, Stephen. *Abbreviations; A Reverse Guide to Standard and Generally Accepted Abbreviated Forms.* Ann Arbor: The Pierian Press, 1971.

Spillner, Paul. *World Guide to Abbreviations* (3 Parts). New York: R. R. Bowker Co., 1972.

Webster's Atlas and Zip Code Directory. Springfield, MA: G. & C. Merriam Co., 1973.

Webster's Collegiate Thesaurus. Springfield, MA: G. & C. Merriam Co., 1976.

Webster's Instant Word Guide. Springfield, MA: G. & C. Merriam Co., 1972.

Webster's New Collegiate Dictionary. Springfield, MA: G. & C. Merriam Co., 1973.

Webster's Third New International Dictionary. Springfield, MA: G. & C. Merriam Co., 1961.

Engineering

Laird, Eleanor. *Engineering Secretary's Complete Handbook.* Englewood Cliffs, NJ: Prentice-Hall, 1967.

Lojko, Grace R. *Typewriting Techniques for the Technical Secretary.* Englewood Cliffs, NJ: Prentice-Hall, 1972.

English Grammar

Gorrell, Robert M. and Charlton Laird. *Modern English Handbook.* Englewood Cliffs, NJ: Prentice-Hall, 1972.

Irmscher, William F. *The Holt Guide to English.* New York: Holt, Rinehart and Winston, 1976.

Keithley, Erwin and Margaret H. Thompson. *English for Modern Business.* Homewood, IL: Richard D. Irwin, Inc., 1972.

Perrin, Porter G. and Jim W. Corder. *Handbook of Current English.* Glenview, IL: Scott, Foresman and Co., 1975.

Human Relations

Laird, Donald A., et al. *Psychology: Human Relations and Motivation.* New York: McGraw-Hill, 1975.

Nirenberg, Jesse. *Getting Through to People.* Englewood Cliffs, NJ: Prentice-Hall, 1968.

Law

Blackburn, Norma D. *Legal Secretaryship.* Englewood Cliffs, NJ: Prentice-Hall, 1971.

Brady, Patricia S. *Legal Secretary's Handbook.* Los Angeles, CA: Parker & Son, 1971.

Grahm, Milton, et al. *Legal Typewriting.* New York: McGraw-Hill, 1968.

Leslie, Louis A. and Kenneth B. Coffin. *Handbook for the Legal Secretary.* New York: McGraw-Hill, 1968.

National Association of Legal Secretaries. *Manual for the Legal Secretarial Profession.* St. Paul, MN: West Publishing Co., 1974.

Prentice-Hall Editorial Staff. *Legal Secretary's Encyclopedic Dictionary.* Englewood Cliffs, NJ: Prentice-Hall, 1962.

Mathematics

Huffman, Harry and J. Schmidt. *Programmed Business Mathematics.* New York: McGraw-Hill, 1975.

Medicine

Alcazar, Carol C. *Medical Typist's Guide for Histories and Physicals.* Flushing, NY: Medical Examination Publishing Co., 1974.

Bredow, Miriam. *Handbook for the Medical Secretary.* New York: McGraw-Hill, 1963.

Bredow, Miriam. *Medical Office Procedures.* New York: McGraw-Hill, 1973.

Davis, Phyllis E. and N. Hershelman. *Medical Shorthand.* New York: John Wiley & Sons, Inc., 1967.

Dennis, Robert L. and Jean M. Doyle. *The Complete Handbook for Medical Secretaries and Assistants.* Boston: Little, Brown & Co., 1971.

Eshom, Myreta. *Medical Secretary's Manual.* Englewood Cliffs, NJ: Prentice-Hall, 1966.

Kabbe, Elaine F. *Medical Secretary's Guide.* Englewood Cliffs, NJ: Prentice-Hall, 1967.

Siegfried, W. *Typing Medical Forms.* New York: McGraw-Hill, 1969.

Webster's Medical Speller. Springfield, MA: G. & C. Merriam Co., 1975.

Office Equipment Systems

Briggs, Robert and Eugene J. Kosy. *Office Machines - A Collegiate Course.* Cincinnati: South-Western Publishing Co., 1973.

Kupsh, Joyce. *Duplicating: Machine Operation and Decision Making.* Beverly Hills, CA: Glencoe Press, 1972.

Pactor, Paul and Mina M. Johnson. *Comprehensive Business Machines Course.* New York: Pitman, 1968.

Office Landscape

Duffy, Frank and A. Wankum. *Office Landscaping: A New Approach to Office Planning and Layout Planning.* New York: International Publications Service, 1969.

Robichaud, B. *Selecting, Planning, and Managing Office Space.* New York: McGraw-Hill, 1958.

Office Procedures

Dallas, Richard J. and James M. Thompson. *Clerical and Secretarial Systems for the Office.* Englewood Cliffs, NJ: Prentice-Hall, 1974.

Place, Irene, et al. *College Secretarial Procedures.* New York: McGraw-Hill, 1972.

Records Management

Johnson, Mina M. and Norman F. Kallans. *Records Management.* Cincinnati: South-Western Publishing Co., 1974.

Kahn, Gilbert, et al. *Progressive Filing and Records Management.* New York: McGraw-Hill, 1971.

Maedke, Wilmer O., et al. *Information and Records Management.* Riverside, NJ: Glencoe Press (distributed by Macmillan), 1974.

Place, Irene and E. L. Popham. *Filing and Records Management.* Englewood Cliffs, NJ: Prentice-Hall, 1966.

INDEX